W9-CHP-972

# INTEGRATED
# MARKETING
# COMMUNICATION

## CREATIVE STRATEGY
### FROM IDEA TO IMPLEMENTATION

# INTEGRATED MARKETING COMMUNICATION

## CREATIVE STRATEGY
### FROM IDEA TO IMPLEMENTATION

Robyn Blakeman

ROWMAN & LITTLEFIELD PUBLISHERS, INC.
Lanham • Boulder • New York • Toronto • Plymouth, UK

Special thanks to Margo Berman of Florida International University for obtaining images and permissions.

ROWMAN & LITTLEFIELD PUBLISHERS, INC.

Published in the United States of America
by Rowman & Littlefield Publishers, Inc.
A wholly owned subsidiary of The Rowman & Littlefield Publishing Group, Inc.
4501 Forbes Boulevard, Suite 200, Lanham, Maryland 20706
www.rowmanlittlefield.com

Estover Road
Plymouth PL6 7PY
United Kingdom

Copyright © 2007 by Rowman & Littlefield Publishers, Inc.

*All rights reserved.* No part of this publication may be reproduced, stored in a retrieval system, or transmitted in any form or by any means, electronic, mechanical, photocopying, recording, or otherwise, without the prior permission of the publisher.

British Library Cataloguing in Publication Information Available

**Library of Congress Cataloging-in-Publication Data**

Blakeman, Robyn, 1958–
    Integrated marketing communication : creative strategy from idea to implementation / Robyn Blakeman.
        p. cm.
    Includes index.
    ISBN-13: 978-0-7425-2964-9 (pbk. : alk. paper)
    ISBN-10: 0-7425-2964-9 (pbk. : alk. paper)
    1. Communication in marketing. I. Title.
HF5415.123B557 2007
658.8'02—dc22                                                                    2006033879

Printed in the United States of America

♾™ The paper used in this publication meets the minimum requirements of American National Standard for Information Sciences—Permanence of Paper for Printed Library Materials, ANSI/NISO Z39.48-1992.

# Contents

# Introduction

STUDENTS OF advertising are introduced to many terms and even more definitions, yet they are often unable to define a term's role in the advertising process. The problem is that a term cannot adequately describe the business or role of advertising and a definition does not represent the creative process. Interpretation of these terms and their multifaceted definitions are the key to understanding how the business of creative works.

Understanding how to tie the business of advertising to the creative of advertising is one of the basic foundations behind integrated marketing communication (IMC). Creative represents the voice of business and can ultimately determine the success or failure of a product or service in the marketplace. Successful advertising understands how to exploit this creative as a business relationship and realizes that the advertising creative process is not an art—it is a marketing function.

Ultimately, the goal of advertising is to generate revenue through information and entertainment. In order to do this, account and creative teams must build an interpretive creative strategy based on a sound business plan. A creative strategy looks at who is most likely to purchase, and what it will take to get them to purchase. A business plan that employs IMC expands the creative strategy's voice by using one visual/verbal message throughout multiple media. This consistent visual/verbal message can be more accurately targeted to reach those most likely to purchase or use the product or service by incorporating a message developed with their specific needs and wants in mind.

IMC requires students to look at the creative side of advertising as a part of the business of advertising rather than seeing the two as separate functions within the advertising process. Although two very distinctive and different mindsets will need to analyze these areas for advertising to succeed or make a profit, they must work together. A creative idea doesn't work unless the groundwork for that idea is laid down in the marketing process, is tied directly to those most likely to use or purchase the product, and is then appropriately placed in a media they are likely to see or hear.

This textbook will attempt to teach the student of advertising (1) how to interpret a business plan to create an idea and (2) how IMC uses a strategic approach to build and sustain brand to target relationships using a coordinated message in diverse media.

# Integrated Marketing Communication

## Here We Go Again

Understanding advertising today requires a look at where advertising in the United States began. Integrated marketing communication (IMC) can trace its roots long before the invention of computers and industrialized manufacturing, all the way back to one-on-one trade between friends and neighbors.

Early in the settlement of the United States, the majority of the population lived and worked in small, tight-knit communities. While word of mouth was probably the first form of communication between seller and potential buyers, it was personalized selling that built and retained relationships between local consumers and merchants.

Local citizens could rely on area craftsmen for handcrafted items such as furniture and boots and shoes that were custom made to meet buyers' individual needs. Household goods such as pots, pans, coffees, teas, ammunition, and tobacco were sold by, or could be ordered through, the resident grocer, while local farmers supplied the community with a variety of meats, fruits, vegetables, and dairy products.

The mid-nineteenth century ushered in the Industrial Revolution, and for the first time mass-produced goods, often manufactured in far-off places, were sold to a wide audience. The custom work of the craftsman was all but replaced with machine-produced products, effectively ending the two-way dialogue between local merchants and residents.

**FIGURE 1.1**

# CASE STUDY:
# DOVE'S "CELEBRATING CURVES" CAMPAIGN

Throughout this and subsequent chapters, case studies examining recent advertising campaigns will be used to determine not only the results, but also how Integrated Marketing Communication (IMC) is developed and employed. These campaigns are presented to assist with laying a foundation for how IMC uses one tone of voice across multiple media to deliver a cohesive visual/verbal message.

Poster courtesy of Ogilvy Düsseldorf and Rankin Photography.

## Discussion

Successfully employing an IMC campaign requires using a diversified promotional and media mix that reflects the same visual/verbal tone of voice. A good example of this is Dove's award-winning "Celebrating Curves" European campaign, created by Ogilvy & Mather, London. By changing how beauty was defined, Dove was able to change not only how the beauty industry defined a beautiful woman, but also how women defined themselves.

Using innovative media choices, Dove re-launched its "Firming" line in March 2004 with the goal of repositioning an aging brand. While other beauty categories pushed physical perfection, Dove's repositioning campaign focused on the inherent beauty all women possess despite their shape or size. Previous advertising for products within this category traditionally featured women younger than the targeted market, and those in perfect physical shape, reflecting a non-traditional user. Dove ultimately chose to use real women in their ads rather than the traditional anorexic-looking model. This cutting-edge approach not only broke new ground by featuring women within the targeted age group, but also featured those most likely to need, and subsequently use, the product in their advertising.

The campaign was so well received that during the next phase, Dove looked into their target mix to find the next group of "Firm Friends." But creative efforts did not stop there. According to an article at www.unilever.co.uk the next group of "Firm Friends" to almost bare all was Dove's own marketing team: "After finally being exposed to real women on poster, the public got to see the real women behind the posters."

## Dove's New Look

Dove's major print campaign included posters that sported a one-line headline stating their message boldly across the top of the page: "Dove Firming. As tested on real curves." The main visual focused on a group of six women, each a different size and shape, standing in a line and leaning one against the other, dressed in various styles of lingerie. A smaller, secondary visual appearing in the lower right-hand corner of the ad shows three Dove products, with the word "new" directly to their left.

## Who Was the Campaign Trying to Reach?

The campaign targeted women in their thirties who were first-time users of firming products and were concerned about obtaining a firmer, more toned body.

## What Did the Campaign Need to Accomplish?

Marketing objectives included:

- Increasing Dove Firming's market share
- Tip the scales on how women perceive themselves
- Changing current perceptions of the brand
- Creating a unique and memorable advertising campaign

Strategically, it was important to develop the brand's image and overall personality while educating the target on the product's ability to firm those troublesome hips, buns, and thighs. Dove went against tradition when it chose to use women of varied sizes to deliver the message both visually and verbally. The underlying premise was that only real women know about these troublesome attributes and only real women can realistically deliver the message. By stepping outside of the traditional advertising box, Dove's creative team took the

*(Continued)*

**FIGURE 1.1**

Campaign Case Study: Dove's "Celebrating Curves" Poster courtesy of Ogilvy Worldwide.
(Continued)

first step to obtaining the campaign's objectives and redefining beauty. The aforementioned
www.unilever.co.uk article reports that Dove's strategy was to engage the press to help
deliver their message. Local newspapers were "given an exclusive on Dove's revolutionary
advertising. The newspaper interviewed the 'real women' who would appear in the new campaign, as well as its famous celebrity photographer, Rankin. Another exclusive [was] on
celebrity role models." But Dove's public relations push did not end here. The team enlisted the
help of psychologist Dr. Linda Papadopoulos, the Unilever article goes on to say, who "was
enlisted to help explain why women feel so disheartened by traditional advertising images. And,
to further emphasize the 'real life' element, TV channels were provided with behind-the-scenes
shots of the shoot itself."

The next step was to determine the proper media mix to employ. Radical ideas, and the
resulting media interest created, required an unusual choice of media. In the case of Dove
"Firming," public relations played a major role in introducing the campaign, along with posters,
out-of-door, TV, and print.

## Exploiting the "Buzz"

This redefinition of beauty caused a "buzz" across Europe and according to an article appearing on adforum.com in 2005, "sparked a debate on how beauty is portrayed in the media."
Dove was able to capitalize on all the media attention surrounding this "new" image debate
and to use the media and public relations to its initial advantage. Dove chose not to use a traditionally heavy print/broadcast media mix. Instead the team chose to use a third of its budget on public relations and related press events, with television playing a lesser role. Posters
were used to broadcast the message within communities where women in the target audience
lived and worked.

## Conclusion

These efforts resulted in Dove's successfully changing its image from old-fashioned to a new-
fashioned beauty product. Marketing objectives were met, and the campaign was successful at
creating a unique position for the product in the mind of the targeted consumer. Creative
efforts and a good media mix assisted with creating brand awareness and successfully developing brand equity. The "buzz" created through the media and public relations efforts gave the
creative message meaning and spotlighted the product's intent, to reinvent the visual/verbal
voice of beauty.

Sources: "EACA EURO EFFIES 2005, 'Celebrating Curves Poster,'" www.adforum.com, accessed October 8, 2005; "Clever
PR Boosts Dove 'Real Women' Campaign," www.unilever.co.uk/ourbrands/casestudies/dove_casestudy.asp, accessed
January 22, 2007.

Taking its place was a generic one-way statement from an anonymous manufacturer to an unknown, uninvolved consumer. Limited competition and media options made advertising efforts simple and wide exposure more or less guaranteed—for a while.

Advances in technology eventually expanded media options and encouraged competition. Product categories once dominated—often for generations—by one brand were suddenly inundated with multiple equivalent products. Features once considered unique or cutting-edge in one brand could now be easily and economically copied by other brands within a category, so that what was once a selling point for a particular brand became a routine product feature within months. Without any distinguishing features or meaningful differences between individual products, brand image erodes—along with consumer brand loyalty. The unqualified number of diverse and often misused or incorrectly used media options contributed to this erosion by splintering consumer attention further—offering too many media options to successfully guarantee reaching a specific target audience—and diluting brand awareness.

Today, IMC has resurrected the relationship between buyer and seller by re-creating an environment of consumer-focused communication efforts. IMC's ability to strategically deliver a consistent message to the right audience, through the correct media, is crucial to the successful implementation of an IMC creative series. To do this effectively, marketers must develop a creative strategy that not only coordinates advertising efforts, both visually and verbally, but also answers the target market's most important question: *What's in it for me?*

## What Is Integrated Marketing Communication?

IMC, also known as relationship marketing, works to interactively engage a specific individual, using a specific message, through specific media outlets. The goal is to build a long-term relationship between buyer and seller by involving the targeted individual in an interactive or two-way exchange of information. Expertly placed media efforts and the use of computer databases play a big role in getting the message to the right target audience, as does the development of a consistent visual/verbal image for the product or service.

It wasn't until the mid-1990s that IMC first began to attract and hold the attention of marketers. Up to this point, most advertising dollars were spent on more traditional mass media advertising, such as print (newspapers and magazines) and broadcast (radio and television), that sent a more generalized message to a large audience. IMC, in contrast, focuses on the use of alternative or promotional media, such as direct marketing and sales promotion, to reach individual consumers with a personalized message. Consumers in today's marketplace are inundated with hundreds of advertising messages daily; consumers must pick and choose which will be remembered and which will be ignored. IMC attempts to ensure that the message will be remembered by replacing unwanted one-size-fits-all tactics by presenting an individualized message to a much smaller target audience in a language they can understand and relate to, and in media they are sure to see and use.

Messages used in an IMC campaign must be tailor-made to fit a specific target audience's needs, wants, and lifestyle. The goal is to reach one individual within the target with a specially designed message that will create a lasting relationship and develop a brand-loyal consumer who will continue to purchase that brand without the need for continuing advertising efforts.

Each brand or product must be as individualized as the target. The enormous number of media options and virtual product anonymity in many categories makes it necessary for marketers to create an identity for a brand or service so it will stand out from the competition.

It is important that the product's image match the target's image of himself, and the advertised message must get and hold the target's attention among the clutter of the competition.

If it sounds like it's more expensive to get a message to individual targets as compared to a mass audience, it is. IMC is often more expensive to employ than traditional advertising methods, but the results can be worth the expense.

Communicating with a target that has a known interest in the product or service increases reach, or the number of interested people who will see the message, and reduces frequency, or number of times an ad or promotion will need to be used. Exposure to the message is more or less guaranteed when placed in a special-interest medium the target is known to use, making purchase more likely.

The initial steps required to attract a brand-loyal consumer are more expensive than those needed to retain a brand-loyal customer. Once the consumer thinks of a brand as her only choice, the need for additional communication efforts can be reduced, minimizing costs.

Traditional advertising, on the other hand, takes longer to build loyalty. Because it is less likely a given target will have repeated exposure to a mass media vehicle, the amount of time it takes to educate the target on the features and benefits of the product or service is increased. The result is a target that is often unable to recall the product's name at the time of purchase.

## Basic Reasons for the Growth of IMC

Technology has changed the way corporations market their product and services. The customer is now in control of what he buys, when he buys, and where and how he buys. Computerized databases have given a name and personality to the mass audience. Advertised messages can be addressed to an individual and feature products he or she has a known interest in based on past purchase behavior. The Internet and other interactive media make it easy to purchase virtually any item without leaving the house, at any time of the day or night, using a toll-free number or Internet site. Consumers are better educated about products and can seek out additional information at their leisure. Marketers realize consumers have many product options from which to choose when making a purchase. Because of this, thinking has gone from being sales oriented to being customer driven in a relatively short period of time.

Before IMC, traditional marketing efforts were simple, aimed at making a sale and increasing profits. This type of tactic, where the seller does no more than deliver a message to a buyer, is known as an inside-out approach. IMC, on the other hand, is consumer driven and understands the consumer has many choices available in any single product category. Marketers are now focusing on an outside-in approach in which products are designed to meet consumers' individual needs and wants.

Successfully employing IMC requires a change in corporate philosophy, or a different way of thinking about, and planning for, strategically effective marketing communications. To be effective, IMC must be looked at as a process for building a relationship with the target and developing a product or offering a service that meets the specific needs of these individuals. Product performance and quality is also a critical component to success. Each time the target repurchases, the product or service must match her expectations and consistently deliver reliable results.

## Why IMC Fails

IMC fails when it is seen as just another communication effort, rather than a corporate philosophy expressed both inside and out.

Most people think of IMC as just a parity of advertising with its one-image/one-tone-of-voice approach. However, unlike traditional advertising, IMC really comprises all aspects and any "interaction points" of planned or unplanned communication between the brand, service, or corporation and the target audience, and is affected by both inside and outside influences.

Planned contact is external and includes outside advertising and promotions employed to reach the target. Unplanned contact is internal, or corporately focused to employees and vendors and is the less controllable of the two. Because of this, it must be the most flexible form of contact in order to adjust to changing market, corporate, or consumer conditions. Corporate philosophy plays a major role in unplanned contact, which includes:

- Employee gossip
- Word of mouth
- Governmental or media investigations
- Management performance
- Customer service initiatives
- How sales associates greet clientele

- Product quality and performance
- In-store and out-of-store displays
- Packaging
- Distribution
- Price
- Store locations
- Uniforms
- Deliveries
- Delivery drivers
- Dress codes
- Sales tactics
- Management style and/or philosophy

All of these will have a direct impact on how the target views the product or service and will affect both initial and repeat sales.

Any change in corporate philosophy brought about by IMC efforts must be communicated internally as well as externally. Even the smallest details affect the success of IMC, and for IMC to work every individual in the company, from the top down, must buy into the message being delivered to the consumer. If this is not the case, the target will receive mixed messages: a disconnect between what he hears in communication efforts and what he actually experiences when dealing with a company representative. Consider the following example: If the message to the public is "Fly the Friendly Skies," every employee with access to the public must be made aware of, and understand, this message. Nothing will kill the momentum of this advertising campaign faster than the target's meeting an angry ticket agent or snooty customer service representative.

## What Drives IMC

To successfully use IMC, corporations must absorb the message into their corporate philosophy to ensure the target receives a consistent message and a reliable product or service. But this is only one of many initiatives that drive IMC. In order to be truly consumer driven, IMC planning must also address several issues.

- Research
- Database development
- Use of the Internet
- Employing correct media tactics
- Building brand-loyal consumers
- Creating an interactive relationship
- Brand development
- Projecting a consistent visual/verbal image
- The promotional and media mix
- Evaluation

## Research

IMC can't work without an intimate knowledge of the intended target audience—those individuals research has determined are most likely to buy the product or use the service. Research is key to understanding what the target audience wants, how they will use the product or service, where and how they live, what media vehicles they use or see, and what are they looking for in a customer-brand relationship. Information gathered in the research phase will be used to determine the best promotional and media mix to reach the intended target audience, and what type of message will motivate purchase.

## Database Development

The growth of IMC can be traced to the development of database marketing. Database marketing uses a computer to store personal information about individuals and their past purchase history. Unlike traditional advertising methods, which focus communication efforts on a large group of targeted members, IMC targets individuals. Every time a consumer makes a credit card or grocery store purchase, visits a website, subscribes to a magazine or trade organization, or fills out a warranty or rebate form, personal information about the consumer is gathered and stored in a database. This information is used to direct future communication to only those individuals known to be interested in a product or service, eliminating advertising waste and allowing for a more personalized appeal.

The ability to talk to a target audience member by name is not all that new. What is new is how much is known about the targeted individual and her special interests. Because messages can be designed to specifically address issues of importance to the target, the question *What's in it for me?* can be answered for every target group or niche market. Database information also plays a role in determining the best media and promotional mix, creative strategy, and overall message strategy needed to reach the intended target.

## Use of the Internet

The use of computer databases to identify targeted audiences and the growth of the Internet as an information source is behind the initial and ongoing success of IMC. The Internet has personalized communication efforts between buyer and seller, moving from talking at the target to talking with the target. As an educational and informational tool, the Internet can persuade and motivate consumers to take the next action-oriented step—such as picking up the phone and dialing a toll-free number to speak directly to a customer service representative, or to request additional information, make a purchase, give feedback, ask for coupons, request sales promotion materials, or enter a contest or sweepstakes—all on their own time from their own home or office, and with few distractions. The use of credit cards and the availability of multiple quick and easy contact options have made interaction and purchase immediate and, more importantly, interactive.

## Employing Correct Media Tactics

It's no longer necessary for IMC to depend only upon traditional advertising vehicles such as print and broadcast media to reach the intended target audience. Modern IMC is about using any type of communication vehicle to reach the target audience.

It's impossible to develop a relationship if the target never sees the message. Students of advertising often think only of advertising when deciding what media to use when developing their IMC program. But the options are much more diverse than that. The IMC media grab bag also includes public relations, direct marketing, sales promotion, the Internet, and, new to the media mix, alternative media sources such as revolving truck-side billboards, manhole covers, or parking meters.

The focus in IMC is on getting a coordinated message out to the right target via the best media. The advertised message must appear in the right place at the right time, no matter how unusual that "place" may be. If the target can see it or hear it, it is a potential advertising vehicle. It doesn't matter if it's a parking meter, a bathroom stall, the sidewalk, a manhole cover, athletic wear, T-shirts, shopping carts, product placement on television or in movies, shopping bags, or a curb—everything has message potential written all over it. This kind of alternative advertising is known as guerilla marketing. The role guerilla marketing plays is small compared to that of the promotional and traditional mass media vehicles, but it is no less important. Although traditional media vehicles are where the majority of advertising is still placed, don't stop there. The times are a'changin', and traditional vehicles might not be the best places to find your target.

If your message doesn't reach the target audience where they are, your budget is wasted and unless it is utterly unique your product will not gain enough acceptance to survive in a cluttered product category. The increasing cost of mass media advertising makes the old hit-or-miss ways of advertising obsolete. Your message must be placed in the media that research have proven to be seen or used by your target market on a regular basis. What media you should use will depend on the target, the objectives that need to be accomplished, and the overall strategy.

## Building Brand-Loyal Consumers: The Long Road to Loyalty

For decades the middleman—the retailer—has successfully silenced communication between buyer and seller. IMC removes this barrier by encouraging consumers to actively participate in communication with the seller.

Individually targeted buyers can easily gather information or shop from the comfort of their own homes at times convenient to them. By picking up the phone or visiting a website, they can place an order, ask a question, or request additional information from a knowledgeable customer service or technical representative. In many cases consumers can order products built to their individual specifications, make suggestions, and give feedback about a product or service or about customer service initiatives. This two-way dialogue between buyer and seller solicits brand loyalty by allowing the consumer to receive a product tailor-made to his needs and be a major contributor to ongoing product and corporate development. Brand loyalty means that not only will the target favor your product or brand over all the others in the category, but she will do so reliably, building the lasting, long-term relationship needed to build brand equity or become the product leader in any one category.

By concentrating communication efforts on a specific group of individuals, you develop an approach that consistently and effectively speaks to the target's needs. Message development based on a target's needs, wants, and special interests sets a product or service apart from its competition, and this is the basis for an effective creative strategy.

## Creating an Interactive Relationship

It took a long time for today's product and corporate leaders to understand that it is less expensive to retain old customers than it is to constantly look for new ones. Communication tactics used in an IMC approach shift communication efforts away from the traditional one-way mass media monologue to a two-way dialogue between buyer and seller. This approach builds a relationship by allowing the target to give feedback, discuss ideas, and register complaints as an involved consumer.

Building a relationship between buyer and seller is a necessary precursor to building a brand-loyal consumer, and brand-loyal consumers require less advertising effort, which leads to rising profit margins.

Relationships are built on dialogue. One feature that distinguishes IMC from traditional advertising efforts is that advertising speaks *at* a group of individuals through mass media vehicles about perceived problems or interests, while IMC speaks *to* (or *with*) a single individual about his known problems or special interests.

## Brand Development

Because today's consumers are exposed to hundreds—if not thousands—of diverse advertising messages on a daily basis, it is important that a product or service have a personality, or brand image. A brand is a product's identity: the name, symbol, image, and use that distinguish one brand from another. A brand's name is something the consumer trusts based on past history with the product. If the product tastes the same, works the same, or fits the same every time the consumer buys, she no longer spends time thinking about or looking for a replacement. This is brand loyalty.

Brand value is the sum of every experience the consumer has—not only with the product but with the company that makes the product. Are the sales associates courteous every time the target enters the store? Do delivery drivers drive cautiously and make deliveries at times that don't inconvenience consumers? Is the product always as fresh, as the advertising says it will be? These are the type of influencers that affect brand image. Every experience between the seller and the target will affect the brand's image and brand equity.

All communication efforts should work to anchor or position the brand's identity and image in the target's mind. If the brand's image mimics that of the consumer, it creates a tie that binds the product to the consumer's lifestyle. A reliable brand offers reliable results and will be the first product the target thinks of, and recognizes, when purchasing. With all the similar brands available in any one category, the goal is to make your brand a familiar face among a crowd of strangers to the consumer.

## Projecting a Consistent Visual/Verbal Image: The Business Strategy behind Creative

Advertising is more than a creative idea: It is the end result of months of planning and strategizing. Advertising encapsulates a study of the product or service, the competition, and the target audience into an effective and coordinated business and creative strategy.

The results seen on television or in print media are just a small part of the business of advertising. At its most basic, advertising is a process that reacts to the client's or marketer's business needs by finding a creative way to sell a product or promote a service. Remember, a successful IMC campaign talks directly to a specific target about a specific point they are interested in and placed in a medium they will be exposed to often.

Traditional advertising is no longer the most strategically effective way to reach a media-blitzed, often apathetic audience. To reach today's savvy and educated consumer with the right message requires a message that relates to the target's life experiences, reflects the target's image of himself, and is repeated enough to develop an identity or relationship with the target.

An IMC campaign is based on a set of objectives that communication efforts need to accomplish. Each campaign focuses on one key benefit of the product or service that research has found is important to the target. This benefit may be unique to the product, or it may feature a creative solution that sets the product or service apart from the competition. Strategy refers to how the key benefit will be creatively delivered to the target. What you learn from your target investigations should be used to build an appropriate message strategy that will talk directly to the target about the product, addressing points especially important to the target.

It is important that all pieces in an IMC creative series have a consistent visual identity and send a consistent verbal message that is easily recognized as the tone, or voice, of the product or service. The visual/verbal identity must talk the talk and look the part consistently from media vehicle to media vehicle. This is not to say the ads should be repetitive—that would be boring—but they do need to have some kind of tie that binds them together visually, such as the layout style or typeface, color, or spokesperson or character representative. Verbally, ads can be tied together through the copy or the headline's voice and style.

The bottom line is that every communicated experience should look and sound familiar. The ability to strategically direct a cohesive message to the right audience, through the correct media, is crucial to the successful implementation of an IMC creative series.

## The Promotional and Media Mix

The ability to reach the targeted audience using the best promotional and media mix available is another of IMC's many strengths. The promotional mix includes public relations, advertising, direct marketing, sales promotion, and the Internet.

Communication efforts are often directed at different audiences, each requiring its own message and promotional mix. Determining which combination of promotional vehicles to use often depends on the target's overall knowledge about the product or service. For example, those who know little about a brand will need a different promotional mix than will those who are more regular users.

The media mix breaks the promotional mix down to specific media vehicles such as newspaper, magazine, direct mail, and so on. The media mix can be either concentrated or assorted. A concentrated media mix places all advertising efforts into one medium. An assorted media mix employs more diverse media. Like the promotional mix, the type of media mix employed will depend on budget, overall objectives, and the target audience and its degree of brand knowledge and/or loyalty.

Let's take a brief look at a few of the major players that make up the promotional mix that we will be looking at in more detail later in this text.

| | |
|---|---|
| • Public Relations | • Direct Marketing |
| • Advertising (including newspaper, magazine, radio, and television) | • Internet and Viral Marketing |
| | • Guerilla Marketing |
| • Sales Promotion | • Personal Selling |

**Public Relations**  The job of public relations is to give a product or service news value. The most common form of information distribution is done by issuing a news release, but news conferences and interviews are also useful. Such exposure is often free, but it is not always guaranteed. Information sent to local news outlets is not always picked up and used, and when it is the news staff often rewrites content. Not all forms of public relations rely on the ability to generate news; others, like event sponsorships and brochures, are paid for, have guaranteed message content, and occur on a predetermined schedule.

Public relations is an effective way to announce events or repair a damaged reputation.

Strategically, public relations can be used to inform, tantalize, or build curiosity around a product or service launch, deliver testimonials, or whet the consumer's appetite for upcoming promotional events.

**Advertising** Advertising is a term often used to generically describe all forms of advertising communication. In reality it covers only communication appearing in print media, including newspapers and magazines, and in broadcast media, including radio and television. Advertising is known as a mass media vehicle that can reach a large, less targeted audience. Advertising must be paid for, so media placement and message content are guaranteed. Advertising is still the best choice to build brand awareness and develop brand image.

**Sales Promotion** Sales promotion uses incentives or motivators as an enticement for consumers to buy or use a product or service. Typical incentives might consist of coupons, rebates, samples, contests, sweepstakes, buy-one-get-one-free offers, and premiums such as T-shirts, pens, pencils, and calendars, to name just a few.

Sales promotion incentives can generate interest, and are best used for new product launches, "try me" opportunities, or when attempting to resurrect an aging brand.

**Direct Marketing** Direct marketing, also known as direct response, employs such media vehicles as direct mail, catalogs, infomercials, and telemarketing. Because direct marketing uses databases to reach an exclusively targeted audience, it is one of the best ways to talk to the target on an individual level and induce an immediate response. The availability of credit cards, toll-free numbers, order forms, and websites makes purchasing from home convenient, fast, and easy. Both sales promotion and direct marketing are considered promotional vehicles, and both are great ways to build brand awareness and encourage purchase.

**Internet and Viral Marketing** The Internet allows targets the opportunity to gather information or to shop from the comfort of their own homes, at a time when they are exposed to fewer distractions. Products can be purchased online, and targets can seek out additional information interactively through chat rooms with other product users or talk one-on-one with customer relations or technical representatives.

Viral marketing, the newest form of Internet word of mouth, is a great way to build brand awareness and reach a large number of consumers. Viral marketing uses interactive and/or entertaining Internet advertising, often delivered via e-mail or secondary websites to inform and "infect" targets with enough interest about a product or service to visit the host website. The success of viral marketing depends on each receiver passing the interactive message along, "infecting" a friend or family member with information about that particular site. Viral advertisements can take many forms, but the most common include amusing streaming video or audio options, interactive games, and text messaging.

**Guerilla Marketing** Guerilla marketing refers to the use of any clean, printable surface for message delivery. Surfaces appropriate for guerilla marketing campaigns include, but are not limited to, sidewalks, cars and transportation vehicles, parking meters, and bathroom stalls. These unique media vehicles often reach the target audience more effectively than advertisements in print or broadcast media, so advertising efforts and costs are minimized, but maximum exposure is achieved. This nontraditional approach looks at the demographic, psychographic, behavioral, and geographic profile of the target audience and determines whether traditional media will or will not reach them.

**Personal Selling** Since this text deals exclusively with consumer promotions and personal selling is usually found in corporate environments, it will not be discussed in detail here. But as a member of the promotional mix, it is worth mentioning. Personal selling is face-to-face selling between a buyer and a seller, the ultimate interactive relationship. However, its very one-to-one nature makes it very expensive, relegating its use almost exclusively to the corporate environment.

In choosing the most appropriate media mix to reach your target, the point is to know your target: where they are and what they see or hear. Employing alternative media opens up a whole range of communications possibilities (see figure 1.2). The right media mix for your client's product or service might include any of the following: newspaper or magazine articles; remote radio broadcasts; outdoor boards; banners; transit advertising, including both interior and exterior options, on buses or taxis; small airplane banners; building signs; caps and cups, a message stuffed in the pocket of a new garment; grocery receipts, packaging, window, or in-store displays; table tents; posters; shopping bags; bill or credit card stuffers; freestanding inserts; text messaging; home pages; and banner and pop-up ads. These are only a few of the alternative media options available for use in an IMC campaign. Which ones are most appropriate for an individual campaign is determined by your target and your product.

## Evaluation

Evaluating the results of traditional advertising efforts is fairly easy: Did we realize a return on investment (ROI)? Very basically, ROI is determined by how much money was spent on advertising versus how much money was made.

Evaluation determines whether all goals or objectives for the IMC campaign have been met. If they were, great—keep doing what you're doing. If not, you must determine what outside or inside influences got in the way, such as competitors' advertising, whether or not the correct message was used, whether the target audience saw and understood the message, and so on.

Evaluation can be a rejuvenator or an annoyance. There are many who feel the evaluation techniques used in IMC are inadequate and do not accurately assess results. However, as it stands right now, evaluation is the best indicator of what worked, what should be used again, where additional attention needs to be directed or backed off on temporarily, and what needs to be changed in order to accomplish the overall objectives.

**FIGURE 1.2**

The "Boom Gate" parking garage gate promotion was created by Bartek Grala, Daniel Piecka, and Jason Romeyko, creative director, from Saatchi & Saatchi Poland for Voltaren Emulgel. This ad appeared in a number of car parks (parking garages) across Poland and was designed to demonstrate the product's effectiveness in increasing mobility of muscles. When the gate was closed, consumers could see the selling line: "The joy of movement." Image courtesy of Saatchi & Saatchi Poland.

IMC is designed to make money, but additional ROI or outcomes require more than a strong profit margin to survive in today's competitive market. It is also important to determine such things as brand awareness, how the target views or positions the product or service against leading competitors in the category, and smaller but no less important issues such as how many new contacts were made, the number of responses resulting from direct mail efforts, and the number of participants in the most recent sales promotion, to name a few.

## Tying It All Together

### The Difference between Traditional Advertising Methods and IMC

Traditional or mass media advertising uses conventional print and broadcast media such as newspapers, magazines, radio, and television to get a message across to a mass audience that may or may not be listening. Because the messages are general, rather than personalized, in nature, this sort of advertising does not build a relationship with the target audience and it takes longer to build brand loyalty.

Successful relationships require nurturing, a component missing in traditional advertising efforts. Without dialogue, information can travel only one way, as a monologue from seller to an often passive and distracted buyer.

With all that being said, when pure message is all you want to get out, traditional advertising methods are still the best way to build awareness or influence consumer attitudes about a product or service.

Traditionally, advertising has always taken a lead role, with public relations, sales promotion, and direct marketing used as support mediums. IMC, on the other hand, analyzes the various options available and chooses only those that will most effectively and consistently reach the target audience. *Advertising is no longer a marketer's first—or even best—media option, and often it is not used at all.*

### The Line That Divides

IMC differs from traditional advertising in the way it chooses media, uses databases to talk to individual members of the target audience, tailors messages to the target's self-interest, and creates consistency between advertising pieces via layout and message delivery.

IMC is everything traditional advertising methods are not. IMC is about communicating the client's message or a key benefit of the product or service both consistently and cohesively. It's about developing an image that is recognizable to the target no matter what medium it appears in.

Traditional advertising knows the target audience; IMC knows the targeted individual and uses a message that relates specifically to that audience member's needs or wants. Unlike traditional advertising, IMC vehicles can be personalized to speak to one person within a target group or to other shareholders such as employees, retailers, or tradesmen.

Media choices are based on the target's lifestyle and IMC messages appear in media vehicles the target is sure to see and use. The brand's overall image should be expressed consistently in the choice of creative strategy, message, and layout style used, as well as reflected in the product name, logo design, packaging, price, and overall layout design. No internal or external customer interaction point should be overlooked. These images will further reflect the image and reputation of both the consumer and the store where the product can be purchased or the service can be used. Often traditional advertising methods do not coordinate these elements, sending multiple or unrelated messages to the target. IMC strategically coordinates these elements, both inside and out, into one consistent brand image targeted to a very specific audience.

Being able to define a product or service for a target requires a communications plan of attack. The business of advertising would go nowhere without a creative solution that can cut through the advertising clutter and not only capture the target audience's attention but reach out and communicate with them. To do this effectively, IMC must develop a creative strategy that not only coordinates advertising efforts both visually and verbally, but also answers the target audience's most important question: *What's in it for me?*

## Defining a Creative Strategy Statement

*Creative* describes a unique and individual idea. *Strategy* is a plan to accomplish that creative idea or concept. Employing an IMC creative strategy is all about sending the right visual/verbal message to the right target audience, through the right media, in order to achieve the overall communication objectives.

A creative strategy statement is an integral part of the marketing communication process. Once you know the goals or objectives set up by the client, you can begin developing an effective creative strategy that will accomplish them. Effective strategies are the slippery yet essential monsters that define advertising direction. Determining the right one requires research. You are not looking at ideas, describing a creative look, or solidifying media outlets at this point; you are looking at solutions to an advertising problem. These solutions assist in the development of a concept or theme that can be consistently executed both visually and verbally within multiple media without losing substance or focus.

A successful creative strategy statement is developed from information found in the client's marketing plan (discussed in chapter 2) and is written from the consumer's point of view. It needs to ask, on behalf of the target, *What's in it for me?* How will it solve my problem or make my life better? The answers should ultimately lead to an idea, unique to the product or service, that will influence the target to act on the message and make the product or service stand out from the competition.

The creative strategy statement will define the IMC campaign's visual/verbal tone of voice and is the foundation for the communication phase of an IMC program. The creative strategy affects every aspect of IMC and will ultimately give the product its image and voice, and define seller-to-buyer contact.

## Who Develops the Creative Strategy Statement and For Whom Is It Intended?

The creative strategy is usually developed by the agency account executive (AE), but it can also be developed jointly with the client. Representing the business side of advertising, the AE acts as the liaison between the client and the agency and the client and the creative team. The creative team includes, at the very least, a copywriter and an art director. This team of "creatives" will use the creative strategy to develop the overall concept or idea. Their interpretation of the creative strategy begins the construction phase of message development.

## The Look of a Creative Strategy Statement

Creative strategy statements can take many different forms, depending on the agency and the overall size and scope of the project. The longer, more explanatory form has two main areas: The first looks at the communication objectives and the second dissects the creative strategy statement into four main sections: the target (primary and secondary), the competition, the key benefit, and the proposed promotional mix. Let's take a brief look at each one (see figure 1.3).

**Communication Objectives**  Creative strategies must accommodate a specific set of objectives, or what the client needs communication efforts to achieve. Objectives are determined by problems the target or product category may have and any market opportunities the product has to solve to overcome these problems.

Objectives describe what it is you want the target to think, feel, and do after exposure to the message, and should answer the target's question: *What's in it for me?* Some of the

**FIGURE 1.3**
Creative Strategy Statement Template

1. Communication Objectives
2. Creative Strategy Statement. Each section should be answered with no more than one or two sentences.
   a. Primary and Secondary Target Audience Profiles
   b. Competition
   c. Key Benefit
   d. Promotional Mix

most common objectives might include creating brand awareness, or what you want the target to think or know about the product or service after exposure to the advertising message; defining a need the product or service can fulfill, such as how the target will feel or how much can be accomplished after using the product or service; encouraging action on the part of the target, such as making a purchase, visiting a showroom, or calling for more information. Determining how these objectives should be addressed will be the first hurdle the creative team must clear before a creative direction is determined.

**Creative Strategy Statement** Each of the following sections should be addressed with no more than one or two sentences. A successful strategy requires the creative team to have a thorough understanding of the target audience, the competition, the product's key benefit, and the media options or promotional mix.

The Target Audience  The primary target is identified based on research as the most likely prospect to buy the product or use the service. Secondary audiences are often influencers whose opinion the primary target audience member trusts or seeks out for advice. Take, for example, a campaign for iPod. Advertising efforts may focus on a primary target of fifteen- to twenty-eight-year-olds, with a secondary audience of the parents or grandparents of the primary target. Messages targeted to the primary audience may focus on image and features, while advertising targeted to the secondary audience may add information on price or purchasing options.

A thorough understanding of both audiences will help the creative team determine the answers to some important questions: What does the target audience want? Are they aware of the product or service? What will influence their decision to purchase? How will the product be used in their daily lives? Are they currently using a competitor's product? If so, what do they like or dislike about that product? What will it take to convince them to switch brands? Are there any major influencers, or secondary target audience members, who also have to be reached?

Advertising to a single target audience no longer has the impact it once had to deliver the brand's image and promise. Many purchases require little or no thought, while others, especially high-dollar purchases, or products that reflect a target's lifestyle, the need to fit in or to be the first to own, are influenced by other individuals trusted by the primary target. These individuals are known as outside influencers.

In his book *Strategies for Implementing Integrated Marketing Communications*, Larry Percy identifies roles a individual can play that can positively or negatively affect their decision or another's decision to buy:

- *Initiator:* the individual who originally decides to purchase a product or use a service.
- *Influencer:* an outside person or group of people who recommends or discourages the purchase of a product or use of a service.

- *Decider:* the person who ultimately determines what will actually be purchased.
- *Purchaser:* the individual who actually initiates the purchase or use of the product or service.
- *User:* the individual who will use the product or service.

It's important to remember that IMC talks not to a target audience but to a single individual within that targeted audience. Every time the target considers a particular type of purchase, he assumes a mindset or plays a role. That role will determine the type of message the target receives. Initiators must be made aware of the product or service and the benefits that come with ownership or use. Influencers, such as family and friends, salespeople who may or may not recommend the product or service, and professional influencers such as doctors or financial advisors, must understand the reason a product or service should be recommended or discouraged. The decider must have the answer to the question *What's in it for me?* before deciding whether or not to purchase. The user must not only use the product but also be willing to recommend and repurchase the product or reuse the service.

The Competition  This is not a list of competitors, but rather a look at what competitors are doing and saying in their advertising and a statement regarding what the client's brand must do in order to compete within the product category, stand out from the competition, and attract the target's attention. Knowing how the product is positioned in the mind of consumers, or what they think about the product or service, will help determine a unique and individualized concept direction. A new product will need to have a brand image and position created for it; an established product will need to have its image and position supported; and a mature or reinvented product may need its position altered in the target's mind, or its image rebuilt or reestablished. It's important to know what leaders in the product category are doing so your message can address or challenge them with its own unique image and voice, avoiding a "me, too" approach. It is also important for the target to know why your client's product is better than the competition.

The Key Benefit  The key benefit is the answer to the target's question *What's in it for me?* It is the one product or service feature and benefit combination that research has shown to be the most important to the targeted audience. All IMC communication efforts will focus on this feature and its corresponding benefit.

It's important that the creative team know enough about the product or service to be able to understand, define, and highlight the key benefit's inherent drama. The successful translation of this drama into a meaningful benefit tailor-made to fit the target's self-image and lifestyle will make the product or service memorable and it will stand out from the competition.

Advertising must be memorable in order to achieve the stated objectives. Memorable advertising will present a key benefit that will solve a target's problem or reflect a creative concept or idea that resonates with the target's lifestyle or self-image. For an ad to be memorable it must:

- Tell a visual and verbal story that can hold the target's attention
- Push one strong idea of special interest to the target: one that is important to the target, fulfills a need or want, and can be delivered both visually and verbally
- Clearly repeat the product name throughout the copy and represent it visually throughout the ad
- Use an appeal that matches the benefit and target audience profile
- Have a creative element or benefit that makes the ad stand out from other competitors in the brand category

**The Promotional Mix**  Once you have a thorough understanding of what you need to accomplish, who your target is, and what his motivation is to purchase, it's time to consider the best promotional mix to reach your target.

This section should give the creative team an idea of where the message will appear, since media choices often affect the overall message to be delivered. Choices beyond—or even instead of—traditional advertising can make it easier to reach your target audience during each step of the decision-making process.

How will you know which media within the promotional mix to use? Ask yourself the following questions:

*Public Relations*
- Is there something newsworthy about the product or service?
- Is it a new product launch?
- Is the product or service sponsoring any charitable events or opening new production facilities?
- How does the company fit into the local community? Are relations good or bad?

*Sales Promotion*
- Why do you need to give something away?
- Do you strategically need to increase short-term profits?
- Is this a new product launch, where samples or "try me" opportunities would increase awareness and/or sales?

*Direct Marketing*
- How well does the company know the target audience?
- Will addressing the target personally increase awareness or induce purchase?
- Is there access to a computer database of target names, interests, and past purchase history to make a personalized message relevant or motivational?
- Is this a product or service that lends itself to creating a long-term relationship?
- Is there a target or prospective target niche that has been overlooked by previous communication efforts that fit the target profile?

*Internet*

- Do members of the target audience have computers? If so, do they use it to seek out additional information and compare products?
- Is this a rational or life-sustaining purchase, like food or clothing, or is this a purely emotional or fun purchase?
- Is this a product that requires interaction with customer service or technical representatives?
- Does this product offer upgrades? Is there a need to update the consumer on product changes or uses, and can this be done through personalized e-mail notices?
- If dealing with multiple targets, can alternative information be delivered with greater frequency and with less expense electronically?
- The Internet takes a product or service global; is the company able to handle this volume of consumers and keep customer service initiatives high and delivery timely?

When used correctly, IMC should successfully integrate all messages throughout the promotional mix into one unified strategy.

## Strategy Statements That Get to the Point

An established client making minor changes to a product's performance or image does not require the same amount of research as a new product or client. Existing knowledge about the target and competition can be easily reexamined and reused to coordinate message and media needs. This type of situation will often require a simpler and more informal type of creative strategy statement that is not more than two to three sentences long and includes:

- The target audience to be reached
- The key benefit
- The objective or purpose of the communication message

Some creative strategies developed for corporate advertising may not use any of the above options and instead rely solely on the company's mission statement as a place to begin idea generation.

Execution of a creative strategy will be discussed in further detail in the discussion on creative briefs in chapter 5.

# 2

# IMC Marketing Plans

## The Role of the Marketing Plan

The marketing plan dissects the overall environment in which the product or service will be used. Before any creative executions can take place, the company must first determine what it is it wants to do, financially, strategically, and competitively.

A marketing plan is your client's business plan; it diagnoses the current market situation by looking at any internal and external factors that could affect a product's success. It is an internal document that outlines the company's strengths and weaknesses as well as the opportunities and threats affecting the product or service. A marketing plan determines marketing objectives, or what is to be accomplished; profiles the marketing strategy, or how objectives will be met; identifies the target audience; compares current competitive strategies; and determines implementation and evaluation tactics.

Without a marketing plan, the client cannot determine overall operating and business decisions or justify advertising spending.

Think of it this way: All advertising begins with a client that has a product or service they need to promote. In order to do this effectively and expeditiously, the client must know a few important facts first. To begin with, a thorough knowledge about the product or service is important when comparing its attributes to competing products or services. Next, the client needs to determine the target audience most likely to buy the product or use the service, and what product attributes the target likes or dislikes about competing products. Finally, the client must decide what kind of message strategy it will take to set its product apart from the competition.

All the questions and all the answers begin and end with research. Each section of the marketing plan must be carefully researched to determine current trends, attitudes, and both market and target needs. Any problematic areas or favorable trends that need to be addressed or exploited will need to be researched further.

## Where to Begin: Research

The organization of research takes place in the marketing plan. Research can be qualitative or quantitative in nature. Qualitative data employs the use of open-ended questions that can be distributed through interviews, convenience polling, and focus groups. A focus group gathers together a representative sample of the target audience, usually ten to twelve people, who will use or try the product in a controlled environment. Information gathered in a session can be used to determine creative development, product design, or the effectiveness of product attributes, to name just a few.

Quantitative data, on the other hand, is comprised of closed-ended or controlled surveys, where participants must choose their answers from a preselected set of responses. There are two types of surveys: formal and informal. Formal surveys include closed-ended questions where participants choose from a predetermined set of responses such as strongly agree, agree, disagree, and strongly disagree. Informal surveys are open-ended, allowing participants to give their opinions.

Surveys need not be completed in a sterile office environment; they can be conducted at malls and shopping centers, in parking lots, online, over the phone, or through the mail. Researchers should not concentrate their efforts on only one type of research technique but should consider using multiple options. Ultimately, the type of research performed will depend on what needs to be accomplished, the product or service to be advertised, and the target audience for the product or service.

Client input determines what type and how much information needs to be gathered. Once researchers know the questions that need to be answered, they have to determine if the information exists or needs to be gathered. There are two types of information available to researchers: primary and secondary data. Primary data does not exist and requires that original research be gathered from a variety of sources such as surveys, interviews, focus groups, observations, or experiments.

Secondary data is already available and can be found from external sources like the public library, websites, trade associations, and the U.S. Census, to name just a few.

Research is the foundation for the development of a marketing plan. The marketing plan solidifies the client's marketing goals or objectives, and serves as the launching pad for creative strategy development and all future communication efforts.

## What Does a Marketing Plan Do?

Simply put, a marketing plan is a comprehensive look at a business' place within its product category. Its primary function is to detail a business' strengths and weaknesses as compared to its competition and determine any opportunities or reveal any relevant threats within the marketplace. It also defines marketing or sales objectives and determines the appropriate marketing strategy needed to accomplish those objectives, defines the target to be addressed and the competition, and determines evaluative measures.

Developing a plan that incorporates input from their customers is the first step in developing a strong IMC plan. For the plan to be truly integrated, it must ensure all messages use the same tone of voice and are reflected in all internal and external communication. So if your client wants to increase sales, profits, and brand equity, it must have a plan that will specifically talk to the right audience, define the product and the competition, and offer a product that is unique and consistently reliable. A typical marketing plan is comprised of seven sections: For a sample marketing plan template see figure 2.1.

Let's take a quick look at the seven basic areas that make up a marketing plan.

---

- Situation Analysis
- Marketing Objectives
- Marketing Strategy
- Target Market Analysis

- Competitive Strategies
- Implementation Tactics
- Evaluation

---

**FIGURE 2.1**
Marketing Plan Template

Marketing plans differ from organization to organization and their appearance can vary as widely as its content. This example is only one way of developing a comprehensive marketing plan. The marketing plan should be as long as is necessary to understand the competition, the client, the target, and the marketing objectives and goals. All business documents should be double-spaced with at least one-inch margins on all four sides. Use either 10-point Helvetica or 11-point Times, respectively, to make reading easier. Be sure to number all pages.
Include the following when completing your marketing plan:

Name:
Date:
Assignment:
Situation Analysis:
Marketing Objectives:
Marketing Strategy:
Target Market:
Competitive Strategies:
Implementation Tactics:
Evaluation:

## Situation Analysis

The situation analysis looks at current marketing conditions and their possible effect on marketing efforts, and how factors in the marketplace can affect outcome. It is here that the product or service, the competition, the target audience, and any environmental, economic, legal, and political situations are dissected and analyzed.

Each of these factors can be broken down and examined further by developing a situation analysis, or SWOT. A situation analysis looks at a company's strengths (S) and weaknesses (W) as compared to the competition and any opportunities (O) and threats (T) to the product or service within the marketplace.

Further studies will compare and contrast current product features with those of the competition, analyze any previous communication efforts, and determine distribution needs.

A thorough look at the target market and any competitors' advertising efforts will help to determine how the situation analysis can be used, if the objectives can be met, or if any modifications will be needed.

## Marketing Objectives

From the data developed in the situation analysis, a set of marketing objectives will be devised to determine what the company wants to accomplish through its marketing activities. Over the next year, client objectives will concentrate on various financial outcomes such as sales or profit issues.

## Marketing Strategy

A marketing strategy determines what steps will need to be undertaken to accomplish the stated objectives. It is here where the marketing mix will first be identified.

**The Marketing Mix**  The marketing mix, also known as the *4 Ps*, is a brand's marketing plan of action and includes product, price, promotion, and distribution or "place." Each will play a vital role in message development.

1. *Product.* This specifically deals with anything that has to do with the product, including quality, features, packaging, servicing arrangements, and warranties.
2. *Price.* Any and all price issues are looked at here, such as payment terms, cash or credit options, and any discounts or sales materials.
3. *Promotion.* This deals with the communication or promotional mix, including public relations, advertising, sales promotion, direct marketing, and Internet marketing. The promotional mix provides a foundation for examining the best promotional options available to reach the target audience with the right message. As a part of the

marketing mix, it looks at what promotional vehicles are available for possible use, such as public relations, advertising, direct marketing, sales promotion, or Internet marketing. No matter how these different vehicles will be employed or combined for use, the goal is to reach the target with the right message.

4. *Distribution or "Place."* This deals with where the product will be available for purchase.

## Target Market Analysis

The more you know about who will be using your client's product, the better you can target your message directly to them. This section breaks down the intended target audience, those people research has determined are most likely to buy the product or use the service, into the following market segments: demographics, psychographics, geographics, and behavioristics. Segmentation can also be based on usage patterns, level of loyalty, and specific benefits.

Good ideas should talk to the target in words they can understand. To do this effectively we have to isolate target attributes in a more personalized way.

Demographics breaks down personal attributes such as age, sex, income, marital and professional status, occupation, education, and number of children.

Psychographics looks at the targets personal attributes that affect lifestyle, such as cultural, emotional, family, health, and social issues, as well as hobbies and overall beliefs. Psychographics affect how the consumer will view the product and advertising.

Geographics defines where the target lives, and how that affects who he is, how he thinks, his goals, and his limitations. Geographics can be broken down regionally, or by city, state, or ZIP code. Where a person lives often influences on the type of product he will buy and where the product should be advertised. A hard-laboring blue-collar worker might have different goals and limitations than a college graduate. They use and are exposed to different media and require different messages.

Behavioristic profiles look at why a person buys: Is it loyalty, social acceptance, brand name, or need?

When determining the correct target audience for your client's product or service, any one or combination of the above segmentation practices could be used. Answers found within these segments will determine both message content and media choice.

Demographic and geographic information is used to determine if the target market has sufficient disposable income available in order to purchase the product. Psychographic and behavioristic data is used in the creative development stage. Demographic, psychographic, behavioristic, and geographic information can be found by purchasing or using existing databases, surveys, or focus groups.

If IMC is to successfully build a relationship and develop advertising materials that are consumer focused, research needs to take a thorough look into the lives of your target audience. As discussed in chapter 1, it is just too expensive and wasteful to advertise to anyone who is not interested in buying or using a particular product or service. Because IMC is intended to develop a personal relationship and build a loyal client base, advertising must talk to those most likely to use the product or service.

In order to personalize a message we need to know what media they are most likely to use and what motivates and interests our target. The success or failure of advertising depends on whether the information gathered will help determine what kind of promotional mix will reach the target audience and what kind of message will solve their problem, address their image or social status issues, or satisfy any particular needs and wants.

Again, there may be times when you will need to divide a larger target audience into smaller market segments or secondary markets. For example, if your client is in jewelry and your primary market is eighteen- to thirty-four-year-old women, a good secondary market might be husbands, significant others, parents, or even grandparents. Each would require a creative approach unique to that market segment.

**How Are Target Audiences Chosen?**  It is important to find a reason a target audience needs the product or service you are trying to promote. What does the target want that is currently unavailable? How can your client's product or service meet that want? What does your client's product or service offer that the competition doesn't? Who are the people who are in need, how do they live, where do they live? What do they buy now? What are their purchase and media habits? These questions and more can be answered through target profiling.

In his book *Strategies for Implementing Integrated Marketing Communication*, Larry Percy lists five potential target audience groups broken down into two categories. Knowing where your target audience falls will decide message development and media choice.

*Noncustomer Groups*
- New category users—those trying the product for the first time
- Other brand loyals—those loyal to competitors' brands
- Other brand switchers—those who have loyalty to no particular brand and will switch based on a sale or promotion

*Customer Groups*
- Favorable brand switchers—those who favor the brand but will consider switching
- Brand loyals—those who are using the brand and will never switch

**Identifying Ethnic and Other Influential Consumer Groups**  When targeting for a new product you have to reflect both lifestyle and buying habits. Different target segments will look at new product launches differently, some more openly while others more skeptically. Each requires an approach that talks to their lifestyle. Knowing how your target audience thinks and acts, what their needs and wants are, what excites them and what offends them, makes addressing their issues and concerns easier. This knowledge helps in building a loyal customer base and allows the product or service to grow and change as the target changes.

Changes may be based on the growth of a specific ethnic group, age or purchasing power, geographic relocation, or a change in interests. No matter what the change may be, issues associated with these changes will affect ethnic and other influential consumer groups differently. In the United States, there are three very distinct ethnic groups beyond Caucasian: African Americans, Hispanics, and Asian Americans. Another influential demographic group is the baby boomers.

Each group, although also often part of a larger target profile, requires a message designed especially for them. Brand loyalty throughout ethnic and other influential groups is higher if communication efforts use members of the target group, are written in the group's native language, and appear in print or on a broadcast media targeted to the specific demographic group. Let's look at how these very different markets break down.

African Americans  According to the U.S. Census, blacks and African Americans make up just over 12 percent of the population. According to the latest edition of *The Buying Power of Black America*, African Americans spend more than any other ethnic group in almost all product and service categories, with a median income of just over $29,000 and rising. Additional statistics show African American women to be the leading force behind this spending growth. More than 17 percent of African Americans have a bachelor's or advanced degree and 72 percent own their own home. Almost half of the black or African American population is married with no children, allowing for discretionary buying. Major expenditures include food and clothing, cars, trucks, home decor, and travel.

Media use encompasses non-prime-time (94.6 percent), prime-time (86 percent), and cable television viewing (71.4 percent). Radio listening is at 84 percent, newspaper readership is at 83.4 percent, and Internet use is at 48.2 percent.

Hispanics  The Hispanic market includes Mexicans, Puerto Ricans, Cubans, and South Americans. The U.S. Census reports the Hispanic population at just over 14 percent. Hispanics are the fastest-growing ethnic group in the United States, with 75 percent of the population under age forty-five. More than 55 percent of Hispanic Americans are married, and Hispanics have the second-largest households overall with 3.25 members. The median household income is $33,103 and almost 12 percent are college graduates. Most, just over 70 percent, are bilingual.

Image is important to Hispanic consumers. They are impulsive buyers who are willing to try new brands, and will switch brands to keep up with current styles or if pop-culture dictates change. The most heavily purchased items include children's products, health and beauty aids, fashion, and personal electronics.

Media use encompasses non-prime-time (94.4 percent), prime-time (81.4 percent), and cable television viewing (69.9 percent). Radio listening is at 85.9 percent, newspaper readership is at 64.7 percent, and Internet use is at 47.4 percent. Young Hispanics, between eighteen and thirty-four, are heavy magazine readers.

Asian Americans  The Asian American population includes Chinese, Filipinos, Indians, Vietnamese, Koreans, and Japanese. The U.S. Census places the Asian American population at 4 percent. Asian Americans are the second-fastest-growing ethnic group and the most affluent ethnic group, with a median income of $52,626. They are also the most well educated, with almost 50 percent having college degrees. Asian Americans often have several generations living under one roof, making their overall household the largest family unit with 3.98 members.

Asian Americans are brand-conscious consumers, generally geographically concentrated, making them an easy and cost-effective group to reach.

Media use is less than other ethnic groups and includes non-prime-time (90.5 percent), prime-time (75.7 percent), and cable television viewing (68.3 percent). More than 78 percent listen to the radio, newspaper readership is at 69.8 percent, and 76.4 percent use the Internet Asian homes are the most "wired" and represent the greatest online use of any other ethnic group.

Baby Boomers  The aging baby boomers make up 28 percent of the U.S. population but have 50 percent of the discretionary income. This underprofiled demographic will make up 45 percent of the adult population by 2015. Baby boomers are the most affluent of any demographic segment, with an average income of $60,000. They hold the majority of all net worth at 91 percent.

This market is open to new brands and is willing to try new products. They purchase 41 percent of all new cars, represent 80 percent of all luxury travelers, and account for 65 percent of all cruise passengers. As grandparents they purchase 25 percent of all toys, and in general they spend more in virtually all categories.

The fifty-plus consumer is living longer, more physically active, better educated, and more financially secure than previous generations at this age. The majority of boomers are married, 80 percent own their own home, and another 80 percent are still employed. The majority of boomers are white, with only 8.1 percent being African American, 2.7 percent Asian American, and 5.5 percent Hispanic American.

The fifty-plus consumer watches more TV than eighteen- to forty-nine-year-olds, and spends more time online than teenagers, spending $7 billion online annually. Baby boomers routinely spend time listening to the radio and are heavy users of all forms of print. They are profuse catalog purchasers, which makes them a great direct mail target.

Baby boomers do not see themselves as old and worn out, but rather as healthy, independent, active, and successful, and advertising efforts should reflect that lifestyle.

As you think about the direction your advertising campaign will go, never lose sight of who your target audience is. They are the ones the advertising needs to reach and affect.

Talking to the right audience doesn't guarantee success if you have the wrong message in the wrong media, but it does highly increase the chances for success. The bottom line is that the creative team should know your target audience so well after reading the research, that they are able to address their creative efforts to an old friend.

## Competitive Strategies

Knowing what competitors are doing with advertising and product development is the difference between being a leader or a follower within a product category. Understanding the similarities and differences between a product and its leading competitors is crucial in order for a product to stand out from the competition in the mind of the targeted consumer.

## Implementation Tactics

Implementation tactics determine if everything can come off on schedule and in the right order, with the right materials in place, and with the proper people available to carry off the marketing efforts. Additionally, such items as scheduling, budgetary items, timelines, and information on enacting the marketing mix have to be discussed and developed.

## Evaluation

Evaluation takes place before the marketing plan is put into effect and again

### Narrowing the Target Down Further

Target audiences can be further broken down into small specialty and/or age groups. Some products never reach mainstream popularity but do have a very strong and loyal group of users. When advertising efforts concentrate specifically on winning the attention of a small group of mostly affluent consumers loyal to one specific product, it is known as niche marketing. The limited number of consumers keeps competitors from competing in the market or trying to copy the product because it would not be profitable.

Target audiences can be further classified into four distinct age groups. These groups respond to different kinds of advertising. Since they have social and financial differences, it is important to keep the group classifications in mind. Differentiating one target group of consumers from another is crucial.

- Matures: born 1909-1945
- Baby Boomers: born 1946-1964
- Generation X: born 1965-1984
- Generation Y or Millenniums: born 1985-present

after implementation to determine whether results in fact reflect corporate goals and whether objectives were successfully met. Evaluation is critical to a successful IMC program.

## The Creative Strategy and the Marketing Plan

Once you understand the corporate goals, it is time for agency executives to begin considering a creative strategy to direct results. Remember, a creative strategy is a synopsis of the product or service and the target audience. It should describe the key features of the product or service and define the overall benefits to the targeted audience.

The marketing plan should answer the target's main question: *What's in it for me?* There should be enough information in the marketing plan to identify a unique product feature or specific target need, and to start imagining creative direction.

# Branding and Positioning

## Defining a Brand, Its Image, and Its Worth

The American Marketing Association defines a brand as a "name, term, sign, symbol, or design, or a combination of them intended to identify the goods and services of one seller or group of sellers and to differentiate them from those of the competition." Quite simply, your brand *is* your product or service. Branding is a product's identity and its legacy. By building a strong brand image for a product or service, you give the product a personality, an image, and the single voice or message for the brand. This ultimately determines how the consumer thinks about the product or service and how it stands out from the competition. The more unique the persona you create, the more memorable the brand will be.

Target perception is only one aspect of a brand's image. Another key characteristic is brand and/or corporate reputation, or the ability to deliver a reliable performance from purchase to purchase. Repetitive results create repeat purchases and builds brand loyalty and brand equity.

Repetitive results relate directly to product performance. Over time, a product or service that has repeatedly proven itself to the consumer creates trust and goodwill. If a product is inconsistent or cannot deliver on the promise made in the advertising and promotional efforts, it can result in unfavorable reviews or bad word-of-mouth, one of the most powerful forms of communication. Think about it: How many people do you talk to in a day, a week, or a month? Consumers trust in the unbiased opinion given by friends, colleagues, or professionals over those they hear in advertising claims. Eventually, these repetitive negative comments will discourage repeat purchases and affect brand equity.

## Brand Equity: What Is Brand Equity?

Brand equity is a company's or product's reputation in the marketplace. Over time, a brand must repeatedly deliver reliable results to create trust between the target and the brand. Trust translates into brand loyalty and repeat sales.

From the consumer's perspective, brand equity means that consumers are familiar with the brand and know from experience that it brings positive results and unique brand associations. So to the consumer, brand equity is made up of two kinds of brand knowledge: brand awareness and brand image.

Brand equity is our perception of quality based on experience, often even before we buy a product. For example, Campbell's is a brand, even though it is not a specific product. We buy Campbell's chicken soup or tomato soup—a product—because we know it's a quality brand, and favor it over, say, a store brand. Consequently, Campbell's has more brand equity in the mind of the consumer than does a grocery store brand.

Once a product or service becomes so well known that its name is no longer its sole brand identity, other aspects of its package design or logo treatment, such as typeface, graphic symbol or color use, can be just as representative as the brand name. For example, most consumers can conjure up the Coke script, the Nike swoosh, or the Bayer yellow in their minds without the product in front of them. This is because those brands have equity or ownership of their product categories.

But being the recognizable face of a product category can have its drawbacks. For instance, a brand's equity can be threatened when its brand name becomes the noun used to describe all products within a category, such as Kleenex for all tissue products, Xerox for all photocopies, or Coke for all soda products. We have all been guilty of using one of the above brand names to represent a generic product. These companies have been almost too successful at building brand equity, setting themselves apart from the competition so well that their equity is being eroded away as the brand name becomes the representative for a product category or task.

IMC can be used to identify and turn around this generic use before a product's name becomes mainstream and loses its brand identity, its trademark protection, and target loyalty to the brand. This can be done by tackling the problem head-on in public relations announcements or through news or magazine feature articles. Advertising or direct marketing efforts can create awareness and reinforce not only product differences, but the relationship with the target.

## Brands: What's in a Name?

A brand is a product's name. Its image is created through advertising and often over a long period of time, becoming part of that brand's reputation. Brands are identifiers: Some are easy to acquire, while others we aspire to obtain because of the status they bring or the success they represent.

## Brand Awareness: Perception Is the Better Part of Advertising

It may seem obvious that before a brand can succeed, the target needs to be aware of its existence. But what is not always so obvious is that the target also needs to be aware of what the product or service has to offer, how it is different from competing brands, and how it can address the target's specific wants or needs. It is important that every product or service, whether new, old, or mainstream, know its own product attributes and perceived image before making any claims against or comparisons to competing brands.

Once your target is aware of the brand, the next logical step is for them to create a favorable opinion, based on the product, service, or corporation's reputation, advertised image, and/or its ability to fulfill a specific need or want.

### Brand Image

A brand's image is its personality and its status as compared to other brands of the same or similar quality in its category. Targets must decide whether they like it or don't like it, or whether they care about how influencers, whose opinions are valued, will think of them when seen using the product or service.

A brand's image is created and maintained by what we think about a product before and after use. Brand image is built in the media and maintained in the mind of the consumer based on quality or lack thereof. Brand image is based on consistency. Every time the product name is mentioned the consumer has an image or specific qualities associated with it.

A brand's personality must be built around the target's needs and wants. It should become a reliable old friend that does not change with each passing fad but can be trusted to bring home consistent results, purchase after purchase.

Most brands in a given product category are the same; it is easy in this day and age for companies to quickly create a product exactly like a successful competitor's, often at lower cost. But reputation cannot be replicated. Advertising should build on that. By creating a brand image or personality for your client's product, you can keep it standing apart from the competition. Make it more distinct through creative ideas, packaging, and logo design; make consumers see, hear, and feel the product before they need it through the use of distinctive typography, color, and slogans. If your client's product is the one they think of first and the one they trust, they will purchase and/or use it because it delivers on its advertised promises.

Image development begins by asking a few questions about the product: Is there anything holding back the brand, such as limited size or color choices? How much does the target already know about the product versus the competition? Is there any confusion that deals directly with the product's visual/verbal identity, purchasing options, or the product's life cycle stage?

## The Visual/Verbal Brand

Before a brand can achieve equity or develop or maintain loyalty, its product must first have a consistent brand image that can parallel the target audience's perceived image of themselves. This consistent identity begins with the development of a logo design that appears in all communication efforts and on all packaging. A product's visual/verbal identity should define not only its personality and/or image, but should represent a solution to the target's problem. Its distinctive look should be one of the factors that make the product or service stand out from its competition.

A brand's identifying symbol or logo design can include a representative typeface, color or colors, and graphic symbol that reflects the brand's personality and/or use. Another, more simple option might be nothing more than a simple black-and-white type treatment. A slogan or tagline representing the corporate or campaign philosophy may also accompany the symbol.

When producing multiple pieces for use in multiple media such as public relations, advertising, direct marketing, and sales promotion, it is imperative that the logo design be visible and consistent. Believe it or not, your target may not remember the name of the product, but he will remember the package, color(s), slogan, or logo and look for that when buying. Obviously, your promotional goal is to encourage name recognition, but color or logo recognition will do just as well.

Once the product or service has an individualized visual/verbal identity, image development must also take into account which life cycle phase the product or service is in: new, mainstream, or reinvention.

**New Brand** A new product will need to have an image developed for it that matches the target market's self-image and reflects their lifestyle. New products are a blank canvas that will, over time, need to develop brand equity and earn consumer loyalty. In order to create a competitive advantage, a new product must immediately distinguish its product advantages from those of its competition.

Determining which product advantage to promote will depend on the target, what the competition is doing, what needs to be accomplished, and the creative strategy used to influence the target. Considering these options, a product's advantages may be implied, found among its features and benefits, or based on price, status, or elitism. Additional advantages might center on the creation of a fad or trend, or they might be based entirely on emotional or rational needs. Creating brand awareness is critical to the success of a new product launch.

**Mainstream Brands** Once a brand has been established, communication efforts must work to consistently maintain awareness, reinforce quality and reliability, and continue building a relationship with the target.

**Reinvented Brands**  Reinvention can occur when a brand is in need of a new or updated image or as a result of a damaged reputation. A product's reinvention means looking past sins in the eye and eliminating outdated approaches that directly affect image and target perception. Products that are reinvented, no matter the reason, will have to prove themselves over time in order to rebuild lost equity and regain brand loyalty.

A product's creative message can focus on any one of, or a combination of, the following options when a product's life cycle stage will play an important role in advertising and promotional efforts.

1. *Brand Image.* How does the target audience view the product or service?
2. *Word-of-Mouth.* What kind of experience did the target audience have with the brand? Whether good or bad, their opinions carry a lot of weight with others within the target group.
3. *Positioning.* What does the target think about the product or service as compared to the competition?
4. *Education.* How will the product be used? Is it expensive, professional, or technical?
5. *Brand Awareness.* What does the target audience know about the product or service?
6. *Promotional Offers.* Do you need to create involvement, through coupons, contests, or samples?
7. *Creating a Reaction.* Do you need to get the target to come in to a showroom to try the product, or visit a website for more information or to make a purchase?
8. *Direct Comparison to the Competition.* Will your point be stronger if a direct comparison of features is made to those of the competition?
9. *Use.* Is the product or service revolutionary? Is it easy or difficult to use?
10. *Product Introduction.* Where is the target's knowledge? Is the product new, old, or considered a reliable old standard?

The bottom line is, no matter what life cycle stage your product or service is in, for it to become or stay successful the target must believe the message and relate to the image.

## Brand Loyalty

Brand loyalty refers to the relationship between the product and the target. Brand loyalty—the target's dependable repurchase of a brand based on favorable and reliable past experiences—is critical to IMC and brand equity. It is important that all advertising and promotional efforts represent the product as it is, not as an exaggeration of what it is. This is the best way to build and maintain brand loyalty, which in turn leads to brand equity.

Band loyalty is built on trust and the knowledge the product will deliver what it promises every time it is purchased or used.

Remember, objectives determine what you want to accomplish with your advertising. The product's position in its life cycle will determine what those objectives are as they relate to brand development, maintenance, or reinvention.

Brand-loyal consumers require less coaxing to repurchase. With the cost of advertising in today's market it is (or it should be) every client's goal to build brand loyalty by targeting their advertising efforts to the right audience, providing consistency of product, and building a brand image consistent with the product's use and/or personality—and then maintain it. The more intimate the relationship between the target and a brand the less likely they are to be affected by competitive promotions.

## Positioning

Positioning relates to how the consumer thinks about and rates your product or service against the competition. Positioning requires highlighting target-relevant benefits for the product's features. Benefits must be tied to uses that will enhance the target's lifestyle or image. The position of a brand is sometimes confused with brand image; a brand's position in the mind of the consumer is created via advertising and promotion, and brand image created based on experience.

Positioning is effective only if fully researched. You must *know*—not think you know—how the consumer thinks and feels about the product or service. Ask yourself a few questions: Who is most likely to use the product or service? What are the benefits to your target of using the product? How does the product stand up against its competition: what makes it unique; what features are duplicated? What is the perceived value of the product within the marketplace? How will the product be made available to the target? Does it come in different sizes, colors, or price ranges? Is it relevant to the target?

One of the ways to break through the advertising clutter is to find out what makes your clients's product or service unique and position the product directly against the competition's image. If communication efforts can prove your client's product is bigger, faster, or longer lasting than the competing brand, it is more likely to be noticed and remembered.

It's important to understand that your client's product is probably not the only product of its kind; it is most probably one of many virtually identical products in the category. To make it stand out from the crowd you must carve out a niche or position for the product. Today, the majority of products are no longer mass advertised, but rather, as discussed earlier, advertising vehicles are more selectively targeted to eliminate media waste.

A strong position is a direct result of a strong brand. This position is built up over a period of time based on reliability of performance. Branding gives a product or service an air of exclusivity and a unique identity from its competitors within the product category.

Successful, memorable advertising begins with an established position. Once a product's identity is established and accepted, consumers remember it and use it as a measurement device for all other competitors within the category. Measurement may be based on quality, convenience, reliability, or service, to name just a few.

Brand image helps to determine the product's position. This is because positioning deals with who the target audience is, what they currently think about the product, who the competition is and what the target thinks about them, and, finally, what features are relevant to the target. Once you know this, you can determine and communicate positioning strategies.

In his article "How to Position Your Product," Luc Dupont outlines the seven ways to position a product or service:

1. *Originality*. Being first at anything is a short-lived boast, but if your client's product is, you can use it to set the product up as unique.
2. *Low Price*. Less expensive does not necessarily mean lesser quality. A low price can be a selling point if the consumer is convinced of the product's value.
3. *High Price*. More expensive does not necessarily mean high quality, so the target must be convinced an expensive product is worth the investment.
4. *Sex of the Consumer*. Not all products are made for both sexes. There are razors especially designed for women and others designed especially for men; fragrances are also gender based, such as colognes for men and perfumes for women.
5. *Age of the Consumer*. Few products appeal to consumers of all ages, so it is important to consider the age of your target audience. Baggy jeans are for teens; Dockers are for the upwardly mobile professional. A Volkswagen Beetle appeals to a younger audience, whereas a Mercedes reflects status and/or success.
6. *Time of Day the Product Should Be Used*. Some products are intended for use at specific times of the day, such as cereal for breakfast, soup for lunch, frozen entrees for dinner, or popcorn as a late-night snack.
7. *Distribution Channels*. This relates to how the consumer will receive the product. Examples include ordering through a website or direct marketing efforts delivered through the mail versus the need to visit a showroom.

Al Ries and Jack Trout, specialists in positioning, sum it up this way: "In the communications jungle out there, the only hope to score big is to be selective, to concentrate on narrow targets, [and] practice segmentation. In a word, positioning."

## Repositioning

A product needs to be repositioned when you want to change the way it is viewed in the mind of your target. Changing perception is much more difficult than working with an existing position or creating a new one. Repositioning should work to define a new or special niche in a consumer's mind.

## Tweaking the Marketing Plan

Successful campaigns can run and should run for years, continually striving to build both brand loyalty and brand equity. Change should be considered only when the product or company significantly changes. Today's advertised messages often change with the seasons, leaving little time for awareness or loyalty to emerge. The inconsistent repositioning of brands or repeated challenges to competing brands can affect the target's image of the product or service. Products that are patient, and work at building loyalty over time, will find competitors' constant change less of a factor in building and maintaining brand equity.

# Creative Briefs

## The Big Influence Inside a Small Document

The creative brief, also known as a copy platform, creative work plan, creative plan or copy strategy, is the next step in the evolution of the creative strategy. Information from the marketing plan is used in the creative brief to outline the communications plan of attack.

A small internal document created by the account executive, the creative brief should dissect the product or service for the creative team. It should redefine the target audience, introduce the key benefit, describe the individual features and consumer benefits, define objectives, address the competition, and outline tactics. It is the encyclopedia the creative team will use to define the integrated marketing communication (IMC) message that needs to be communicated. Think of it as a set of building blocks, meticulously laying the foundation for the concept or idea that will become the visual/verbal message.

The creative brief is not a document that speculates or generalizes; it needs to be detailed and concise enough that the creative team of art directors and copywriters can develop a creative solution for the client's communication problem. A creative brief also ensures that the creative team, the account executive, and the client all have a thorough understanding of exactly what objectives communication efforts need to accomplish.

First and foremost, the creative brief is a business plan that provides the guidelines for developing the creative message. It is not a creative outlet: you are not writing copy or defining or determining what creative should look like. It is a road map for idea generation and visual/verbal development.

There is no exact length for creative briefs. The only absolute is that it must contain all the information the creative team needs to inspire ideas and keep them focused on what problems need to be solved.

# What Makes Up a Creative Brief?

Overall length, information content, and format vary by agency, but most creative briefs contain at a minimum the following.

- Target Audience Profile
- Communication Objectives
- Product Features and Benefits
- Positioning of the Product
- Key Consumer Benefit

- Creative Strategy
- Tone
- Support Statement
- Slogan or Tagline
- Logo

**FIGURE 4.1**
Creative Brief Template

The purpose of the creative brief is to provide a blueprint for creating an effective ad or campaign. Preparing a brief forces you to learn essential information about your brand and its situation and can inspire your creativity. There are a number of ways to present a brief; our example brief is in two columns: one for headings, the second for information or instructions. Place one inch of space between columns, with one-inch margins on all four sides. The creative brief should be double-spaced. Information about the product, target audience and competitors, and so on must be gathered before you can write a good brief. If you don't collect the necessary information, the brief is useless and your ad is unlikely to be successful.

Target Audience Profile:    Define your target audience in terms of

- Demographics
- Psychographics
- Geographics
- Behavioristics

Identify common key internal and external factors in your target audience's frame of reference. Profile a typical target audience member.

Communication Objectives:    Describe what the ad is supposed to accomplish in terms of what the consumer should

- Think
- Feel
- Do

Is the ad intended to build brand awareness (think)? Are you trying to change consumers' attitudes toward the brand (feel)? Do you want the consumer to seek additional information by calling a toll-free number or visiting a website or make a purchase (do)?

These are communication-based objectives. Explain your choices.

**Product Features and Benefits:** List every attribute of the product (feature) and the benefit that results from each. Attributes can be inherent in the product (e.g., ingredients) or be aspects of the image of the brand (e.g., Rolex). List as many features and benefits as are needed to educate the creative team about the product or service. Set up each benefit and feature within this section in the following way:

- Feature: In one sentence, tell me what the feature is.
- Benefit: In one sentence, tell me what the benefit of the above feature is to the target audience.

Repeat this format for each feature and benefit.

**Positioning of the Product:** Briefly compare and contrast your client's product to its major competitors. Describe any advertising messages used currently or recently for competing brands.

**Key Consumer Benefit:** Choose either a USP or a big idea. Justify your choice based on everything you've mentioned above. This section should be no more than one to two sentences in length.

**Creative Strategy:** Explain how the ad will convince the audience to select your client's brand over others. Spell out how the objectives will be met. Select a strategy appeal or appeals and one or more approach(es) and explain your choice(s).

**Tone:** How will you execute your strategy? What execution technique will be used? Will it be humor, emotions, facts? Explain direction based on what is presented in USP/Big Idea and Strategy sections.

**Support Statement:** Based on your benefits and features section which point is second in importance to your USP or big idea. This benefit/feature combination should directly support your key benefit or USP or big idea.

**Slogan or Tagline:** Include the company's slogan or tagline here. It represents the company's or ads image and philosophy. Knowing it can help with creative direction.

**Logo:** Place the name of the client, product or service here.

## Target Audience Profile

Redefine the target audience here. Remember, the target audience consists of those consumers determined through research to be the most likely to buy or use your client's product or service. They should be characterized in living detail through demographics, psychographics, geographics, and behavioristics.

The goal of advertising is not only to inform but also to find just the right way to inspire your target to act. When developing a creative direction it's important that the creative team never lose sight of who the target is. Your target audience is the reason you are developing communication efforts. You must know how they will react to your message in order to successfully advertise any product. Just knowing what the target thinks, what he finds important and how the product or service can fulfill his needs and wants, makes creating the right message a lot easier. You can strike out by communicating to the masses with a generalized message or you can hit the ball out of the park with an individualized, consumer-focused message.

## Communication Objectives

Communication objectives, or goals, clearly define what the communication efforts need to accomplish. Objectives should pinpoint what you want the target to think about the product or service, what you want the target to feel when using the product or feel toward the product overall, and what you want the target to do, such as make a purchase or request additional information.

There is a limit to what can be accomplished with one ad or even a campaign. On the average, no product or service should have more than three to five obtainable objectives. Each objective needs to focus on communication-related issues. Communication-based objectives give consumers usable, personalized information, as opposed to marketing-based objectives that are sales related. Primarily, creative efforts will focus on positioning objectives that inform and educate the consumer about the product or service as compared to its competition. It is important when determining objectives to know your target's level of knowledge abut the product or service. A look at the product or service's life cycle stage will also be beneficial when determining what needs to be said or shown; what needs to be introduced, maintained or expanded; and what needs to be overhauled completely. This will affect whether objectives can be accomplished over the short or long term.

Think of it this way: If you have a new product launch or are reinventing a brand, a relationship must be built first on image and then trust. So the first thing you need to accomplish is to position the brand in the mind of the consumer while working to build brand awareness. Over time, the objective is to achieve loyalty, and eventually, brand equity.

This type of traditionally based or mass media advertising is known as brand image advertising. To be successful, all objectives must translate to results.

## Product Features and Benefits

The features and benefits section looks at product attributes and attaches them to target needs and wants. One mistake young account executives or designers often make is to sell a product's features and not its benefits. A feature is a product attribute; a benefit answers the question *What's in it for me?*

Features are lovely, but have no point. The point that needs to be hammered home is what the feature can offer the consumer. Determining a benefit for each of your product's features helps break down the product information into smaller, more manageable bundles, giving concept development a visual/verbal starting point.

Look at figure 4.2 for an example of features and benefits for a toaster. If the product comes in five colors (feature), the creative brief should inform the creative team by listing all five colors. Research gathered on the target audience might suggest to the creative team that the target is upwardly mobile and might have just bought a new home, is on a budget and will be remodeling, or is trendy and just likes to keep up with the most current look in decorating. A benefit that informs the target there's a color that matches any decorating scheme or considers family size by featuring two-, four-, or six-slice models talks to the consumer's current needs.

Benefits can deal with either product feature/benefits or consumer feature/benefits. Features can be inherent in the product (e.g., ingredients) or imply that the status or image of the brand (e.g., Rolex) can affect the consumer's personal image or lifestyle.

Everything the creative team needs to know in order to write and design the visual/verbal message needs to be included in this section. That includes pricing issues and any detail copy such as address, phone, fax, e-mail, hours, or credit card information. This is also where any specific information covering coupons or order forms should be included.

**FIGURE 4.2**
Sample Features/Benefits

| | |
|---|---|
| Feature: | It comes in five different colors: red, green, blue, yellow, and orange. |
| Benefit: | Makes coordination with your kitchen color theme easier. |
| Feature: | Comes in two-, four-, or six-slice models. |
| Benefit: | No matter what size of family you have to feed, there is a toaster size that makes it faster and easier. |

## Positioning of the Product

Next, the creative brief should briefly discuss the brands that represent direct competition to your client's brand. Compare and contrast each product's similarities and differences as compared to your client's brand, and explain how your target audience sees each brand. Rate your client's brand against its direct competitors based on brand image, positioning, and so on. Describe any advertising messages used currently or recently by competing brands.

This section will help keep the creative team from duplicating what competitors are saying and doing with their promotional efforts. In order to chose a key benefit and determine the best way to make a product stand out from the competition, it is important to know what competitors are doing.

## Key Consumer Benefit

The key consumer benefit is the one feature/benefit combination that either is unique to your client's product or can be positioned as big or important. The key benefit will be the point that screams from every ad, either visually or verbally, positioning the product as the one that meets your target's internal and external needs. It will become the one voice of your IMC message and should be chosen because research has determined that it is important to the target audience and will speak directly to their interests and lifestyle, encouraging some sort of desired action.

There are two types of key benefits: the unique selling proposition (USP) or the big idea. The big idea or USP is determined by analyzing the target market and determining which key benefit can accomplish the stated objectives. It will be the tie that binds all advertising and promotional efforts together. Along with the strategy, the USP or big idea will help determine the visual/verbal direction the communication efforts will take.

**A Unique but Big Selling Idea** Determining whether to use a USP or a big idea depends on what the product or service has to say about itself as compared to the competition and whether the target audience thinks its benefits will enhance their lives. If the product or service speaks of individualism or uniqueness, or is the first to introduce a product or feature, the best key benefit to use would be a USP Products that have no outstanding or unique characteristics to differentiate it from the competition will need a big idea. A big idea takes the feature/benefit combination and turns it into a memorable idea that sells.

A USP has a feature/benefit combination that is unique or exclusive to your client's product or service. USPs are also used in promoting a commonplace feature as unique. If competitors have products with an identical feature but are not advertising it, make the feature unique by making it important to the target and use it to stand out from the competition. For example, all microwaves may have a plug, but no one has found a unique way to make their product's plug a creative symbol. Differentiation can come from a creative idea touching a known interest with the target, fulfilling a need, or creating a status symbol.

**The Big Idea** A big idea is a creative solution that sets your client's product off from the competition while at the same time solving the client's advertising problem. This does not mean the competition does not have the identical feature, only that they are not pushing it in their advertising. Big ideas that are consumer focused or based on lifestyle will have more longevity than product-oriented ideas. This is because concepts based on lifestyle are more difficult for the competition to duplicate. When using a big idea, creativity is the key to success.

Finding inspiration for a big idea is a little more difficult than determining a USP. The big idea most often has to create something unique and interesting out of nothing in order to attract attention and create a relationship with the target. But by focusing on the consumer and his lifestyle, you can make even a generic product feature alter a target's existing view of a product. The key is to shape it into an unusual, different, or interesting benefit that will catch the target's attention. There are several places to look for a big idea:

- Life (your imagination)
- Creative Strategy
- Product Name
- Product Use
- Product Appearance
- Product Features
- Product Comparison
- The News
- Pop Culture (books, movies)
- Historical Reference

A product or service will never stand out from the competition or build brand loyalty if the USP or big idea has a "me, too" message or "been there, done that" creative. A product must have an identity and offer personalized benefits the target can relate to and a creative approach that offers the target a reason to try it.

In the next step, the creative team will combine the big idea or USP and the strategy to get an idea of what needs to be accomplished creatively in order to create a consistent, memorable, informative, and beneficial idea that touches the target and can transfer easily between media vehicles.

## Creative Strategy

The creative strategy is the foundation for the creative direction or concept. Strategy tells the creative team how it will talk to the target and accomplish the stated objectives, and the best way to feature the key benefit. The strategy's main objective is to discuss how advertising and promotional efforts will position the brand and how it will compete against other products in the same category. Your client's product must be made to step up and away from the competition in a way that is important to your target. If research, media, and creative efforts reflect the strategy, a successful outcome is within reach.

The strategy employed by communication efforts is critical to accomplishing brand differentiation. Brand positioning engenders brand awareness by creating a brand image that is important to the target. Only through research can we determine what these influencers or specific factors are. Advertising clutter can influence these factors.

One of the best ways to make a brand stand out from competing products is to employ a positioning strategy. This is, quite simply, how the product is looked at as compared to its competition. In order to favorably position the product in the mind of the consumer, you must determine what factors or benefits are important to your target and build your message around that. Another option is to use a brand strategy. Branding develops a personality for a product or service that creates a favorable relationship between product value and target need. Building brand loyalty through quality or reliability ensures the product is the only purchase option in the mind of the consumer, leading to repeat purchase.

There are several decisions you need to make before deciding on a strategy direction. The first is what approach will be used to determine how the product or service will be positioned, the second is what kind of appeal will be used to reach the target, and the third is the execution technique or tone that will be used to make the appeal.

Many factors can affect the creative strategy. One of the most important is the life cycle stage of the product or service. Many communication obstacles can be overcome and opportunities can be exploited by considering and using this information. During a product launch, building brand awareness is one of the most important steps; as interest in the brand grows, building awareness plays less of a role.

The next phase outlines the product's benefits over the competition. As the product's status and/or reputation solidifies, building brand equity or owning a large share of the product category is important. It is also important to keep the target up to date on any product or technological changes associated with the brand. Finally, ensuring brand loyalty takes repeated efforts to deliver a quality and reliable product.

The creative team uses the creative strategy section to determine the approach and the appeal combination that will be used to determine the look and overall tone the creative message will take. The approach chosen can focus on the product, the consumer, or the objectives, while the appeal looks at whether the product or service will fulfill an emotional or rational need. Every concept will be built around the choice of approach, appeal, and tone or execution technique.

We will focus on two different types of strategic approaches. The first concentrates on using either a consumer or product-oriented approach. The second uses the think/feel/do model to define objectives.

**Product or Consumer-Oriented Strategic Approaches**  Once you determine whether the focus will be placed on the product, the consumer, or the desired consumer reaction, you can begin to flesh out the concept direction. There are several different ways an ad's message can be approached; most can be categorized as having either a product- or consumer-oriented focus. The appeal used will be based on the approach that will be stressed:

- A product-oriented approach focuses on one or more feature(s)/benefit(s) of the product.
- A consumer-oriented approach focuses on shaping consumer attitudes about new and existing products and demonstrating how the product can solve a problem.

**Product-Oriented Strategy**  A product-oriented approach can focus on four different areas: generic claim, product feature, USP, or positioning.

- *Generic Claim*. Pushes a product category rather than a specific product.
- *Product Feature*. Pushes one specific feature of the product—ideally one unique to the product—in all advertising and promotional efforts.
- *Unique Selling Proposition (USP)*. Pushes a unique product benefit important to the target market.
- *Positioning*. Focuses on how the target thinks about the product or service as compared to the competition.

**Consumer-Oriented Strategy**  A consumer-oriented approach can focus on three major areas: brand image, lifestyle, and attitude.

- *Brand Image*. Creates an image or builds a personality for the product.
- *Lifestyle*. Affiliates the product with the lifestyle of the target.
- *Attitude*. Affiliates the product with feelings, attitudes, and overall benefits of use.

It is not uncommon to use a combination of approaches. Strategies under each approach can be used individually or combined.

**Think/Feel/Do Strategic Approaches**  Another way to define the strategic direction is to work directly off the desired consumer reaction defined in the objectives.

***Think Message Strategies*** Think message strategies are used to evoke identity, image, or message and can focus on three different areas: brand identity, generic, and positioning.

- *Brand Identity.* A product or service is so established and well known that it can be identified solely by its logo treatment or package alone.
- *Generic.* If the product or service has no unique characteristics to set it apart from the competition, it is important to take a feature/benefit combination not being promoted by competitors and make it appear unique to the product and important to the target.
- *Positioning.* Deals with how the target currently views the product or service as compared to the competition. These views may need to be created, enhanced, maintained or reinvented depending on the products life cycle.

***Feel Message Strategies*** Feel message strategies are used to create emotional or fact-based responses and can focus on six different areas: brand image, association, lifestyle, attitude, respectability, and significance.

- *Brand Image.* What do you want the target to think about the product?
- *Association.* What association does using this product or service create between the product's image and the target's self-image?
- *Lifestyle.* What can this product do for the target?
- *Attitude.* What feelings can be created through use of the product to create an emotional tie with the target?
- *Respectability.* What do users of the product have to say about it? Testimonials are a great way to highlight the quality of new products, to alleviate fears about products with potential risks, or to repair a bruised or damaged image.
- *Significance.* What features and benefits are relevant to the target? This approach is useful for brands that are unique from the competition or that offer features and benefits not inherent in the competition. Creative solutions are the key here. This is a great way to build status or to give importance to previously ignored features. Creative solutions could be used to build status or introduce uses to features never before seen as relevant.

***Do Message Strategies*** Do message strategies are used to incite action and can focus on four different areas: promotional response, memorable reaction, incentive programs, and interaction.

- *Promotional Response.* The competition has one-upped your client. To bring the target's attention back to your client's product, you offer an incentive to create immediate purchase, offsetting the competition's position of power.

- *Memorable Reaction.* Used to remind the target audience of their past history with a mature brand.
- *Incentive Programs.* Offer a reward to the consumer with repeat purchase. Incentive programs are great for building brand loyalty.
- *Interaction.* Create dialogue between the manufacturer and the target. The target is able to get additional information, give feedback, or make a purchase directly from the seller.

The strategic approach you decide to use will depend on the product or service, the target audience, the key benefit, the overall objectives, and the appeal and execution package employed.

**The Appeal of the Message**   Once you have determined whether you will be using a consumer-, product-, or objective-oriented approach, the next step is to determine the appeal or feel.

An ad's job is to persuade. Whether it is successful or not depends on the type of appeal used. There are two types of appeals: emotional and rational. Consumer response depends upon whether the product fills an emotional need or a rational need. Many advertising efforts will employ the use of both appeals.

Emotional needs include lifestyle enhancers such as cars, iPods, jewelry, and fashion. Emotional appeals target image and are used on status-related products. These ads appeal to the target's need to fit in, be a trendsetter, or stand out from the crowd.

Rational needs are life sustaining, like food and clothing. Rational appeals are information based, using facts, charts, or expert opinions to back up claims. These ads are meant to educate the consumer on the product's use, quality, and value.

Appeals are used to attract consumer attention and influence the perception of need for a product. The focus is most often placed on the consumer's need for or use of the product and/or how it will affect the consumer's lifestyle. Message content reflects on the features and benefits of a product or service. Often emotional appeals will work better on brands that have little or no differentiation from competing brands, since communication efforts are more creative and memorable and build image based on the target's psychological and/or social needs.

Since emotional appeals deal with how the target views self-image as compared with the product or service's image, both the strategy and message content can be more creative and less rational or functional, focusing on personal pleasure. If the message will focus on lifestyle or feelings, consider the following options: achievement, affection, ambition, comfort, excitement, fear, happiness, joy, love, nostalgia, pleasure, pride, safety, security, self-esteem, sentimentality, or sadness. Strategies focusing on social or image based emotions might focus on acceptance, approval, belonging, embarrassment, involvement, recognition, rejection, respect, and social status or class.

Rational appeals can take several different forms: feature, competitive, price, news, and image appeals. Feature appeals focus on the most important trait of the product or service. Competitive appeals make comparisons to other brands in order to point out important or differentiating features. Price appeals use a products price as a differentiating feature. News appeals give some kind of news about the product, perhaps a new and improved version or a technological advancement or upgrade. Image appeals stress a brand's status or popularity within its category or among other users. Some of the most common informational or rational motives for purchase include comfort, convenience, dependability, durability, economy, efficiency, health, performance, and quality.

If the product or service doesn't fit snuggly into either the rational or emotional appeal categories, there are alternative appeals to consider. Reminder advertising is used to maintain brand awareness for more mature products. Teaser advertising is used mostly for new product launches to increase curiosity and building interest in a new product before launch. Information is used to tease consumers about the product without showing it.

## Tone

An extension of the creative strategy section, the tone or execution technique defines the personality and overall voice or style you want your advertising message to portray. The only rule is that it should reflect the key consumer benefit.

Once the approach and the appeal have been solidified it's important to determine how the information will be delivered. The execution style or technique is the development of the visual and verbal tone, what it will look and sound like or the overall way the ad will be presented to the target.

The tone should be outlined in a couple of sentences that describe the product's personality and the attitude, mood, or spirit of the ad or campaign as presented in the key benefit and strategy sections. This personality can be either stated or visualized in the advertised message. It is important to remember that the style of language used flags or attracts consumer attention based on quality, fun, or status as much as any visual can.

Questions to consider when determining tone include: Will the overall visual/verbal message be conceptually emotional or rational in tone? Will the focus be on the product or the consumer? What role if any should the competition play? Where is the product or service in its lifecycle? Should the tone of the message be hard sell, soft sell, or more visually enticing in nature?

The visual/verbal tone used to address the target audience has to be very effective because if the target audience does not connect with the product, there is a good chance that they will not be buying it. By now the creative team should be able to determine how that connection can be developed and how the target will respond to humor, facts, or testimonials. Is the product or service newsworthy, can it teach the target something, or will consumers be more interested in a demonstration? Whatever tone you take, it should work toward creating or supporting the brand's image, promoting the key benefit, and advancing the strategy.

The technique chosen should be the tie that binds the approach and appeal together. In order to visually and verbally get your key benefit across, consider some of the following techniques.

---

*Rational Tone*
- Straight Sell or Factual Message
- Technical or Scientific
- Demonstration
- Comparison
- Testimonial
- News Event or Educational
- Authoritative
- Reminder
- Teaser
- Instructional
- Talking Head
- Dialogue
- Lifestyle and Narrative

*Emotional Tones*
- Humor
- Fantasy
- Animation
- Slice-of-life
- Fear
- Sex
- Fantasy
- Scarcity

*Combination Tones*
- Character Representative or Personality Symbol
- Product Feature or Product as the Star
- Inherent Drama
- Music

---

It's important to note that the appeal and execution technique may change depending on whether communication efforts are talking to the primary or secondary targets or influencers. The key is that they must consistently focus on the key benefit each time the specific audience sees the communicated message.

## Support Statement

The support statement is one feature/benefit combination that can be used to directly support or advance the key benefit. Consider the toaster example used in figure 4.1 with regard to color and kitchen decor. If this becomes the key benefit, then the support statement for the two-, four-, or six-slice toaster could address how much counter space is required for use or how it's stylish design is contemporary enough to complement any decorating scheme.

## Slogan or Tagline

Often used interchangeably, the slogan and the tagline are associated with the logo and appear either above it or below it. A slogan deals with the company or corporate philosophy and a tagline defines the campaign or ad philosophy.

## Logo

The logo is the product or corporate symbol. It could be a simple graphic, a line of text, simple initials, or a combination of both a graphic and text. Always be sure to put the logo on the creative brief. It is helpful for the creative team to know for whom they are working.

When all is said and done, the job of the creative brief is to summarize goals, facts, features and benefits, and strategic goals for the creative team. No creative direction should be offered, but the facts will help define creative direction. The next step is conceptual development or the idea stage. How will the information presented be used to meet the stated objectives? What will be said, how will it be said, how will it be shown, how will it be laid out on the page? The creative brief is a blueprint; it is the creative team's job to build the house and organize the details.

# Left- and Right-Brain Selling Points

## Left Brain versus Right Brain: A Thought

By understanding how consumers think, act, and feel, we can more accurately target our communication message to meet their needs. These needs are controlled by the brain, which is divided into two halves, the left and the right.

The left side of the brain controls reading and verbal skills, as well as logical and rational thought processes, making an individual's outlook more conservative. This is the side that tells you not to step out in front of a moving vehicle or that you need a parachute when jumping from an airplane. The left side of the brain is also responsible for math skills and the ability to remember facts, names, and vocabulary.

The right side of the brain is the more passive, liberal, emotional, and visual side. Its strengths include a vivid imagination, musical and artistic abilities, and a more open-minded outlook.

The right-brained individual needs to see a message repeatedly, in multiple forms of media, before reacting to that message. The left-brained individual often responds to a message by researching a product or service more thoroughly through customer service calls, annual or consumer reports, or the Internet. Most of us are neither completely right- or left-brained; rather, we use some abilities of both sides of our brain.

It is critical that these left- and right-brained attributes be taken into consideration when creating visual/verbal relationships in advertising design. The more left-brained individual relies on facts to make a decision, making copy important. The more right-brained individual relies more on the visual aspects of the ad. The overall creative message needs to appeal to both kinds of individuals within our target audience.

Initially, the basic needs for each of these individuals differ. If, for example, you are advertising a car, the left-brained consumer will be more interested in facts such as gas mileage and safety features, whereas the right-brained consumer will be more interested in aesthetics. It's not that right-brainers don't care about safety or that left-brainers don't care about what the car looks like; they're just not the first or most important things they consider.

---

### Selling a Car to Both Sides of the Brain

| Left Side | Right Side |
|---|---|
| Mileage | Color |
| Safety | Style |
| Reliability | Upholstery |

---

One way to create a strong visual/verbal relationship that immediately attracts the attention of both types is to use a strong headline explaining a consumer benefit accompanied by an answering visual, attracting the left-brainer with words and the right-brainer with pictures. Another option is to attract the right-brainer with copy that paints a visual picture; if you intersperse relevant facts within the visual copy this will also attract the left-brainer. This type of approach is particularly important for new product introductions, additions, and upgrades.

The more knowledge you have about the product, client, target, and competition, the more ammunition you have for creative ingenuity.

## Word Lists

The best place to start when trying to develop a great idea is to begin with what I refer to as a word list. A word list gets both sides of your brain working. Believe it or not, there are multiple ideas amid your gray matter; you just need to get them out of there and into reality. It's also important to realize that great ideas, for the most part, do not just pop into your head. They often come in bits and pieces that come at the most unlikely of times and places—in a business meeting, the subway, or the shower.

A word list starts the brainstorming process. This is the best way to experience how consumers think; at the same time, it helps build your conceptual skills. A word list is composed of three columns or parts.

See figure 5.1 for a complete example of a word list, using an orange as the product. The first column represents the left-brain. Here is where you list the facts about the product or service.

**FIGURE 5.1**

Example of a Finished Word List

| Orange | Sunshine | HOT, HOT, HOT, TASTE. |
|---|---|---|
| Round | Navel | Show a human navel, talk about the connection to Mother Earth. |
| Sour | Face Contortion | Show varied people's reaction to their first bite of an orange. |
| Slice | Saw<br>Knife<br>Teeth | No matter how you slice it . . . Show the options being used on an orange. |

*Fact Column One:*
Orange
Round
Sour
Slice

In the second or middle column, choose a descriptive or visual word to represent each product/service fact used listed in column one. (A thesaurus works great for assistance and can be a big help with column two.). This column should lead to previously "unthought-of" directions. Here is where "been there, done that" or old ideas go to die.

*Fact Column Two:*
Sunshine
Navel
Face Contortion
Saw
Knife
Teeth

The third column is where you describe how the combinations of the first two columns might be used in an ad. Ask yourself questions. Consider the five Ws—*who, what, when, where, why*—and don't forget *how*. Create a scenario for use either visually or verbally.

*Fact Column Three:*
HOT, HOT, HOT, TASTE.
Show a human navel, talk about connection to Mother Earth.
Show varied people's reaction to their first bite of an orange.
No matter how you slice it . . . show the options being used on an orange.

This column, representing right-brain traits, should create something we can feel, taste, or just genuinely experience. Set up your word list so the words are aligned across the page from left to right; one or more ideas can be expressed in any column for any word.

## Are Word Lists Really Useful?

Why do a word list? It opens up your imagination and teaches you to think visually and relate verbally. Word lists help you spark an often dormant imagination while at the same time building your word power. This is a way to communicate to both sides of your target's brain. A good word list should include twenty to twenty-five words and visual representations.

The goal of all creative is to develop an image or express an idea that is unique to your client. "Been there, done that" creative is eliminated when you explore some of your infinite options. That means conservative views must sometimes step aside and let the liberal ideas step up. For instance, would you have chosen a duck to sell insurance or used Frankenstein to sell joint cream? Would you have chosen instead to use a pitchman talking about protecting your family or show a bunch of athletes sitting around talking about pain? Exercising your infinite options really puts a new spin on "never been there, never done that," doesn't it?

Breaking concept ideas down to one or two words helps you to focus on the point you're trying to make. One way to break out of "been there, done that"—the conservative approach to advertising syndrome—is to create and live a little inside your word list.

## Visual/Verbal Relationships

By working with a descriptive word list you will learn to hone your imagination and gain an understanding of just how much thought needs to go into bringing a product to life both visually and verbally.

In a nutshell, visual/verbal relationships answer the question *Does what you're showing in your ad have anything to do with what you're saying in your ad?* If so, both the left- and right-brained consumers in your target audience will understand your message and act upon it by calling a toll-free number, surfing the Web for more information, and ultimately making a purchase. If not, you have an ad that is not speaking in the integrated marketing communication (IMC) model of one voice used both visually and verbally.

Knowing about how the brain works is important to the communications process because both kinds of users will be a part of the target audience. Some will be more visual while others will be more fact or verbal based. Every message in every medium will need to communicate to both types of thinkers.

Remember, for the left-brained consumer the copy is more important than the visual. These consumers want details, not generalities, about the product or service you are promoting. The right-brained consumer, on the other hand, is drawn to the visual or bright colors. It's not that these consumers are not interested in facts, it just won't be what grabs their attention. Alternately, the left-brained consumer will want to know what the car would look like before buying, it's just not as important as gas mileage, warranties, or performance statistics.

So how do you appeal to both in promotional efforts? The easiest way is to write statistical copy to reach left-brainers and show interesting and/or colorful visuals to attract right-brainers. But the most creative way is to write copy that tells a visual story about how the product performs, or feels, with statistical information weaved in throughout. The visual should *show* the visual/verbal copy in action. This inspires the target to think about how the car will affect or influence his life, how it will fit into his budget, and what it will feel like to drive, as well as concerns such as reliability, additional colors, interior specifics, and so on, thus moving him to acquire additional information.

## Visual Cues versus Verbal Cues

Words by themselves or visuals without direction cannot sell anything. Both the left- and right-brained members of your target need to be hit by the one-two punch of a cohesive visual/verbal message. Even if you have little or no copy on the page, the logo, slogan, or tagline must speak volumes. Once you decide what the product's key benefit is—what will be stressed in the ad—and what your strategy will be, you must write a headline that creatively presents that idea. The visual chosen for the ad must represent that idea. It is the visual/verbal unit that will powerfully and successfully knock out the competition. The key benefit strategically represented by a cohesive visual/verbal message will become the advertising concept.

It is also important to consider what part of its life cycle the product is in when deciding on the most appropriate visual/verbal message. Is it a new product launch, a current product favorite, or a struggling wannabe; is it a mature or well-known old friend; or does it need to be repositioned in the consumer's mind as a result of product inconsistencies or consumer bias that it is old-fashioned?

## Constructing Visual/Verbal Cues

The construction of a visual cue rests with one very important design principle: eye flow. Where do you want the target's eye to land within the ad, and where do you want it to go next. This requires knowing what you want your target to focus on in the first place, and what kind of relationship you want the visual to have with what is being said in the ad. Let's take a look at some possible visual cues.

- *Key Benefit*. The key benefit is the one product feature that will be stressed in your IMC efforts.
- *Framing*. The visual cue can be highlighted by placing it within horizontal and vertical lines, such as a doorway or window. The frame need not be traditional; any

kind of line—curved, wiggly, or angular—will work, so long as it can enclose or pin-point the image.

- *Placement.* Placement deals with where the product is in relationship to the camera. Is a close-up required to show detail, or a long shot to show scope? Will a profile work, or will a head-on shot tell the consumer more? Placement defines how much the consumer needs to see to understand what is being said.
- *Arrangement.* Arrangement deals with composition, or where the product is placed in relationship to other items or other people in the ad. There are three levels to all images: the foreground, the middle ground, and the background. Making use of these areas can help to place a product in a setting, physically tie the image to the copy, or create ambiance. The key is to use what you have and create what you need to produce the required environment to help project an image, feeling, or use.
- *Lighting.* Light reflects emotion. Sunlight is happy, sunsets are romantic, and a dimly lit room is relaxing. Pools or streaks of light create natural eye flow and can be used to draw the eye to some important point, like the copy, product, or logo.
- *Color.* Color also reflects emotion. Soft colors relax; bright colors energize. Red is hot, green is earthy, and black is elegant. Strategically placed color can draw the eye to an important spot, such as the product or logo. When black-and-white photographs feature a spot of color, the result is referred to as spot color. This is an excellent way to highlight the product by making it stand out in contrast to the rest of the photograph. Spot color can give a visual the illusion of three-dimensionality. The lack of color can also draw the eye, such as with a black-and-white photo used in a medium heavily saturated with color visuals, which creates a striking contrast.

Now that we have discussed the visual cues, what can be done to tie them to the verbal message?

- *Logo.* One verbal message that crosses the boundary into the visual arena is the product or company logo. A logo is the symbol (visual) that represents a product or company name (verbal).
- *Slogans or Taglines.* The logo can also have an accompanying slogan or tagline (verbal) that represents the company's philosophy (slogan) or the campaign's key benefit (tagline).
- *Headline.* What the visual shows, the headline needs to explain. The headline is the largest piece of copy on the page. It needs to grab the target's attention by screaming out a consumer benefit associated with your key benefit. It should talk directly to the target market and should play a huge role in tying the strategy together.
- *Body Copy.* The body copy will continue the story began in the headline. If you can keep your target's eye moving through the ad to the body copy your ad has done its

job: It has grabbed the attention of those most likely to buy or use your product or service. Body copy is ultimately where the sale will be made.

The visual you choose should radiate the concept and product personality. The concept will further be developed by the type of visual presentation you choose to use, such as an illustration, color or black-and-white photograph, or line art.

The headline's visual punch should relate the message in its entirety with the details left to the copy. At a glance your target should know *What's in it for me?*—what the product or service offers her personally.

Your visual approach will depend on your target market. Visuals that show the product alone, in a setting, or in use will get the job done without a lot of creative flair. Use visuals that interest your target and look to your psychographic and demographic profiles to find ones that will both grab their attention and support the headline. Keeping your target audience in mind will keep your visual/verbal message on target.

If the headline is what stops a left-brainer, the visual will draw the right-brainer. The overall layout of the ad should combine elements attractive to both sides to draw them into the ad and thus into the body copy to complete the sale.

## Cause and Effect

Consumers purchase products for any number of reasons. The verbal left-brainer spends time doing research before undertaking any purchase. The visual right-brainer is more impulsive and buys based on feelings and/or need.

Consumer behavior can be defined as the response to a message or visual that ignites a need, want, or emotional interest in any attainable product or service.

Ideally, purchase decisions are made in a logical manner with the study of a product's features and an understanding of the benefits they will bring to the consumer. Satisfaction with a purchase is the ultimate outcome, with the product supplying an answer or solution to the target's perceived problem.

Triggers that affect purchase decisions include:

- Need
- Research
- Purchase
- Reflection

## Need

The need for a product or service can be either rational or emotional. Rational needs deal with life's most basic issues, such as food and shelter. Emotional needs deal with lifestyle issues, often involving image or status, and are made to make the target feel or look better to themselves and others.

## Research

Information gathering begins with an interest in a product or service and the hope that it can fulfill a need or solve a problem. Research can be undertaken in any number of ways: through expert or professional advice; advice from colleagues, friends and/or family; product comparisons; or the Internet.

## Purchase

Beyond emotional or rational needs, purchases can also be triggered by factors such as price, purchase options, location, color, size, and so on. The ultimate goal of all advertising efforts is to get the target to take some kind of action, such as to call, write, or come into the showroom or store for more information—or, best of all scenarios, to make a purchase. If the product or service can solve a problem for the target, the right brain will kick in to purchase or the left brain will be motivated to seek out additional information.

## Reflection

Was it worth it? Remember, building brand loyalty is the ultimate goal of IMC, so the product must live up to the consumer's expectations and encourage repurchase. The more expensive the product, the more reflection will take place. Buyer's remorse is often an expected outcome, known as cognitive dissonance. Cognitive dissonance is the guilt or anxiety associated with decisions concerning extravagant or excessive purchases. It is the role of advertising to anticipate and alleviate these fears by addressing them pre-purchase in copy or guarantees, and post-purchase via follow-up customer service calls or surveys.

## It's Cluttered Out There— How Do I Get Attention?

This is a good question. To break through the jam-packed advertising highway, advertisers must address the important visual/verbal cues that attract left- and right-brained consumers. How do these two types of cues affect purchase?

Peripheral cues are what catches our attention. Some examples include jingles, creative graphics, abundant use of white space, character-based spokespersons (human or animated), and humorous situations. Factual clues give the target relevant information or research that will solve a problem.

For low-involvement products such as light bulbs and band-aids, peripheral clues will address visual involvement. For high-involvement products such as cars and jewelry, factual clues will address verbal involvement.

What are the visual/verbal cues used in IMC?

- *Culture.* Culture reflects lifestyle. It includes such visual things as clothing trends, hairstyles, and traditions.
- *Values.* Values might be expressed both visually and verbally in terms of family, society, or political issues.
- *Rituals.* Rituals are a systematic, visually symbolic set of events that take place at predetermined intervals, such as turkey at Thanksgiving and party hats and noisemakers at New Year's.
- *Social Class.* Not all target groups or products are created equal. Social class can visually be represented by layout style or price or place of distribution.
- *Family.* Any and all purchases made are based on necessity, lifestyle, or standard of living, such as food or clothing, rather than want alone.
- *Influencers.* Those people the target might turn to for advice or see as role models, such as family, friends, professionals, or celebrities.
- *What's "In"?* Advertising sets trends for the public and gives personality and social status to a brand. What's "in" for this season begins with advertising.

The more you know about how your targeted audience will react to visual/verbal cues, the more effective your message will be at inspiring the target to act upon the message and begin the process of building a lasting target to product relationship.

## Building Target/Product Relationships

Building a relationship between the target and a product or service is like building a personal relationship. On the one hand, the target must trust the product to do what it says it will, and considers it reliable. On the other hand, the target will ask, "What's in it for me?" The answer may be that the product or service will build or sustain personal image, increase self-esteem, address a special interest, reinforce an image of success and wealth, or create a sense of belonging. Whatever it is, it must exist and flourish within the product. There are four possible ways to build a relationship with your target.

- Prolonged Inquiry
- Minimal Inquiry
- Customary Inquiry
- Repeat Purchase or Brand Loyalty

## Prolonged Inquiry

Prolonged inquiry is usually associated with higher-priced products or those affecting social status. The first step is to acknowledge a need and the second step is to determine a foundation for purchase. Once the target has determined a need, he will exhaust all research options before deciding to purchase.

## Minimal Inquiry

Minimal inquiry requires little or no thought or research and usually deals with everyday types of products. Without motivation or personal involvement, the target will usually select the first product she encounters that will fill her need or solve her problem.

## Customary Inquiries

Customary inquiries are typical when the target has a history with the product, and thus little thought is given or required for a repeat purchase.

## Repeat Purchase or Brand Loyalty

The repeat purchaser, or brand-loyal customer, knows and has developed a relationship with the product, and automatically repurchases it.

Delivering an informative visual/verbal message determines how the product or service will be positioned in the mind of the target audience. It is the first step to laying the foundation for repurchase by eventual brand-loyal customers.

# The Creative Process

L ET'S TAKE a break from all this business and strategizing and take a look at the
creative process.

## The Creative Brief Is the Inspiration behind a Good Idea

There is no document that outlines the creative concept or idea development stage. The
documents we have looked at—the marketing plan and creative brief—concentrate on
marketing assessments and an overall communication profile.

Creative, its interpretation and its ultimate ability to produce a sale, is the driving force
behind any integrated marketing communication (IMC) ad or campaign. If creative efforts
fail, it is because the marketing plan failed. The fate of an ad or a campaign is sealed during
the development of the creative brief.

Everything creative—copy and layout—begins and ends with the creative brief. Before
any brainstorming takes place, before any copy is written or any concept laid out, the creative team needs to thoroughly study the creative brief.

The creative brief lays an informational foundation for the creative team to build upon. It
outlines what the IMC creative efforts need to accomplish and is the rationale behind creative
direction. The creative team will use the knowledge about the target to define the audience they
are talking to. Objectives will determine what the creative efforts will need to accomplish; the
strategy and positioning will help determine how the message will be delivered and the image
and position needed to stand out from the competition. The key benefit will become the voice
of the IMC promotion and must dominate all creative executions, both visually and verbally.

A great idea can usually be stated in one sentence: the key benefit. It is what you do with that sentence to bring the idea alive that creates memorable ideas.

## How Do You Translate Business Thought to Creative Execution?

The best place to start when trying to develop a great idea is to begin with a word list, as discussed in chapter 5. A word list gets both your left- and right-brain working. It is important to realize that for the most part, a great idea will not just pop into your head. Great ideas most often come in bits and pieces that will come together at the most unlikely of times. It pays to be prepared and have pen and paper available to corral brilliance when it does come.

All creative efforts must be written and designed specifically for your target audience, in a vernacular, or language, they can understand about problems or situations they can relate to, and appear in a medium they frequently see.

There is a lot of bad advertising out there, with no direction, no strong brand identity, and no defined target audience. This kind of advertising usually carries what I call a "been there, done that" creative label. This means the idea has been used before—sometimes many, many times. How many times do consumers have to see creative teams animate the Statue of Liberty—or worse yet, make the Mona Lisa smile—for yet another product?

When you've seen something once, it's interesting; when you've seen it two or three times, it's boring. Once consumers are bored, they stop paying attention to the message.

Today's consumer is bombarded with hundreds of advertising messages each day. A good creative team recognizes this and looks for an innovative way to make their product stand out among the clutter. GEICO did it with the "Gecko" campaign, and Aflac did it with the "Duck" campaign.

## The Soccer Game of Idea Teamwork

Once the creative team has decided on a creative direction, the next step is determining a visual/verbal solution that will bring the idea to life. Coming up with that extraordinary idea is not as easy as most people think it is. It involves using both sides of the brain effectively. As the left side sorts out all the research you've collected or digests the creative brief, the right side begins the imagination process.

An active imagination is commendable, but it is fallible, and not every idea will be a good idea. However, believing your ideas are the best ideas is the only way to approach the creative process. Fortunately—or unfortunately, depending on how you look at it—there are always other people around to deny or confirm our brilliance. An idea needs to bounce around in your head, and once you've got it under control, it needs to be bounced off a colleague before it can be molded into a good idea. This may seem a little like a soccer match, with balls hitting everyone in the head a few times. You need a partner to play the idea game; this is why creatives often work in teams.

The creative team is made up of an art director—a visual right-brainer—and one or more copywriters, the verbal left-brainers. This team is responsible for developing the idea, writing the ad copy, and designing ads that bring the key benefit to life. The creative team takes these ideas and designs them to each media vehicle's strengths and limitations. When left- and right-brained people work together, visual and verbal communication becomes a powerful problem-solving combination.

## Who Are the Creatives?

Creative as used in this text is a broad term for the conceptual process. A creative is a person who is involved in creative activity, especially, in this context, involving the creation of advertisements. The creative team is comprised of some very eclectic personalities. Job titles, which are as diverse as the personalities that fill them, depend on where you are in the country and on the size of the agency. I will talk here only about the most common and generally accepted titles.

- *Creative Director.* This title probably varies most across the country, but basically this person is the boss or team leader. He or she handles administrative and/or management functions and is most often involved with television and other high-profile projects.
- *Art Director.* Job titles range from junior through senior levels. This person is the workhorse of the advertising agency, with their hands in everything. On any given day the art director could be working on newspaper, magazine, point-of-purchase (POP) advertising, direct mail, or television for any number of clients. The person in this position needs to know a lot about the creative process, from conceptual development to photo shoots to production.
- *Copywriter.* These team members write copy, and, like art directors, may have a range of titles. Copywriters can find themselves writing copy for multiple media vehicles and even more diverse types of products.

The art director is the visual idea person. The copywriter is the verbal idea person. These two diverse minds sit down together with the creative brief in what are known as brainstorming sessions. These sessions are used to generate multiple ideas that will solve the client's advertising problem. Hundreds of good and bad ideas are presented for discussion; most will be discarded but many will be worked on and developed further.

Anyone associated with a creative team must be open-minded and well versed in social behaviors, current issues, politics, movies, music, and the classics. They should be able to use anything from historical references or present-day slang to sell or represent a product or service. These brainstorming sessions are critical to getting boring "been there, done that" ideas out of your head and get down to the new, the unusual, and the eventually successful ideas.

New ideas set a product apart from its competitors and can be the catalyst to building lasting brand images and an ultimate and essential position in the minds of the consumer.

The key to a good brainstorming session is to never be afraid to look and feel stupid and to come up with a really, really bad idea. It's humbling but necessary in order to ignite the ideas of others in the session: One really bad thought voiced aloud can spark another—hopefully better—idea in another.

Stale advertising begins and ends with stale ideas. Most young creatives believe their first idea is their best idea, but it's only their best idea because it's their *only* idea. Test the waters stretch your legs, you will be surprised where you end up.

The creative cylinders that must be firing to be a successful copywriter or art director include the following:

- Be able to see what is not there. If a product comes in six colors, what does that represent: a canvas, an oil spill, a sunset?
- Never linger in one place too long. A creative solution is often elusive and must be chased down through the clutter of one's own mind. Staring off into space, acting out, or borrowing the actions from the guy on the subway might evoke new ideas.
- Know your profession. What is old can be made new again, but it should not be copied if it is already associated with another product. Using nostalgia in your message can make a point; copying a competitor can be confusing.
- Be a student of media. Watch TV; go to mainstream and independent movies; pick up a book, newspaper, or magazine and read up on current and historical events; watch for fads and trends; watch the fashion wheel of fortune; listen to the radio. Knowing and interpreting what's going on in society helps you set new trends rather than having to follow them.
- Watch the human species. We're interesting, we're unique, and we can relate to each other's mannerisms, body language, style or lack thereof, eye movement, and hand gestures, or how different personalities and age groups move, eat, sit, stare, and read.
- Know your product. If you haven't used the product, do so. If you are unfamiliar with competing products, use them and compare. You can only sell well a product you are intimate with. Knowledge is power, so empower yourself and you will be able to ignite action and interest under your target audience.
- Understand that advertising is a business. Creative is based on a business plan, it must be on strategy and meet the stated objectives, and be on budget. You will never get to do what you want. Accept that great ideas are not hindered by limitations, but challenged by them.
- Excellence should come with the territory. If you can't spell or lack grammatical skills, copywriting may not be in your future. If you are visually impaired and have never had an interesting or unique thought, art direction may not be the profession to pursue. Clients pay out large sums of money for the expertise advertising brings to the table.

Because of this the competition is fierce, the life span short, and the stress high. It's what makes the profession a compelling one.

- Cry a little, laugh a lot. The creative process is a tough one. The chance of anyone liking your ideas in their original form is slim to none. Changes are a fact of life; rejection of ideas is right up there with death and taxes. Get over it. When an idea does take form and fly, it's like birthing a baby: initially you don't want to do it again, but once you see its personality, you can't wait to start all over again.

Creative doesn't happen in a vacuum, it takes long hours and a lot of reworking before an idea can be presented, first internally to the team and then eventually to the client. Because the creative process takes place toward the end of the advertising process, time is limited. Brilliance may have as little as a few hours, to as much as three to four weeks, to show itself. Any creative team member must be able to turn on the creative juices in a moments notice and for long hours at a time. You must be willing to fight for what you believe in, but also be able to let those ideas that just don't measure up go, and live to fight another day. Stress should be considered a creative catalyst, not a paralyzing force.

Because of these unique challenges, creatives are pretty well left alone to come and go as they please, and to work in as creative and individualistic environment as possible.

## Are You On Target?

An effective IMC creative series must be on target both visually and verbally throughout the promotional mix. The creative team must ask themselves throughout the creative development stages whether the creative is still on target with the stated objectives. Is the creative strategy effectively reflecting those objectives? Does the tone, approach, and appeal decided upon for copy and visual images used reflect the strategy? Has the creative brief successfully dissected the product or service in order to understand its features and benefits? Is the visual/verbal message screaming out the key benefit? Does the concept position the product or service away from the competition? Are consumers being reached in a language they can understand and with an image they can relate to? Is the key benefit clearly apparent across all media? Does the promotional mix reflect media the target is sure to see? If you answered yes to all of the above questions, you are on target. If the visual look and the verbal message are inconsistent, and the key benefit is not apparent on all pieces, the creative is off target or off strategy.

Great concepts and successful creative must be on target. Advertising that is off target can be very entertaining, often even brilliant, but if it doesn't create sales and raise awareness, it's useless.

If staring out the window or shooting baskets in your office motivates you, more power to you. Perhaps darts or Nerf basketball is more to your creative liking. Whatever gets the creative juices squeezed can be found in any creative department.

## Where Does a Good Idea Originate?

The creative brief begins the idea generation stage. All great ads begin with a good idea. A good idea can come from an overactive imagination, pain, observation, experience, or just plain luck. It is the thing that drives concept. All good designers need to be culturally diverse, open-minded, and have an overactive imagination. This realm of endless possibilities, this dream state, is the place to define and build ideas. Go beyond the MTV culture and look at the world as it once was and as it is. What was is very important in defining what is.

Go outside your immediate likes and dislikes. Start with music, and experience new sounds like those from the archives of rock, jazz, blues, or country. Music is a powerful weapon; everyone relates to it in one way or another. Music makes listeners active participants, whether they're reminiscing or singing along.

Next, go to museums and art galleries to see how art, like advertising, marks history and defines cultures and attitudes. Attend independent film festivals, another cultural marker; note how your peers speak and represent culture, both past and present. Go to the park or the mall and people watch; play with a child; talk to the elderly. Don't define or label anything you see: just experience it. After all, if we want our advertising to touch our readers', viewers', or listeners' taste buds or fashion consciousness, we need to understand their world.

Readers and viewers alike respond to stimulants, whether they're reminded of something from their childhood or college days, or something they haven't yet experienced but wish to. If you plant the thought, the consumer will decide whether or not to experience your idea.

Your imaginative thoughts will eventually lay the groundwork for an idea. That idea will need to be developed into a concept direction for your client's product or service. All great ads begin by developing, producing, and then eliminating hundreds of ideas that just didn't measure up. Open your conservative mind, and your liberal imagination will follow.

Daydreaming and role-playing are a designer's first line of defense when struggling to solve a client's advertising problem, and is actually an important part of the design process. Those carefree dreams acted out in the backyard—when you imagined yourself a pilot, astronaut, explorer, princess, clown, or juggler—are just waiting to be resurrected. Feel free to act up and act out. Jump aboard that broomstick horse; rebuild that impenetrable fort made of boxes, sticks, and whatever was leftover from Mom and Dad's last home improvement idea. Or run outside or look out the window and excavate that passing cloud for a recognizable image. As an adult, you'll find these are the kinds of thoughts and acts that inspire award-winning ads and memorable slogans.

All that said, the problem is that most of us have had imagination beat out of us in the formative years of our schooling—the years when our imagination is the most active and inventive. Reignite your imagination and pump up your dreams, because creativity requires a bizarre and innovative thinker, a trendsetter and fad developer.

It's time to reacquaint yourself with your inner child. Instead of feeling ridiculous acting out your innermost creative thoughts, feel inspired.

## The Creative Concept

Creative concept is an idea that imaginatively solves the client's advertising problem. Coming up with a brilliant and effective idea takes a lot of hard work. Before you can isolate one great idea, you must pursue many mediocre ones. Conceptual development or "brainstorming" is a process that starts when you kick your imagination into overdrive and expose the "unthought-of."

### Brainstorming

Brainstorming is your imagination at work. In the process, good ideas, partial ideas, and bad ideas are considered, developed further, or thrown out.

Brainstorming is still done the old-fashioned way—from gray cells to mouth to paper. Brainstorming sessions may be comprised of a creative team of copywriters and art directors, or they may involve a solitary session in which you allow your thoughts to mature. Nothing is set in stone, apart from the product's features, so as not to limit the number of ideas the session may generate.

There is no set way that creatives brainstorm ideas; the main goal is to discuss the creative brief and imagine a way to solve a problem. Within the key benefit lies the product's inherent drama. What makes it tick? What aspects are interesting or unusual? How will it benefit the target audience? Brainstorming isolates that benefit and places it within various scenarios that have meaning to your target audience. The result should cause them to think. People don't pay attention to abstract ideas; they pay attention to realism, and they want to know *What's in it for me?*—how the product or service can solve their personal problem or need.

A traditional brainstorming session may begin with a copywriter throwing out a headline to promote the key benefit while the art director, with drawing pad and marker in hand, quickly roughs out a visual that supports the headline. On the average, a creative team can come up with anywhere from fifty to one hundred ideas per session. Of course, not all of these ideas will be brilliant. Some ideas are weak, some too complicated, others just plain stupid—but each one inspires another direction or even the possible combination of ideas.

The next step is to search for quality in the quantity. Ideas with potential will eventually be reworked and narrowed down to three to five ideas or concepts that are presented to the client.

**How Do You Know a Creative Idea When You Think of It?**  Here's another good question. The short answer is that if you've seen it done before, it's no longer creative. It's that "been there, done that" thing again. Once an idea becomes mainstream, it won't hold the target's interest the way a new and innovative approach will.

You will recognize a good idea when it comes along, basically, because it doesn't stink as bad as the rest. It's also dead-on strategy, features the key benefit, and meets the goals laid out in the objectives.

Ideas can come from anywhere. You might see something relevant on the street, or overhear a devastatingly good conversation on the bus or at a coffee shop. Cocktail conversation is often enlightening, and nothing can compete with basic personal experience or a good discussion about the product itself. Talk about it, think about it, question it, position it, brand it, place it in a relevant setting (or even an irrelevant one), let it stand alone, compare it to the competition, show before-and-after results, twist it or bend it—but make it your own. When enlightenment finally does come—and it will come—pounce on it.

**Enemies To Creativity**  The biggest enemy to creativity is the lack of exploration. If you take shortcuts, failing to fully research both your client and the competition, your ideas will lack focus and be unimaginative.

Great ideas take a lot of work, and once you think you've found a direction that will solve the client's problem, you'll do a lot of reworking to perfect it.

## The Image behind the Layout Style

An ad's personality can be expressed through the layout style, or how its elements are featured in the design. What does your concept say about itself? Will you be using lots of white space, for an elegant feel? Will you insert a dominant photograph to draw the viewer's attention? Are you incorporating multiple small illustrations, scattered throughout the copy, to instruct the viewer how to use the product or service? Do you want to section off the ad to show the viewer multiple benefits?

Think of layout styles as the clothes for your concept. Does it shout sporty, sophisticated, or modern? Does it demand attention through words, or is a visual worth a thousand words? When you're designing, it's doubly important to consider what you want the ad to project visually to the consumer as well as what it says. Let's look at nine of the most commonly used layout styles.

| | |
|---|---|
| • Big Type | • Multipanel |
| • Circus | • Picture Window |
| • Copy Heavy | • Rebus |
| • Frame | • Silhouette |
| • Mondrian | |

**Big Type**  The big-type layout style is used when the headline is the focal point of the ad. If the product or service can boast a definitive consumer benefit, then the ad should shout that benefit from the rooftop in very large type. Visuals play a secondary role here. The ad's beauty and appeal are defined by the typeface and what it says. The size and weight of type will often vary, but it should project a distinct pattern. The static appearance of this layout style is very clean and concise. Type works as a graphic, creating mood. If pictures are included, they are small and do not compete with what is being said. If you love the shape, texture, and movement of type, the opportunities to use it as a graphic, verbal element are wide open in this layout style.

**Circus**  The circus layout style uses everything from the designer's arsenal in the ad. It is not unusual to see multiple type sizes and faces, with assorted snipes and bursts (bold, black callouts) touting grand openings and sale dates in brazenly reversed text. In this layout, there are always too many unrelated visuals to even think about grouping them in an organized fashion. These ads scream chaos; the key to making it work is controlling that chaos. Consider using a grid layout, combining or grouping elements to focus on one dominant image. Try to create as much white space as is humanly possible. This attempt at structure aids in manipulating the viewer's eye movement in a more controlled fashion, guiding them to move from element to element without missing anything. Structure also alleviates that floating look and grounds the design, giving it more power.

**Copy Heavy**  Headlines and visuals take a backseat in the copy-heavy layout style. Instead, the focus is on the body copy. A large amount of body copy is used to introduce a product or service. Visuals, if present, are small and are used to show the product or logo.

**Frame**  Frame layouts are most often featured in newspaper advertising, where it is important to isolate the ad from surrounding text. Frames or borders can be of any weight or design, and often define ad size. Frames can be simple, unobtrusive lines, pinstriped, detailed, created via colored backgrounds, or illustrative. Frames can also be used around small photographs or copy points to draw the viewer's eye to them.

**Mondrian**  Following the style of the works of Dutch painter Piet Mondrian, the Mondrian layout style screams sections. Here, multiple geometric blocks of text, graphic shapes, color, and/or shaded areas are used to separate parts of the ad and guide the reader through the ad. Each geometrically or organically shaped section focuses on an element within the ad. This layout style uses bold shapes and color to stand out among the clutter of other ads. By isolating single elements, the designer ensures that each element is viewed independently. Solid geometric shapes, such as circles, squares, rectangles, triangles, and lines, are used to further isolate specific sections, but give the ad an almost three-dimensional feel when they are strategically placed near large areas of white space. By placing bright colors within selected shapes, or reversing text out of a colored background, you can draw the reader's eye—so show or say something important here.

**Multipanel**  The multipanel layout style uses pictures with captions to tell a story or feature multiple products in boxes of equal size. These boxes are placed side by side, either butted up against each other or separated by a small amount of white space. Smaller inset photographs can be placed over one large photograph to point out details. Body copy often is replaced with copy captions, located either within the panels or under each picture. This layout style works very well when showing is more important than telling, when comparing one product to another, or when bringing a television storyboard to print.

**Picture Window**  The picture window layout style features one large photograph, often with the headline overprinted. Type can be a solid color, or it can be reversed out of the background. This layout style is best used when you want the reader to participate in the photo, such as when using a headline that helps to place the reader in the photograph. For example, you might have a visual of a lake with a sailboat and a headline that asks "Wish You Were Here?"

**Rebus**  The rebus layout style is usually crammed full with visuals. Working in tandem with the body copy, visuals are often placed within the text to help illustrate the story. Pictures can also be used as substitutes for words within headlines. This is an elegant layout style and lends itself well to instructional copy, where a picture can be used to demonstrate copy points. Text can be wrapped around images, visually isolating the content from what is being shown. Visuals can be repetitive in size or alternate from small to large in order to create focal points.

**Silhouette**  The silhouette layout style relies on the grouping of visual elements within an ad. The group of items becomes the dominant element within the ad. A large amount of white space usually surrounds the grouped items, setting them off even more. This layout style works great when you are featuring multiple products within an ad. By grouping elements in pleasing and even irregular shapes, you give weight to the visuals and create a logical path for the viewer's eye to follow through the ad.

   If you have type that must accompany each element, consider using callouts. A callout is a small amount of copy appearing alongside or below an individual image and connected by a small line. The text is descriptive and might feature price points. This works well when the visual breaks up the headline or the copy, or when type is slightly overlaid on a visual, or vice versa. White space is at a premium when items are grouped together. At times the silhouette layout style can just be too static; to alter its symmetrical appearance, consider allowing items to touch the edges of the ad in opposing spots.

## Elements That Make Up an Ad: What Goes Where?

There is no right or wrong answer to the question of what goes where in an ad. An ad can be nothing more than a visual, or it can be extremely copy heavy. As long as it is informative, advances the product's image, and creates interest in the minds of the consumers, you're on the right track.

An ad can be made up of the following five elements: headline, subhead(s), visual(s), body copy, and logo. Not every element needs to be present in every ad; however, the order is somewhat predetermined.

The order in which elements appear depends on the concept being emphasized. If the headline has a great consumer benefit or is extremely important to the ad's direction, then it must go first; place it at the top of the design. If the visual says more than words can, then place it at the top of the design. This thought process will also help you to determine which element should be the dominant element on the page.

Controlling the order of what the target sees and reads aids him in understanding the advertised message. Figure 6.1 shows the different ways visual/verbal elements can be laid out in a print ad.

## Type Is a Personality Thing

The typeface used in an ad is as important as the message itself. Understanding the visual message of type is critical to building or maintaining a brand's image.

The choice of typeface should reflect the personality of the product or the company. Type is not a whimsical or temporary choice. Like layout

### So Which Layout Style Should You Use?

There are no rules dictating which layout styles are best suited to specific media. To decide which style to use, look first to your concept, and then consider how that message will be delivered and perceived. Readability and legibility issues will play a key role in your choice of layout style, typeface, or visual. Readability is achieved when a viewer can read an ad at a glance. Legibility refers to whether, in that short look, the reader understood the message.

Many of the elements appearing in the ad are of equal importance; it is the art director's job to organize elements into a cohesive package. Elements might include a screaming headline, sale dates, grand openings, new locations, and multiple products—each needing descriptive copy and/or price points. Usually several photographs or illustrations will be needed to show the product. You may also need to add detail copy and a logo that will not get lost along the way. These components will help you determine which layout style to use.

Organizing elements is the key to success in any medium. Remember that even though an ad might be cluttered, there must be one dominant image. Additional images can be smaller and placed lower in the ad in a grid or as a part of the body copy. It is the art director's job to decide what that one dominant element should be, based on information found in the creative brief. A large headline personalizes the message, showing the product alone, in use or in a setting, allows the consumer to interact with the product.

**FIGURE 6.1**

Visual/Verbal Layout Options for the Five Most Common Elements Found in a Print Ad

| Head | Head | Visual | Head |
|------|------|--------|------|
| Subhead | Visual | Headline | Visual |
| Visual | Subhead | Subhead | Subhead |
| Body Copy | Body Copy | Body Copy | Visual |
| Logo | Logo | Logo | Body Copy + Visual Logo |

style, once a typeface is chosen, it should appear in every ad—no matter what the media vehicle. The typeface should become a representative device for that product or service. Type is an art form of shapes, curves, circles, and lines. Making these elements your own, and thus your client's, is an extension of the conceptual process. An ad's type should also reflect your target audience. Bigger type and less formal layouts work well when attracting younger consumers, whereas cleaner, more structured layouts work well in attracting older consumers.

## Type Styles and Identifiers

There are two distinct varieties of type styles, serif and sans serif. A serif typeface has feet or delicate appendages that protrude from the edges of the letters, as in the type you're now reading. These appendages can appear at the top and/or bottom of a letterform. Sans serif type has no appendages.

Type is categorized by its typeface. Typeface refers to type of a specific uniform design. A typeface is part of a larger type family, which includes all the sizes and styles of that typeface. A font consists of a complete character set in one typeface and style: for example, all italic upper and lowercase letters, numbers, and punctuation.

Almost every typeface comes in varying weights. Weight represents the thickness or thinness of the typeface's body. These weights include ultra light, light, book, medium, demi bold, bold, ultra bold, and ultra black.

## The Language of Type

Different type designs reflect different images, moods, or even genders. Serif typefaces, because of their delicate lines, have a more feminine appeal. Sans serif typefaces boast straight, unadorned lines that give them a more masculine appearance. This masculine/feminine appeal can sometimes be achieved using differing weights of the same typeface. For example, the sans serif typeface Helvetica comes in so many weights that Helvetica Light—a stately, tall, and thin typeface—bears little resemblance to the bulky, stout-looking Helvetica Ultra Bold. Serif typefaces such as Goudy—a round, elegant, yet squat typeface—can represent both masculine and feminine products. The best place to begin when determining which typeface and style to use is to match likely candidates to the creative strategy, the product's personality, or the tone of the ad, and experiment from there.

## Type Design Rules of Thumb

When designing, the number of typefaces used in an ad should be controlled. The basic rule of thumb is two typefaces per design. The headline, subhead(s), announcement devices, and any prices are usually set in the same typeface; the body copy and descriptive copy are set in another.

As a rule, smaller copy blocks such as body or descriptive copy are set in a serif face for ease of reading. There is no limit on the different weights that can be used within a design, but common sense should rule the day.

Although there are no hard-and-fast rules about mixing serif and sans serif typefaces within an ad, it is best to use one style throughout the ad. The number of point sizes in an ad should also be controlled. An ad with multiple faces in various styles and sizes takes on a circus feel and is perceived as junky or low-end. However, any device, if used consistently and/or repetitively, avoids the need to play by the rules.

Logos are a graphic element and are not considered a typeface; they do not need to necessarily match the style of the advertised message.

## Type Alignment

The way type is aligned on the page can also affect brand image. There are several ways that type can be laid out in an ad. The first is center on center, where type is set with one line centered above another. Alternating the length of lines can create more white space within the ad.

The next most common alignment is flush left, ragged right. This is where all lines of text begin in the same place—along the left margin of the ad. The right side of each line is varied. You can also set type flush right, rag left. This alignment is most often used when working with two columns of type that wrap around a centrally placed visual.

The last type alignment option is justified. This is where each line of text begins in the same place along the left margin and ends in the same place on the right margin. This option is not used often in advertising design, because type has to be designed to fit within this type of format. Justified type often leaves large gaps between words, stretches out long words, or creates multiple hyphens at the ends of lines. Justified type is great for newspaper articles, but it does not look good and is difficult to read in advertising copy.

Type size directly affects readability. Catch the audience's eye with large text, whet their appetite with medium-sized text, sell the product with smaller text, and tell them what they need to know about where and how to shop with the smallest text. If you're using any secondary subheads or banners, they should be slightly smaller than the main subhead.

Look out for widows and orphans. A widow is a single word or short line that appears at the top of a page or at the top of a new column of copy. An orphan is a short line that appears at the bottom of a page, or a word (or part of a word) on a line by itself at the end of a paragraph. The first line in a paragraph should never end up at the bottom of the page or column all alone.

## Type Faux Pas

Readability and legibility can be adversely affected by several design faux pas. Let's look at a few of the most common.

**All Caps**  The use of all capital letters anywhere in an ad should be avoided. Consider it for a headline only when it is no more than one to three words long. Most people are not familiar with an all-caps format, and as a result must read more slowly.

**Reverse Copy**  Traditionally, type is set with black letters on a white background. Reverse text uses white or light-colored text on a black or dark-colored background. The use of reversed text in large blocks of copy should be avoided. Readability is minimized because the format is unfamiliar. Reverse text works best for banner announcements, like those advertising grand openings or sale hours.

**Italics**  Italics should also be avoided because of readability issues. Use italics sparingly; their best use is for emphasis or to set off a special word or phrase, a quotation, or a foreign word.

**Decorative Faces**  Fancy or froufrou typefaces have no place in advertising. Their elaborate flourishes and decorative appearances make readability and legibility almost impossible at a glance.

## Type as a Graphic Element

If you look at type—*really* look—you will see its beauty beyond content. Its form alone is a graphic device. Each typeface portrays a personality, an individualism that takes shape via content. The very randomness of the letterforms creates a uniform message with character and flair. Whether it's childish, traditional, expensive, or shabby chic, each typeface awaits the shape and expression given it by the designer.

A typeface's personality should match the image projected by the product or service and that of the target audience. However you decide to manipulate type—whether you alter the face by condensing or expanding it, or by increasing or decreasing letter, word or line spacing, type size, or line length—readability and legibility should take precedence over design.

Readability and legibility are also affected by the color and direction of type. Type does not have to be black. It can be any dark color, such as brown, navy, forest green, or maroon, to name only a few. Light or pastel-colored type lacks contrast against the stark white of the printed page, making it difficult to see and slowing readers down, making them reread in order to understand the message.

## Type as a Design Element

The typeface you choose should reflect the personality of the product or ambience of the service or store. The openness or tightness of line and letter spacing can promote this personality further, creating a signature look for the product or service. Work with type; make it the client's and, in time, the product's.

## Putting Ideas on Paper: The Stages of Design

In this section, we'll look at the four stages of the design process.

- Concept
- Thumbnails
- Roughs
- Super comprehensives

## Concept

The first stage in the design process is brainstorming or concept development. As discussed earlier, concept refers to your thoughts and ideas about how to creatively solve the client's advertising problem. Concept sets the tone and direction for a single ad or a combination of ads. This is where bad ideas come to die, and good ideas get a second look and perhaps an overhaul and facelift. It's also where daydreams begin to see the light of day. Here, the creative team hammers out sometimes hundreds of ideas, only 10 percent of which will bear further development.

All those daydreams come out as ideas, many of which will be rejected. Others may stand the test of development; all are worth sharing. It is important when you have an idea to present it to others, whether they're other professionals or your classmates. Don't worry about whether you think your ideas are stupid. I guarantee that you will excel in the realm of the ridiculous, you will be teased, and you may never live it down—but you will inspire ideas in others by sharing your not-so-fabulous thoughts as well as those brilliant ones.

## Thumbnails

Thumbnails, or thumbs, are the second stage in the design process. Word lists, as discussed earlier, play an important role in thumbnail development. Ideas generated there become a reality at this stage.

Thumbnails are small, proportionate drawings, ranging in size from 2 x 3½ inches up to 3 x 5 inches, that are used to place concept ideas down on paper. Each thumbnail should reflect a different concept direction, headline, subhead, and visual; no two should be alike. Try to use a different layout style for each concept. Further development should inspire alternative concept approaches.

The word "doodle" best describes what a thumbnail should look like. Random headlines, visuals, and layout styles should offer varied solutions to further develop your concept.

Thumbnails can have any number of combinations and components, but usually will consist of one or more of the following: a readable headline and possible subhead(s), a recognizable visual or visuals, body copy indication, and a logo. Each thumb should be enclosed in a box, representing the final size and shape of the ad, and should be tightly drawn and consistent in size.

Thumbs should be done in black marker. Color may be added when working within a color medium. Right off the bat, get into the habit of working in marker. Avoid pencils. Markers allow you to work and rework without the benefit of an eraser. When you can erase, you can obsess on one thumbnail idea. If you make a mistake or just don't like the way the idea is going, cross it out and move on; that's erasing, designer style.

Thumbnails are an internal design process, rarely, if ever, seen by the client. Headlines, subheads, slogans, and logos should be written out cleanly and placed in position on the thumb. It is important that other members of the creative team be able to read your thumbs; this helps them understand the concept direction. Visuals should be quickly sketched or traced into position. Body copy should be indicated with parallel lines. These lines represent the placement and the amount of room the copy might take up.

You will rarely have a single thumb that ends up as the final design choice. It is more likely that two or more will be combined to create the overall look of the final ad. The point is to have multiple options for the creative team to discuss.

Thumbnails allow you to work anywhere; it is difficult for even professional designers to be creative on demand a few hours before a deadline. Think about what you need to accomplish and let it fester a few hours, or even a few days if time allows.

Being able to work fast is critical in design. Developing a thought and then quickly sketching a thumbnail wipes out the pressure and anxiety associated with a blank page. Get all your ideas down on paper; thinking ahead makes the creative process a bit easier.

## Roughs

Roughs, or layouts, are the third stage in the design process, and they are chosen from your best thumbnail ideas. Professionals usually use roughs as their idea-generation stage. Roughs are often presented to the client, especially an established client. Roughs are done full size, or the size of the final piece, and are done in color if relevant.

If you are presenting concepts to a new client who has no representative typeface or wishes to change the image of a product or service, offer alternative type choices on each rough. This allows the client to see the typeface on the page, within the design, and with any visuals or the logo. The image or personality each typeface projects for the target, company, service, or product plays an important visual role in the development of an identity or brand image. If your client already has a signature typeface, continue to use that typeface on your roughs.

Each rough should include a different headline, using your key benefit for guidance, with a supporting subhead if required, as well as visual(s) and layout style if presenting multiple concepts. If you are creating a campaign series, each series should include at least three pieces, and the concept based off the strategy and the key benefit should be evident in the headline, theme, character representative, repetitive layout style, and/or typeface.

Because clients see roughs and review all ideas, they should be tight, clean, and accurate. It is important they be checked against the creative brief to be sure they are on target before they are presented to the client. Professional-looking layout and conceptual skills should shine here. The AE will present the client with three to five design options at this stage. However, it is rare for any ad to make it past the client in its original form; most likely it will be sent back to creative for minor tweaks—or worse, a major overhaul. Final client-approved ads will be reproduced on the computer.

## Super Comprehensives

The fourth and final stage in the design process is known as super comprehensives, or super comps. Although not technically a part of the design process, super comps are created from final roughs. They are generated on the computer with all headlines, subheads, photographs and/or illustrations, a logo, and—for the first time—completed body copy in place, simulating exactly how the finished design will look and read.

Ideally, the super comp will mimic the rough as closely as possible; however, this is where most minor changes made by the client will be addressed.

## Visuals, Options, and Decisions

The visual chosen for any creative piece is important. It should take into consideration the medium to be used as well as the product or service to be advertised. The visual the target eventually sees is a representation of the client's product or service. As the designer, you can decide how to present that image—perhaps through the reality of photography or with the artistic expression of an illustration or graphic design. A more simplistic approach can be achieved with black-and-white line art, or budget constraints might call for clip or stock art. Whatever image becomes the visual voice of your client's product, it should support your strategy, headline, and concept, and reflect both the target's and the product's image.

An ad's visual options are diverse. There are five possible visual options the art director might consider using.

- Photographs
- Line art
- Illustrations
- Clip or stock art
- Graphic images

We will also look at logos as representative of image. Choice ultimately depends on budget, media, and image.

## Photographs

Believability is one reason to use photographs. Unfortunately, photography can be expensive, especially color photography. The decision to include a photograph instead of an illustration or line art depends on the concept being used, the image of the product or service, and the medium.

Photographs offer an exclusive viewing opportunity. Paper quality and printing issues will affect how clearly the consumer can see what the product looks like and/or how it is used.

The visual reality offered by photographs allows readers to see patterns, textures, quality, and color as if the product were sitting before them. The idea of visual variety offers designers the option to showcase the product alone or in use, placed in a relevant setting, or being compared to a similar product. Size is also a visual variable; images can be enlarged to dominate the page or reduced in order to show multiple views or options.

**What's in a Photograph?**  The photograph should be something your target is interested in. If it is, any visual will work, but here are some guaranteed attention getters:

- Brides
- Infants
- Animals, especially young animals
- Celebrities
- Outrageous costumes
- Outrageous situations
- Romance
- Scenes of Tragedy
- Current Events
- Slice-of-life

Gender plays a small role in the choice of visual images: for example, men are attracted to animals, whereas women are attracted to images of infants or children. But no matter the sex of the target, in the end the visual must be relevant.

There is no better way to create a mood or conjure up emotions than with photographs, especially those with people in them. Although photographs take time to set up and shoot, consumers prefer them in ads promoting services such as banking and investing, or products such as food. Photographs can more easily show the product being used, and they allow consumers to envision themselves using the product or service.

Using a photograph gives credibility to your product, as do the models you choose for them. Don't use anyone who appears unlikely to use the product or service. Be sure models are suitably dressed and are the right age and sex.

**The Pop of Black-and-White Photographs**  Why use black-and-white photos when you can use color? One reason is price. It is much less expensive to use a black-and-white photograph than a color photograph. Another reason is that a black-and-white photograph stands out against a lot of color. This independence in appearance attracts readers' attention.

Black-and-white photographs are also excellent mood or attitude setters. Issues such as drinking and driving and the results from such behavior are often difficult to take in color. Sadness or isolation, even the passing of time, can be represented best in black and white—especially with all the bright colors on adjacent pages or in other locations.

Some organizations, especially charities, do not wish to look too affluent or wasteful when soliciting donations. They might prefer black-and-white photography to color. Fashion ads in black and white are certainly a surprise. They stop readers, making them spend just a minute longer on this anomaly.

**Spot Color**  An excellent alternative to full-color photographs is a black-and-white photograph featuring one element in color. This is referred to as spot color. This is an excellent way to highlight the product, making it stand out in stark contrast to the rest of the photograph. Spot color can give a visual the illusion of three-dimensionality. By adding a spot of color to the photograph, the designer can control eye flow, drawing the viewer's eye directly to the product.

The use of photographs, especially color photographs, requires a large budget. However, color photography at any level, such as spot color, is often worth the price. It brings an ad alive and helps to create interest and involvement from the consumer.

## Line Art

Black-and-white line art consists of a line drawing that has no tonal qualities. A drawing is a great choice when your ad is spotlighting a product with small details, such as a lace tablecloth or a delicate china pattern. Drawings simplify a design and create a strong black-and-white contrast on the page.

Products presented as line art can be grouped, yet retain their individuality through the strategic use of contrast, shadows, highlights and details, and varying textures. A strong black-and-white drawing retains details without muting quality.

## Illustrations

Illustrations, unlike line art, have tonal qualities, so they are more like a photograph. But, unlike photographs, illustrations are created rather than reproduced. With illustrations, advertisers can take a more analytical approach by presenting charts and graphs, or a lighter approach by creating characters to represent the product.

The choice between using an illustration or a photograph is an interpretive one. Photographers capture reality, but if you want something more imaginative, an illustration can create reality. If you are looking for a nostalgic, homey look, you might choose an illustrator with a Norman Rockwell style. If your concept calls for a more modern approach, you may look for someone who uses a Peter Max or Andy Warhol style.

Illustrations can create a mood or trend as easily as a photograph does. Depending on the style and color usage, they can represent a laid-back or upbeat approach.

The choice between an illustration or a photograph also depends on the product or service. For an ad that features customer services, emotional appeals, or a food product, consider photographs. To create personality, think illustration. For ambiance, it's a toss-up. One thing is for sure: illustrations and graphics are less expensive design options than a four-color photograph.

## Clip or Stock Art

Using either clip art or stock art is a great option when money is tight. Clip art are existing line art drawings. Stock art are existing photographs of all varieties that can be purchased and used. These terms are often used interchangeably. The only problem with using clip or stock art is the small chance it may have been used in another ad. To make your clip or stock art unique, try combining one or more and removing or cropping unwanted areas.

## Graphics

Graphics have great potential when color is an option. If your client's product is youthful or modern, consider using a more upbeat or graphic approach. Graphic design looks at life and situations abstractly. Bright colors, often chosen for their symbolic meaning, are combined with both geometric and organic shapes to create modern and bold designs. These shapes, when used together, are often disjointed, and they are used to create an alternative view of life. When set off by a lot of white space, this design style screams new, bold, or eclectic, especially if the other advertising surrounding it uses a more traditional approach.

If you need something simpler, a graphic can also be nothing more than a single divider line between columns of copy, a graphic box used to highlight copy points, or a logo.

# Color's Representational Role

## The Mood of Color

Effective color choices can be used as design elements. Certain colors evoke specific emotions and can be used to set a mood or attract the eye. In the unfortunate event the target should forget the product name, often the use of unique color combinations on packaging can help with recall when determining which product to purchase.

## The Meaning of Color

Color can make us feel warm, cold, stressed, or lethargic. We know the sun should be yellow and the sky blue. The elegance, reassurance, or casualness of a color comes from our life experiences; we see life in color and use it to describe an event, an emotion, the passage of time, or life and death.

When using color, be sure it does not compete with other colors on the page but instead complements the mood you are trying to create. Elegance is portrayed with more white than color; red and yellow are hot; blue, cool; and green, alive. Be careful not to use too much color, or the ad can become stressful or look gaudy to readers.

## Color and Its Emotion

**Red**  Red is a dynamic and dangerous color with great strength. It can signify passion, lust, and heat as well as blood, fire, and revolution. Whether reflecting positive or negative emotions, it is full of action and reaction. Red is great for men's products or any product requiring a warning label. It also works well for impulse products such as candies.

**Orange**  Orange reflects the autumn harvest, fire, and the heat of the sun. Orange is a weighty color, suggesting depth and volume. It evokes intense feeling, energy, and inspiration. Products that work well with orange include pasta, precooked entrees, and insect repellants.

**Yellow**  Yellow is welcoming, open, and vivacious. Yellow is a light, warm or comforting, upbeat color suggesting laughter. Yellow takes on more weight and stands out when combined with a dark color. Most products will work with yellow or yellow highlights, but some of the obvious include vegetables, fruits, sun products, hair products, or paper products.

**Green**  Green is a relaxing color. It is the color of nature, cleanliness, good health, and money. Green is a good choice for products such as vegetables, garden equipment, tobacco products, pickles, and pasta.

**Blue**  Blue is an earthy color, signifying water, the sky, and ice. Blue, depending on its hue, can be light or depressing. Blue is a relaxing and refreshing, youthful color that supports make-believe ideas and intelligence. Blue can represent such products as soups, cold beverages, travel, or frozen food products.

**Black** Black symbolizes sadness, isolation, and death, or the need to set something apart or end something. Black can also denote elegance, honor, and dignity. It is often used for expensive products such as jewelry, cars, perfumes, or liquors. Black can also be used as an accent color to pop lighter, more vibrant colors off the page.

So where does creative fit with what we know so far? Let's review:

*Phase one includes:*
1. Research.
2. From the research we developed the marketing plan.
3. From the marketing plan we developed the creative strategy statement.
4. From the marketing plan and creative strategy statement we developed the creative brief.

*Phase two includes:*
1. From the creative brief we can begin the brainstorming phase. Here is where we determine our theme, creative concept or big idea.
2. Be sure your concept is on strategy/target with the creative brief.
3. Prepare copy and layouts.

*Phase three includes:*
1. Adapting your creative approach for use in each of the media that make up the IMC or promotional mix: public relations, advertising, (print, broadcast), sales promotion, direct marketing, and the Internet.

# Copywriting

Writing copy is one of the first steps taken when moving from business thinking to actual creative brainstorming and eventual execution. In a perfect world, the copy would be written first and would be the inspiration for an ad's design. However, advertising is not a perfect world. It is most likely that copywriting and design will be happening at the same time. Because of this, it is critical that the copywriter and the art director be on the same page creatively.

A copywriter deals with both the imagination and development processes of brainstorming and writing headlines, subheads, body copy, slogans, and/or taglines. Copywriters must use what they learn during the brainstorming process to produce copy that attracts and motivates the target audience to not only read the entire ad, but to act on what they have read.

Every piece of copy, no matter what medium it appears in, must relate to and complement the visual message, attract the target's attention, build a relationship with the target, and inspire the target to act.

Successful, memorable advertising is a consequence of a little luck, some good interpretive powers, a few great ideas, and the targets audience's ultimate capacity to reflect, digest, and connect to the visual/verbal message.

## The Components of Copy

The copy's voice is the direct result of the creative brief. Once a creative direction or concept has been decided upon, the copywriter must determine what needs to be said, how much copy it will take to say it, the tone and style appropriate to project the concept, and how to adapt that copy to a particular media vehicle. Copy for print can be broken down into four main copy areas: headlines, subheads, body copy, and slogans and taglines. The headline, subhead, and body copy all need to function as a unit to build, present, and explain a single message.

## Headlines

**Headlines That Steal the Show**  A headline is the largest piece of copy on the page and is most often the first piece of copy the viewer will notice. A headline's job is to stop attention, stand out on a crowded page, and be unforgettable by either shouting out the key benefit or supporting the visual. Whether it is a single phrase or one or more complete sentences, a headline must answer the target's question *What's in it for me?* This not only helps to differentiate the product or service from the competition but it also becomes an excellent tool for creating brand awareness or defining a brand's identity for the target.

A headline needs to seduce. It should create enough interest to make the target stay with the ad instead of turning the page. An advertised sales message is not a chosen read; it's what I refer to as an enticed read. The target audience is enticed into the ad because the key consumer benefit is informative, instructional, thought provoking, imaginative, or even suggestive. It lets the target know how the product or service can benefit daily life.

Sometimes headlines are not the best choice for promoting the key benefit. Sometimes it is easier to show the key benefit in action, placing the headline in a supporting role. No matter how the key benefit is disclosed or shown, it is important that the headline relate to the visual. There is no visual/verbal relationship if the head and the visual deliver separate messages. W. Keith Hafer and Gordon E. White put it best in their book *Advertising Writing*: "The visual and headline are indivisible."

If your headline can communicate both visually and verbally, you may not even need body copy. "Tear. Wipe. Done. Cleaning Is So Labor Intensive." It doesn't get more visual/verbal than that.

Writing effective headlines requires writing and rewriting so that the key benefit says just the right thing, in just the right tone, to the target audience. The key is to be original, and to do this, all the "been there, done that" ideas must be exhausted before the headline can assume the product's identity.

Brainstorming sessions exile a lot of ideas to your computer's trash can. But before you decide to empty the trash, consider holding on to some of these refugee headlines. Many can be reevaluated for possible use as slogans, subheads, and opening body copy paragraphs.

**Headlines That Talk the Key Benefit Talk**  Most consumers don't get past the headline, so it's important that the headline can be read at a glance and understood. If you have a lot to say, push just the key benefit in the headline, and consider supporting information in a subhead.

Often a headline's length is directly related to a product's life cycle. New products and reinvented products require a longer headline in order to introduce the key benefit and establish or reestablish a brand image. Mainstream products that already have an established brand identity will continue building on, or maintaining, an existing campaign theme.

Powerful headlines catch and keep the target's attention and pull him into the ad. If you want to make sure your target pays attention to the message, consider some of the tried-and-true "benefit" words or phrases listed in figure 7.1.

Selecting the right words is as important as the tone of voice and style the headline uses to express the strategy. The tone of voice deals with how the message is expressed. Style deals with how the headline portrays the message. The following list of styles is suggested only as a place to start. The way a headline is delivered should not fit a prefabricated mold but should adapt to reflect the brand's image and/or concept and message direction. Consider the following headline styles as another way of brainstorming ideas.

- *Direct.* A direct headline delivers the key benefit with little or no creative flair.
- *Indirect or Curiosity.* Indirect or curiosity headlines tantalize with just enough information to make your target curious for more information. One great way to do this is to ask questions or test existing knowledge.
- *Major Benefit Promise.* A major benefit headline is best used when the key benefit is a unique selling proposition (USP).
- *Play on Words.* If you are going to mess with the English language, be sure to have a point. A play on words manipulates words, often giving special meaning to words to match a campaign theme. This headline type can attract a reader's attention and give an ad a personality all its own. But, as with all messages, be sure your word play advances your key benefit.
- *Question.* A question headline style asks the target a question. This headline style requires your audience to think, and thus participate. Be sure the question is thought provoking and cannot be answered with a simple yes or no, so the more open-ended and less specific the question, the better. Questions can help tie the headline to the visual by showing an immediate benefit through problem solving.

**FIGURE 7.1**

Suggestive Words and Phrases That Help Create Attention-Grabbing Headiines

| | | | |
|---|---|---|---|
| 1. You | 7. Product Name | 13. How-To | 19. Guarantee |
| 2. Free | 8. Love | 14. Why | 20. Results |
| 3. Discover | 9. Offer Guidance | 15. Sale | 21. Proven |
| 4. Last Chance | 10. Introducing | 16. Bargain | 22. Save |
| 5. New | 11. Now | 17. Quick | 23. Health |
| 6. Announcing | 12. Just Arrived | 18. Easy | 24. Safety |

- *Metaphors, Similes, and Analogies.* Metaphors, similes, and analogies compare your client's product to something else. A metaphor looks at two dissimilar objects to make a point of comparison, for example, "He is a snake-in-the-grass." A simile uses the word "like" or "as" to make a comparison, for example, "sick as a dog." An analogy compares two characteristics that are perceived as similar, for example, dry skin compared to sandpaper.
- *News or Announcement.* A news or announcement headline tells the reader something newsworthy about the product. Maybe it has received a patent or is new and improved, or perhaps a new use has been found for the product. This style works well for announcements or introductions.
- *The Reason-Why.* The reason-why headline style gives the target a good reason, or list of reasons, to use the product or service.
- *How-To.* How-to headlines tell the reader how to do or find out something. These work well when tied to psychographical information, for example, how to save money or lose weight.
- *Product Name.* Headlines that feature the product name work best for new product launches or reinvented products. These headlines often do not promote a strong product benefit and so do not build or reinforce the brand image.
- *Testimonial.* If a member of the target audience who has had a favorable experience with your product or service, let her do the talking. Her experiences with the product are more believable than the advertised message to the target. Placing quotes around a headline highlights the fact it is an actual quote.
- *Command.* A command headline firmly tells your reader what to do: "Get to the zoo."
- *Practical Advice.* The practical advice headline tells your target how to do or achieve something: how to make cleaning easier, how to stay healthy, how to make money on investments. Consumers love practical and/or helpful information.
- *Problem/Solution.* Sell the solution, not the problem. Don't waste the target's time discussing the problem; he already knows the problem, so if you offer a solution you will have his attention.
- *Flag.* Talk to a specific group—for example, new mothers or people with bad backs—by calling out to them in the headline to catch their attention.
- *Warning.* As the name implies, the headline acts as a warning to the target audience: if you don't do X, Y will happen.
- *Personal Benefits.* A personal benefits headline promises something to the target, such as beauty, health, quality, adventure prestige, and so on.

**Headline Length**  A visual headline may work with one word, whereas a fact-based headline may require more than one sentence. Five to seven words are typically required to promote a consumer benefit. Length also depends on the media vehicle. When working with limited space, such as on a transit sign, poster, or billboard, the key benefit is about all you have room for.

## Subheads

There are two basic types of subheads: overline and underline.

An overline subhead is used as a teaser or attention getter and appears above the headline. If your headline appears too long or will have to be reduced in size to accommodate everything that needs to be said, consider using an overline as an announcement device.

An underline subhead appears below the headline and explains in more detail what the headline is saying, elaborates on the statement or comment made, or answers the question posed in the headline. Ideally, the main underline subhead should not be another statement, but one or two complete sentences. Remember, the headline's job is to stop attention; once you've got it, the subhead should whet the reader's appetite, enticing them into the body copy.

Because the headline and the subhead work as a unit, no other copy should appear between them. It is acceptable to break up the unit with a visual if it strengthens the bond between the headline and subhead and further promotes the message.

Additional subheads can be used to clarify or explain in further detail what the headline is saying or to break up long blocks of text. Subheads appearing in the body copy should read like bullet listings and need not be complete sentences. A consumer should be able to quickly glance through the subheads and know where the copy is going. Each subhead should relate to the content of the copy below it. Multiple subheads can break long blocks of detailed copy into easily digestible bits of information while adding visual interest.

Use subheads like chapter breaks, with each new subhead signaling a new benefit, highlighting copy and creating interest. Readers can scan the subheads in the same way they might scan the chapter listings in a book. Even if your target can't read the copy now, her interest is piqued and she will read it at a later time.

## Body Copy

The paragraphs of text in an ad are known as body copy. The message of the body copy is the nuts and bolts, and heart and soul of your concept.

The body copy's story begins in the headline. It must speak in the same tone of voice as the headline, explaining and backing up any claims made. If the headline asks a question, the body copy will answer it; if the headline is humorous, the copy will have a humorous tone.

Copy continues the key benefit's story by educating the target on the facts, features and benefits, and any supportive points associated with the product or service.

Body copy is essentially broken down into three areas: an opening paragraph, an interior paragraph, and a closing paragraph. The opening paragraph needs to finish the thought introduced in the headline and developed further in the subhead. If your target has gotten this far, those two sections must have gotten his attention.

The interior or body of your copy is where the actual selling will take place. This is where supporting features/benefits will be presented that will enhance the key benefit and overall lifestyle of your target.

The closing paragraph needs to ask the target to do something: come into the store, pick up the phone, or go online for more information. Advertising is about making sales, don't be afraid to tell consumers what they need to do.

It is very easy to bore your target market by droning on with a continuous list of the product's features and benefits. Entertain them instead by creating a story, something that is fun or interesting to read, that flows toward a climax. That climax is what you want the target to do. Think of your copy as a novel that has a plot (concept): that plot is advanced by events (features/benefits), and those events affect the characters (your target).

As a general rule, body copy should use short sentences and simple words. It should not offend or use slang. Be sure to include a time element into copy to get your target moving toward the desired action. One way to do this is to offer some kind of guarantee, removing any perceived risks associated with purchase, especially if done over the Internet, or through a catalog or direct mail.

Things to remember when writing copy that will reach out to the target audience.

- When writing, talk to just one member of the target market in his own language or vernacular. A conversational tone allows the copy to speak to the target or ask questions of the reader. It's impossible and inappropriate to address your message to a group. Always talk in the first person: use "you" instead of "them." Do not say things like "people" or "they will," but rather "you will." This personalizes the message for the target and allows him to relate the message to his own lifestyle.
- Appeal to the target's rational and emotional sides. In other words, present the information factually and tie the facts to how the product or service will make the target feel, change her life, or solve a problem.
- Write about the benefits of the product or service based on its individual features. Your client's product is not special because of its features; its competition either already has them or will have them in a couple of months. Carving out a niche that features the product's benefits or solutions ahead of the competition will make consumers identify certain features/benefits with it, which is a great way to propel the consumer away from competitors.
- If the copy is long, use multiple short paragraphs and subheads to break up the copy. If the message is broken up into multiple short paragraphs of no more than three to four sentences each, the target is more likely to read it.

- Be sure the opening paragraph continues the discussion on the key benefit first introduced in the headline and explained further in the subhead. Think about what it takes to keep you reading; it must grab your attention and be important to you.
- Keep it simple, and stay on target. Even the most dynamic body copy will not succeed if it is off target.
- When writing, avoid abbreviations and technical jargon unless you are writing copy for a particular profession.
- Avoid using exclamation points anywhere. If you have to use them to make your point, you obviously didn't make your point.
- Get to the point and avoid exaggerated claims. Bragging is great only if you can back it up with facts. It is the facts that make a product claim believable and inspire the target to act.
- Close the sale. Every ad should close by asking the target to do something. If you want the target to make a purchase, include a toll-free number or information about where to purchase. Supply a Web address for those seeking additional information.

**Copy Length**   How long should body copy be? The answer is simple: long enough to inform and entice your target market to action. The length of body copy depends on how familiar the target is with the product and whether the advertising or promotional efforts are to change or maintain the position in the mind of the consumer.

Copy length is also affected by:

- *The Medium*. Reminder advertising, such as a billboard, requires little more than a headline or statement to promote the key benefit. Direct mail, on the other hand, requires long copy in order to explain the key benefit and move the target to action.
- *The Target Audience*. Better-educated older targets, will wade through longer copy in order to find out more about the product or service. Younger readers will respond better to large, colorful visuals, spending less time on copy points.
- *The Product or Service*. If the product or service falls in the rational category, more information will be needed to set the product apart from the competition. Products or services falling into the emotional category have few, if any, distinctive features from those of the competition that will need to be explained in any detail.

Too much copy can keep the target from getting involved with the copy. This is the best time to insert multiple subheads, or visuals demonstrating copy points, within the copy, to break it up into smaller more readable chunks. Too little copy, on the other hand, may not set the product apart from the competition, or strengthen or build the product's image.

**Expressing the Copy's Tone**   As we have already learned, every concept has an individual approach, appeal, and tone or execution technique that defines its personality or image.

How it is expressed depends on the execution technique, or tone of voice employed to communicate the key benefit. Ask yourself what kind of image the product or service should project. Can that image be developed with a sexual tone, through an emotional tone, or a humor-based tone? Is it newsworthy, or should a specific feature be promoted? Should you remind or tease your target, or will a demonstration or instructional tone do the trick? Whichever tone you use to express the key benefit, it should work toward building up the brand's image and successfully promoting your key benefit.

**Formats for Expressing a Message's Tone of Voice** A message's tone can take either a rational or emotional direction, or can be a combination of any of the following from either category.

## When to Use Longer Copy

- New product introductions
- Technical copy
- Repositioning or reinventing a brand's image
- Expensive product purchases

## When to Use Shorter Copy

- Mainstream products
- Rational products
- Reminder advertising
- Inexpensive product purchases

*Emotional Tone of Voice* Emotional tone-of-voice messages might use one or a combination of the following:

*Fear.* Since fear scares us and triggers an emotional response, it is memorable and a guaranteed attention getter. There are no rules about how much fear the consumer can take before being turned off, so common sense in relationship to product benefits or problem/solution should be taken into consideration.

*Humor.* A humorous tone looks at the product and the target and places all in an unusual or outrageous situation in which the product solves a problem.

*Sex.* Sex is another proven way to attract the consumer's attention. It is still possible to intentionally shock viewers with the blatant and often controversial use of sex in advertising. However, for it to be successful at any level it must have a point, not just sex for sex's sake or shock value.

*Music.* Music elicits emotion. Use it to set the scene for use or lifestyle enhancement, or to create product association with a certain mood-setting song. If what needs to be said is boring, consider setting it to a catchy tune known as a jingle: another way to make an unimaginable, unremarkable, indistinguishable feature stand out from the competitive pack.

*Scarcity.* If it's hard to get, it will attract certain types of consumers. Scarcity appeals encourage action and want increases the need for, or the value of, a product. The need to be first or one of the few to own something creates status.

*Slice-of-life.* Slice-of-life is the ultimate problem/solution appeal in which the ad presents a problem only this product can solve. There are four stages to a slice-of-life approach: problem, introduction, trial, and solution.

*Fantasy*. Fantasy takes the consumer on an imaginary adventure. It takes the reality out of an otherwise predictable product and makes it fun—and usually memorable. Many fantasy ads are foolish and fantastic, and deal with predictable themes such as food, sex, vacation getaways, and love and romance.

*Animation*. Animated characters are used to tell the product's story. The characters and the situations they find themselves in are usually very sophisticated and created by computer-generated means.

**Rational Tone of Voice** Rational tone-of-voice messages might use one or a combination of the following:

- *Authority*. Use an expert such as a doctor, scientist, dentist, or engineer to point out product attributes. Other official devices that might be employed to back up claims include scientific studies or survey results.
- *Factual Message or Straight-Sell*. A factual or straightforward approach works on a consumer's needs and wants as well, but instead of selling to the emotions or imagination, the sale is made based on the facts associated with the product. This approach relies heavily on the key benefit and any relevant supporting benefits and features associated with the product or service.
- *News Event or Educational*. News event or educational tones are used when the product is in the news. Perhaps the client or the product has won an award for quality or service. Being first at anything is not only newsworthy but a great sales device.
- *Product Feature or Star*. A feature-based approach concentrates on the key benefit associated with the product. It is nice if the feature is unique to the product, but even an appliance's plug can be made unique if the competition is not pushing plugs and your concept is unique and memorable.
- *Reminder*. The reminder tone keeps well-known products such as table salt or seasonal products in the mind of the consumer.
- *Teaser*. A teaser approach is used to create interest in a product that is not yet on the market. This approach should build curiosity and entice the consumer by talking about a product but not showing it.
- *Demonstration*. A demonstration tone of voice compares the product to the competition; each product's strengths and weaknesses are compared.
- *Instructional*. An instructional tone teaches the consumer how to do something or explains how the product or service can solve a problem.
- *Inherent Drama*. Inherent drama differentiates a product or service from the competition by creating interest around the key benefit. This works well for products that have few, if any, unique characteristics.
- *Talking Head*. A character, spokesperson, or consumer tells the product's story or his personal experiences with the product.
- *Dialogue*. Dialogue copy focuses on a conversation between two people, a group of people, or between characters.

- *Lifestyle or Narrative.* Focus is placed on the target and the role the product plays in her life, rather than on the product itself.

Additional strategic message approaches might compare your client's product to the competition or create a spokesperson or animated personality, creating a personalized approach to your ad. You never can go wrong with a testimonial or endorsement. In a testimonial, a celebrity or an average consumer endorses your product by telling their personal experiences with the product. Endorsements are a little different; the announcer or celebrity often does not personally use the product and is being paid for his time.

These tones or execution techniques are just a starting place for conceptual development. They are meant not as a template, but as a jumping off point. Consider combining one or more ideas together, or envision an entirely new and different way to say something about the product or service.

**The Detail of Copy**  When writing copy don't forget the detail copy. Detail copy is the small copy placed near the logo or the bottom of the ad to inform the target about locations, phone or fax numbers and/or Web addresses, or maps, if applicable. Other items to include might be store hours, parking, and credit card information as well as lay-a-way options and gift certificates. Not all may be applicable for all ads.

## Summing Up a Philosophy or Concept in a Few Words

**Slogans**  A slogan represents a company's philosophy or a product's image. It is usually placed either above or below the logo. The two are a unit and should always be used together. A slogan is usually three to seven words in length and can either be a statement or a complete sentence.

The slogan must aid in positioning the product. It must say what you want the target to know about the company or product. Good slogans have longevity and add to a product's brand image, thus building brand equity.

One of the ways to make a product memorable is to tie the slogan to a product or service's image. It should make an association through visual/verbal cues. Consider how a product works or when the product is used: Some kind of word association, pun, or rhyming scheme may be memorable and representative. By using visual/verbal cues, the slogan represents a products image and message.

**Tagline**  A tagline is not the same as a slogan, although the two labels are often interchanged. A tagline generally represents a current strategy or concept. Like a slogan, a tagline is three to seven words in length and can be either a statement or a complete sentence. Taglines do not have the longevity associated with slogans and often change to match the brand's life cycle stage or current campaign efforts.

## Visuals: Tying the Verbal to the Visual

Creating a visual/verbal message is critical. What you say in your copy must have a corresponding visual. Remember, you have two kinds of viewers in your target market—left-brainers (copy) and right-brainers (visuals)—and each one has a preference for receiving the message either visually or verbally.

The product's key benefit should be screamed out in the headline, developed in more detail in the copy, and represented visually through either a photograph, an illustration, or a graphic element. By creating a strong visual/verbal relationship, you can tap into a reader's left- and right-brain tendencies by allowing the consumer to see the product as well as review safety information and warranties. Other considerations include the headline itself. If the headline copy creates a visual/verbal relationship—for example, "Is This You?"—and the visual shows a tired, worn-out working mother, then a direct relationship is formed between what is being said and what is being shown.

It is important that you have a visual in your head when writing your copy. You want to create the image you want to project in the copy. Your visual choices should help verify that the art director can see what you're talking about.

It is just as important that your copy create a visual image for the art director. This guarantees the right side sells what the left side is reading. The visual is the way to make sure your client understands the copy.

It isn't hard to create confusion. If you're trying to sell the nutrition of dog food and you show a baby, it is difficult to understand your point without the headline's explanation. No one will understand what in the world dog food and babies have in common unless you create the connection both visually and verbally. Consider this connection: If the concept is nutritional value, you want to show that dog owners need to give their puppy a good start, just as they would a human baby. For the consumer to understand your analogy, the visual and verbal messages need to work together.

The layout style used also plays a role in copy. These visual directions or cues will be worked out during the brainstorming sessions or concept development stage. For example, a picture window layout style requires a headline that draws the reader into the photograph, a rebus works great for copy that tells a story or gives the reader directions, and a Mondrian layout has a youthful feel and works well with copy that is upbeat or energizing.

## The Logo as a Symbol

A discussion about visual/verbal relationships would be incomplete without a discussion of logos. A logo is the symbol—and ultimately the image—of a company or product, and should be prominently displayed on any creative piece. A logo can consist of nothing more than the company or product name represented typographically; it can also be a graphic symbol or a combination of type and graphic. A logo needs to close every ad, even if it's used in the headline. It needs to be the last thing the viewer sees. A logo's graphic means nothing until meaning is given it through positioning.

## Visual/Verbal Parts

The purpose and aim of the verbal/visual parts of an ad can be summed up by what each part (feature) needs to accomplish, (benefit) and by recognizing a problem and offering the solution. Every ad needs to accomplish the following:

Problem or Feature ⟶ Benefit or Solution
Attract Attention ⟶ Headlines and Visuals
Create Interest ⟶ Subheads and Opening Copy Paragraphs
Generate Excitement ⟶ Interior Body Copy
Induce Action ⟶ Closing Paragraphs or Detail Copy, Logos, Slogans/Taglines

Once the key consumer benefit is determined, copywriters give it both entertainment and informational value. Headlines promote it, subheads defend it, and body copy develops and highlights its many virtues. Copy is the product's tone of voice. If you can't write copy that visually and verbally tells the product's story, then you can't solve your target's problem and successfully compete against the competition.

## Writing beyond the Ad: Promotional Devices

Many ads have some kind of promotional device, such as coupons or order forms, attached to them. The copywriter is also responsible for preparing promotional copy.

### Coupons

All consumers like to get a break, and coupons are a way to offer something in return for their patronage or loyalty, or as an introduction to a product or service. A coupon is an effective, temporary sales device. Coupons should be easy to remove from the ad and should clearly point out the offer.

The design of multiple coupons must be consistent. Headlines need to be the same size, as do percentages or cents-off claims, on each and every coupon. Alternatives can be used when heads are not of the same length, structure, or consistency. For example, if you are working with three coupons, two with fairly long headlines that will break into three lines and a third that is only two lines in length, consider placing the two longer coupons one and three in the lineup, with the shorter coupon in the middle. This maintains continuity without altering type size. All headlines, price points, visuals, expiration dates, and logos should appear in the same place and be the same size on each coupon. Consider placing a dashed line around the coupon to visually encourage the consumer to cut or tear out the coupon.

Finally, it is imperative the overall appearance be carried through with some kind of repetitive element such as logo, slogan or tagline, color, consistent visual, or spokesperson or animated character. Tie the message, whether verbal or implied, to the visual appearance; make sure the timing works, so that one supports the other; and make the placement match the image.

## Freestanding Inserts

Freestanding inserts, or FSIs, are one-page, full-color coupon ads that are inserted into the newspaper. These inserts are often double sided and usually feature coupons or announce a special sale or promotion. These nationally distributed inserts are also known as supplemental advertising.

## Order Forms

An order form requires the target to do something: perhaps place an order, express an opinion, or relate an experience with the product or service. Additional uses might include an opportunity to ask for a free sample or additional information. If the advertising or promotional goal is to get consumers to ask for additional information or to place an order directly from the ad, you will need to write and design an order form for them to use. Order forms are used most often in advertising, direct marketing, or sales promotion. They are often attached to or found in magazines or

There are several elements to consider when designing a coupon:

- Size can vary, but it usually depends on how many coupons will be appearing in the ad.
- The headline should clearly state the offer: "Buy One Taco Burrito Platter And Get A Second Free."
- If the offer is a cents-off or a percentage-off deal, use a larger typeface and point size to make it stand out.
- If the offer can be redeemed at the grocery store, a small amount of body copy is needed to tell the grocer how to redeem the used coupons.
- Grocery coupons also need to have a UPC code so they can be scanned at the checkout stand.
- Don't forget the product or store logo. Once the consumer tears the coupon out of the ad, she needs to know where to redeem it and on what brand it can be used.
- Most coupons have an expiration date. This time limit should be prominently displayed at the top of the coupon or in bold or italicized type within the body of the coupon.
- If the product comes in more than one size or flavor, or any other variation that might cause confusion for the consumer, add a picture of the product to make it easier to find the correct item.
- Coupons may also include a marketing code. This code tells the retailer where the coupon came from, assisting with future media placement.

in direct mail pieces. However the target comes in contact with them, they must be well written and well designed.

Information gathered from an order form will be used to develop a database of current and past users and to keep track of anyone who requests additional information. This data will be used in future advertising or promotional efforts, mailings, or sales promotions.

An order form should include the following:

- Step-by-step instructions on how to order at the top of the form.
- A headline to call attention to what is being offered.
- A reintroduction of the offer/benefit. Even if mentioned in the body copy (and it should have been), sum it up here again and briefly tell the target what you want her to do. This should be no longer than one to three sentences. Restate it creatively; this is no time to bore the target.
- Blanks for name, address, apartment number, city, state, ZIP, phone, fax, e-mail, date of birth, and intended use for the product.
- A request to "Please Print"—consumers don't always have the most legible handwriting.
- A box for appropriate titles such as Mr., Mrs., Miss, Ms. and what to do next: (Circle One).
- If the product comes in sizes or colors, or requires a monogram, provide blanks or boxes the target can check off. Make it easy, and be sure it is clear enough that the target will be sure to get what was offered.
- If the consumer is asking for more information, additional questions are needed to ensure appropriate information is sent out. For example, a form for more information about life insurance might include questions about current coverage and dependents.
- Any relevant guarantee information. Tell how the product can be returned, any steps that need to be taken or applicable conditions, and how long it will take for a refund to arrive.
- Prices.
- Ordering options such as toll-free numbers, fax numbers, and website addresses.
- Payment options such as credit cards accepted, money orders, or checks.
- How long it will take for the product or information to arrive. List any shipping and handling costs, and be sure to tell how the product will be shipped.
- If there is a self-addressed envelope attached, instructions to place the form in the envelope. If not, the address the target will need to mail in the form. If a self-addressed envelope will be included, you need to write the copy for it separately (usually after the order form copy on the copy sheet) and label it appropriately.
- Repeat the logo and include the slogan or tagline.

The order form closes the sale. No matter how creatively you delivered the key benefit, if the order form confuses or angers the consumer, everything else was a waste of time. It should be not only an order form, but a decorative and creative sales device. As a sales device, it is a call to action, the last step the target makes when purchasing. Make it an easy step.

## Guarantees

Offers such as guarantees and trial offers are interactive devices that all but eliminate buyer skepticism and ensure consumer satisfaction. The guarantee is important, so accentuate it in the copy. If the product or service does not offer a guarantee, be sure to stress the return policy or customer service options. A brand-loyal customer is a repeat purchaser and a word-of-mouth warrior concerning all positive and negative contact points.

Good guarantees remove any risk for the consumer and places responsibility for consumer happiness squarely on the client's shoulders. Consumers will gravitate toward those products that have guarantees and away from those that don't.

A guarantee is one of the "little things" the client can do for the target. It is expected, appreciated, and remembered. A guarantee can replace, substitute, or fully reimburse the consumer if not fully satisfied, and hopefully with no questions asked. It should be easy for the consumer, not time intensive or embarrassing.

## Copy Sheets

Copywriters submit completed copy on a copy sheet (see figure 7.2). Every piece of copy that appears in an ad, such as the headline, subhead(s), body copy, tagline or slogan, logo, and any guarantees, coupons or order form information, will appear on a copy sheet. If it does not appear there, it will not appear anywhere. Each piece of copy should be appropriately labeled and placed in the proper order in which it will be seen in the ad. The client, account executive, art director, and computer artist use the copy sheet as both a visual and verbal guide.

There is no standard format for a copy sheet; most often this is determined by the agency. The example presented in figure 7.2 is only one of many options for presenting copy.

Set the copy up in two columns, double-spaced, with all labels placed in the left column and all copy confined to the right column. Use 10- or 11-point Times or Helvetica. There should be approximately one inch of space between columns and one-inch margins on all four sides. Do not run columns together. Be sure to tab over so that all copy remains in the right column.

Coupon or order form copy appears below the logo on the copy sheet. Taglines or slogans can appear above or below the logo depending on the logo design.

**FIGURE 7.2**
Copy Sheet Template

Name
Assignment Number or Product Name

| | |
|---|---|
| Headline: | The headline should appear here. |
| Subhead: | The subhead should appear here, if applicable. |
| Body Copy A: | Tell the product or service's story here. |
| Subhead: | Multiple subheads are great when making a transition or to break up a copy heavy page. |
| Body Copy B: | Continue the copy here. |
| Subhead: | You need not use multiple subheads if your copy is short. |
| Body Copy C: | Continue the copy here. |
| Slogan: | This could also be a tagline and can either appear above or below the logo. |
| Logo: | The logo should appear here. |
| Body Copy D: | Consider placing detail copy here. |
| Coupon Copy: | Write all copy for coupon(s), including the need for the logo, etc., here. |
| Coupon 1: | If more than one coupon, place copy for the first coupon here. |
| Coupon 2: | Place the copy for the second coupon here, and so on. |
| Order Form: | Write all copy for the order form, including the need for the logo. |

## Selling the Client on the Creative Idea

It would be remiss to close this discussion of copy and layout without discussing what happens next. Once copy and layout are done, the entire concept will have to be sold to the client.

The account executive may present anywhere from three to five ideas for the client to consider. Ideas are usually pitched to the client by the account executive who heads the account. A new product pitch will be done with super comps that feature the headline, subhead, visuals and body copy to promote the concept. Pitches to existing clients may be a little less formal, with roughs. Layout will show only headlines, subheads, and visuals with the body copy not yet written and depicted with lines. There may or may not be a member of the creative team present.

The first step is to be sure the account executive understands the idea, where it came from, and how it relates to the client's communication goals. It's also helpful if you can back the idea up with research. It is especially important to be able to back up how the idea addresses the objectives, reaches the target, and reflects the key benefit; how the product will be positioned in the marketplace; and the brand image you are trying to build.

Once an ad is accepted the client needs to sign off on it. Once it is signed off on, it is ready to go to publication with this copy and/or this layout.

# Campaigns

## The IMC Campaign

Integrated marketing communication (IMC) campaigns differ from traditional campaigns in the way they are managed and in terms of overall outcomes. (See figure 8.1 for a sample campaign.) Like a traditional campaign, an IMC campaign has one unifying message and image, and talks to a specific target audience. Here is where the similarity ends. Unlike most traditional advertising campaigns, an effective IMC campaign focuses on long-term results that build brand image and brand equity, and works toward building a brand loyal consumer. An IMC campaign talks to an individual via a two-way dialogue, creating interactive opportunities to connect directly with the targeted individual. IMC campaigns employ more diverse media vehicles than traditional efforts, and choose media based on the target's lifestyle and media usage. Conversely, traditional advertising campaigns talk at a mass target audience in a one-way monologue, and use fewer media outlets. Finally, in an IMC campaign all members of the promotional mix, beyond advertising, are working together to strategically accomplish the same objectives, rather than as individual contractors.

So an IMC campaign can be defined as one that uses diverse media to deliver a strategic, cohesive, centralized collection of planned messages that focus on a single idea or concept. Campaign development can be broken down into four distinct steps.

- Planning the campaign
- Isolating a single idea or key benefit
- Developing a cohesive visual/verbal message
- Selecting media

---

**FIGURE 8.1**

---

# CAMPAIGN CASE STUDY: ESURANCE

Today the insurance industry is in a battle for consumer attention—not based on rates or options, but on creative strategy.

## Discussion

The newest insurance carrier to entice us with creative ingenuity is Esurance, a direct-to-consumer auto insurance provider. Esurance, a division of New Hampshire–based White Mountain Insurance Group, is only five years old and comes to us via the Internet. Oddly enough, in the insurance world, they own no brick and mortar buildings and offer no face-to-face agent care, just "aggressive online marketing tactics," reports Alex Miller in *OMMA*/MediaPost Publications. In today's world of advertising overload, the big idea can and must capture attention, create interest, and make the product stand out from the competition. So if buying insurance isn't on the top of your list, you're not alone; it's nobody's favorite sport. That's why Esurance has focused on creativity to generate awareness and worked to simplify the online buying process.

## The Idea

Using a small marketing budget, with television making up the bulk of it, the idea was to make the Esurance name stand out and bring attention to its services through the use of a sexy cartoon super-spy. In 2005 Esurance launched a television campaign about a pink-haired secret agent known as Erin Esurance who is tough, savvy, sexy, and good enough to outrace the bad guys, making her escape in various types of motorized vehicles.

Esurance was careful to be sure its website visually and verbally matched the message seen by consumers on television, to not only tie the media and messages together, but to avoid any confusion.

## Using a Character Representative in an IMC Campaign

Part of this consistent visual/verbal message is Erin herself. Esurance set out to create a humorous, visually interesting TV commercial that would hold the viewer's attention and not turn anyone off. Erin may not be realistic, but she is memorable. When she's on the air, the website is buzzing with fact-finding activity. Because of this, it is unlikely we will see Erin's demise any time soon.

## The Interactive Target

Esurance is interested in attracting young auto insurance shoppers, who are Internet junkies, price conscious, and less interested in additional or add-on packages. Internet surf-aholics love Erin and have taken more than a passing interest in her welfare and escapades. Interaction is an outcome of Erin's popularity since many fans e-mail and check the website to find out what her next adventure will entail.

## Media Mix

For Esurance to compete, it had to branch out to larger media outlets such as television to build much-needed brand awareness. Esurance focuses on using national cable TV. In addition to building brand awareness, TV's purpose was to move people online to their website, the foundation of their marketing strategy.

To keep awareness high, in 2006 Esurance continued to run television spots in conjunction with their online presence. In an additional attempt to progressively build brand awareness, they added both radio and direct mail to the media mix. "While online and TV drive the bulk of the company's marketing plan," Alex Miller reports, "[Esurance's Kristin] Brewe says the media mix includes radio in local markets featuring vignettes from Erin's adventures; sponsorships, such as Esurance's involvement with the San Francisco Giants; and 'pride marketing,' which has Esurance running print ads in gay magazines such as *Genre*."

## Make It Interactive, And Stay Awhile

Esurance's website focuses on providing policy and company information making purchasing auto policies as fast and easy as possible. But before the consumer rushes off, Esurance encourages lingering on the site for entertainment value. For Erin enthusiasts, the site contains the section "Erin's World," featuring the Erin Cam, Erin's Secret Diary (a blog by the fictional character), an Erin Art Gallery, and more. Fans of the commercials can also replay various TV and radio spots.

*Sources*: Alex Miller, "Cross-Media Case Study: Secret Agent of Change," *OMMA: The Magazine of Online Media, Marketing & Advertising*, March 2006, MediaPost Publications, http://publications.mediapost.com, accessed January 23, 2007; Esurance website, www.esurance.com, accessed January 23, 2007.

---

# Planning the Campaign

The planning, construction, and launch of a campaign doesn't happen overnight or in a vacuum. It takes a team of dedicated individuals working across many disciplines to bring each phase together on time, on budget, with the right message, placed in the correct media, and addressed to the right target.

In the planning stage, the account executive and the client will look at the marketing plan and review several key areas, including the target audience, the features and benefits of the product or service, the competition, and the communication objectives.

## Target Audience

Knowing what the target needs and wants from this product category, and how your client's product fits into or addresses those needs, is critical. In order to develop a consumer-focused approach, you must know as much about the target as you do about your own product or service. Their experiences, thoughts, ideas, and uses for the product are what will assist with message direction and positioning.

## Features and Benefits

It is important to know more about the product or service than just the key benefit. Knowing the product's attributes, capabilities, and limitations makes it easier to find a creative direction.

Questions you will need to ask include: How is the brand currently perceived? How does its current image affect what needs to be accomplished? Does the brand need to be strengthened or corrected? How many features does the product have? How is it manufactured? What is the quality of materials used and how is it reflected in the price, packaging, store layout, and so on?

Today's educated consumer is armed with enough product knowledge to compare brands and make purchasing decisions based on more than just price. The product must offer some kind of tangible benefit either not offered or not recognized by the competition. It is important to know the answers to the questions your target audience will ask before they compare products. The target audience is not attracted by a great idea alone; they are looking for concrete answers that offer a relevant benefit or solve a real problem. They want to know *What's in it for me?* Why do I need it? What problem can it solve? What are the benefits of ownership? How does it work? Where can I buy it? What does it cost? Is it easy to use? If you can answer these questions before they are asked, the product or service will appear more relevant than the competition's product or service.

## Competition

As with target and product knowledge, you can't know enough about the competition. How does your client's product measure up? Does the competition have studies or professionals backing up their claims or recommending the product? Do you? What is their image, slogan, concept or theme, and is it different enough from your own? Does the competition offer accessories to go with the product? How long have they been in business? How is their reputation? How well does their product perform as compared to your product?

Knowledge is endless when used to support a concept. Use this knowledge to build the product's image, develop a strategy and concept, and determine how the product should be positioned.

## Communication Objectives

Once the target, the product, and the competition have been reviewed, the next step requires another look at the communication objectives, or what the client wants to accomplish with its communication efforts. As discussed in chapter 2, most marketing objectives deal with sales. The conversion to communication-based objectives concentrates on what you want the target to think, feel, or do after exposure to the message. These objectives should be clearly stated, measurable, defined as long- or short-term in nature, and relate to the product's position in the product category.

## Isolating the Key Benefit

Determining the key benefit is easier once you know the product, the target, and the competition. With product knowledge, you can determine how the product or service—as opposed to the competition's product—can affect the target's lifestyle. The decision about which feature/benefit will be used as the key benefit will define the campaign.

The key benefit is the target's motivation to buy. It should fulfill a want or need, create excitement, or make the target feel better or more relaxed. In an IMC campaign the key benefit becomes the voice of the entire campaign. How it is delivered will depend on the strategy and the choice of tone, approach, and appeal used to define the visual/verbal message. Together, these will lay the foundation for how the brand will be positioned and the development of the brand's image. And of course, it should answer the target's million-dollar question: *What's in it for me?*

## Developing a Cohesive Visual/Verbal Message

IMC campaigns must appear and speak with one cohesive and consistent tone of voice across the promotional mix. The visual/verbal message is the common thread that will bind all the communication efforts together. A key benefit alone, if clearly stated and properly targeted, should be enough to bind a campaign together—but does not create a lasting visual/verbal identity on its own. The ability to create a visual/verbal relationship between pieces not only assists with brand-name recognition and image development, but also attracts both left- and right-brained target members. The diverse choice of visual/verbal ties should reflect both the strategy and the brand's image and may include typeface and style, layout style, headline and body copy style, color usage, spokesperson or character representative, jingle, package design, logo, and slogan and/or tagline.

Whatever is used to bind the ads together, it must become synonymous with the product or service—the first thing that comes to mind when the product is mentioned. If a product or service is associated with a catchy statement or phrase that becomes a part of mainstream conversation—like "Whassup?"—or a catchy jingle consumers can't get out of their heads—like the Oscar Mayer Wiener Song—raises awareness, and gives lasting impact to a campaign.

# Why Multiple Pieces?

By this point you may be wondering why you need a series of ads: Why won't just one or two do? Repetitive visual/verbal ties are what differentiates a campaign from a single-view message. Single-view means the message is seen one time and is not associated with any other advertising used currently or previously. One ad with one message, or even a once-in-a-while message, is not a campaign, and does not offer a synchronized message. Individualized message delivery has no repetitive identity reinforcement and does not build or strengthen an existing brand image.

Because consumers are exposed to so many messages, a single-view ad does not create a memorable identity. It takes consistent visual cues and a repetitive message in order for the viewer to give an ad more than a passing glance. Without repetitive consistency, the experience goes into short-term memory and is quickly forgotten. For a message to be stored in the target's long-term memory, it must be repeatedly seen or heard.

So why do single-view ads at all? There are several reasons why an ad may only be seen once, but the two most common reasons are poor planning and overstock or sales-related opportunities. Poor planning is a problem that can and often does affect brand loyalty and brand equity. If the consumer does not receive the correct information, stock is not available, or the message is placed in the wrong media, both the target and the product are affected. Overstocks, on the other hand, provide a great incentive to purchase. Additional stock usually means that lower prices are passed on to a motivated consumer.

No matter the reason, the goal is to use the same campaign-uniting devices that were used in previous advertising and promotional efforts to make a single-view ad fit within the campaign pattern seamlessly.

## The Promotional Mix

Once you know whom you are talking to and why, and what needs to be said, determining the correct promotional mix will be much easier. What media mix will reach the target? Will you need to use a more personalized, interactive media mix, such as direct mail or a website? Do you need to woo the target back or get her to try the product with some type of a sales promotion? Or will mass advertising in print or broadcast do the trick? Remember, in order to get the target to act, she must first be made aware of the product or service and see the product positioned as different or unique from the competition.

It is also important that campaign ideas translate well from medium to medium. Once the concept is solidified, the final promotional and media mix will be critical to the visual/verbal message. The concept may have the benefit of being expressed in hundreds of words, or in only a few, or it may be heard and not seen. Knowing each medium's strengths and limitations will keep the concept from losing its visual and verbal integrity. IMC is not cohesive if the visual or verbal message cannot stand alone.

An IMC promotional mix includes public relations; newspaper, magazine, radio, and television advertising; direct marketing; sales promotion; and Internet marketing, also known as cybermarketing. We will look at each of these individually in chapters 10–16. In whatever medium a piece appears, it must consistently use the same tone-of-voice and repetitive appearance that is used to represent the key benefit throughout the campaign.

## Synergizing the Promotional Mix Message

Synergistic visual/verbal development is the backbone of IMC. Synergy happens when all messages to the target speak with one tone of voice and project a common image, giving the message more impact than any single message could by itself. Without the synergistic coordination of messages you will not deliver a cohesive, consistent message to the target that repeatedly reinforces the key benefit. Multiple uncoordinated messages appearing in multiple media not only create confusion about what the product stands for, but keep the consumer from retaining the message. For example, if public relations works independently of advertising it is not privy to the strategy being employed to deliver the key benefit, and coordination of efforts are not possible. Public relations may mistakenly announce a new product, highlighting one feature/benefit, months before advertising is ready to launch a campaign focusing on a completely different feature/benefit. Inconsistent messages can successfully erode a product's competitive edge. Consequently, brand image and brand loyalty are affected when sales personnel or customer service representatives are flooded with questions to which they have no answer.

## Types of Campaigns

Campaigns typically fall into one of four distinct varieties: national, service, corporate, and retail. Let's take a look at each one.

### National Campaigns

National campaigns use a diverse promotional mix and can be seen or heard across the country. Campaigns of this size are very expensive and are most often undertaken by the corporate giants. Established brands, large budgets, and a diverse promotional mix drive national campaigns.

Students of advertising often mistake large budgets as the key to making a campaign stand out while assuming those with smaller budgets will languish or even fail. Nothing could be further from the truth. A big budget does not make a great idea, but it can sure help one along. Memorable advertising is idea driven and target focused on the key benefit.

### Service Campaigns

Service campaigns are no different from product-based advertising. Although everyone needs and uses services such as health care, banking, or insurance, the goal is to make your client's service stand out from the competition as the one everyone wants. One of the best ways to do this is talk about service issues, such as customer service, no health screenings, easy claim service, or no waiting, to name just a few. The key is to offer the same service as the competition but to make it seem more important to your service organization. Then, when the target opens the phone book to find a representative or location nearby, he will see your ad and remember the visual/verbal message from television or the newspaper—and a bond is created. Your message may directly offer a solution to a problem he is having.

Service is about comfort. You cannot touch customer service, but you can experience it every time you enter the bank or need compassionate health care. Giving your ads a similar appearance and tone of voice reminds the target of who your client is and what it has to offer, every time they see an ad. Service campaigns need to emit "warm fuzzies" such as security, trust, and reliability. The very word "service" means more than one thing, so be sure to tie your key benefit to the overall philosophy of the service provider.

## Corporate Campaigns

Corporate advertising is basically a company tooting its own horn. Here, a corporation takes the opportunity to let its target know what it has been up to, such as cleaning up the environment with new product developments or building homes for hurricane victims. Service to the community creates goodwill, contributes to a brand's equity, and tells environmentally or socially minded targets that this company is helping society or the environment in some meaningful way—an excellent key benefit source. Corporate advertising can raise employee morale as well because it talks about the company's community and national contributions or involvement, which ultimately affects the employees.

When repositioning is needed to address target needs or to compete with competitors, it is important that the direction the campaign is taking be communicated not only externally but internally as well. Internally, other shareholders such as employees, retailers, and tradesmen often will be asked to adjust or adapt to corporate changes. Internal communication is important to how successful the external advertising efforts will be. For example, if the message to the public is "Avis: We Try Harder," employees with access to the public must understand this message. Nothing kills advertising momentum faster than retailers or customer service representatives who don't know—and thus can't act upon—the corporate message.

The worst kind of corporate advertising results from bad publicity, where a company must repair its image in the mind of the consumer. This is a very costly and time-intensive process. The corporation must prove itself all over again to the target in order to build back consumer loyalty. Politics also plays a big role in corporate advertising when corporations use advertising to influence political leaders on upcoming legislation.

## Retail Campaigns

Often referred to as the ultimate real estate sale, retail campaigns can push individual products but more often than not promote a store or business over individual products. The campaign is usually based on price but can also be based on reputation. A business's reputation foretells price and quality, whether the target is dealing with Tiffany & Co., Zales, or Billy Bob's Jewelry Emporium. Each will approach advertising differently: Some will push price, while others exist on image and reputation alone.

Retail campaigns rarely stand out creatively since price is generally the name of the game. However, uniformity is still critical to memorability and status versus product relationships. Because price plays such an important role and constant change is a fact of life, a sense of urgency is always present. Whether the sale lasts a weekend, a week, or a month, the goal is to get consumers into the store.

Unlike the other campaigns we have looked at, retail campaigns have a lot to do. They must initiate attention, create interest, announce prices, direct buyers throughout the store, demonstrate or showcase products, and encourage purchase through price or quality. A retail campaign never stops selling, from the signage outside to the shopping bag purchases are placed in.

All points of contact during the target's shopping experience should reflect the campaign's tone of voice and overall appearance (see figure 8.2). Here are some of the ways a retail-based IMC campaign can sell the key benefit throughout the entire shopping experience:

- Presale advertising or direct mail announcements, with or without coupons
- Window displays
- Window signage
- Interior displays or kiosks
- Shelf and rack announcements
- In-store credit card promotions
- In-store signage
- In-store announced promotions
- Promotional buttons or T-shirts for sales personnel
- Unique, attractive, or colorful wrapping tissue and coordinated shopping bags or boxes
- Table tent promotions for restaurants
- Receipt coupons
- Credit card stuffers

These are just a few of the techniques an IMC effort can successfully employ to build image through its communication efforts. However, image is more than advertising; promotional efforts, internal changes that deal with sales personnel, and decor should be adapted to match communication efforts. Even a discount department store can deliver discounts without looking or acting like it: Well-stocked store shelves; a clean environment; friendly, nicely dressed salespeople; and attractively displayed merchandise can give the illusion of quality at a bargain price.

Taking dry research and seemingly unrelated objectives and turning them into a message that speaks directly to the target across multiple media is not an easy task. The success of creative efforts will depend on how well it mimics and delivers the research found in the creative brief. Since the creative brief is limited to statistical information, it is up to the creative team to turn that information into a viable creative solution that is on target.

Staying on target requires finding an appropriate creative direction. For a good place to start look at the brand name, the packaging, and the product's uses. It is the creative teams job to develop connections to the product or service. Consider doing the opposite

**FIGURE 8.2**

To promote the annual Joffrey Ballet gala, Saatchi & Saatchi created a ballerina doing pirouettes in a revolving door. Image courtesy of Saatchi & Saatchi. Year: 2005; Category: Ambient; Title: Ballerina; Advertiser: Joffrey Ballet School; Product or Service: Ballet School; Advertising Agency: Saatchi & Saatchi; Country: USA; Creative Director: Tony Granger/ Barbara Boyle; Copywriter: Jens Paul Pfau/Glen Levy; Art Director: Menno Kluin/Paul Kwong; Account Supervisor: Mark Rolland

of what the target expects—like a surprise ending in a movie, lead them in one direction only to land somewhere else. Consider using plays on words; although advertisers are often criticized for exploiting the English language for their own creative purposes, it is a memorable way to present a message. The only limits is that you must not deviate from the brief, reach the wrong audience, or talk to them about something they don't care about.

The message cannot be implied or it will not accomplish the stated objectives or receive the needed recognition and sales throughout all media. Consumers do not want to work at understanding the message; if your message is not clear, they will choose a competing brand where the information is clear and the benefit is immediately apparent.

## Concept Components

IMC campaigns consist of three interrelated components that affect concept development and overall appearance: campaign uniformity and visual and verbal uniformity.

Campaign uniformity means that the overall look and message are consistent no matter the media outlet used or the final appearance of any creative piece. Visual uniformity means that all creative materials have a unique appearance or look. This happens when layouts, representative characters, slogans/taglines, or even representative color combinations are found on all pieces. Verbal uniformity takes place when all creative pieces promote one idea or key benefit. For the campaign to be successful it must strategically accomplish the objectives developed in the creative brief and spotlight the key benefit. A diverse promotional mix using the same verbal tone of voice and visual appearance increases the likelihood that the target will see and remember the message, positioning your client's product away from the competition.

The components affecting campaign development emerge from the creative brief to form the campaign's overall creative foundation. Before any concept direction can be successful, it must be able to address and accomplish each of the following:

- Every campaign is driven by a key benefit in the form of either a big idea or unique selling proposition (USP).
- Strategically, all ads work to accomplish the stated objectives.
- The campaign's message must speak directly to the target audience's needs and wants.
- Overall appearance may be based on a specific message or idea, layout or headline style, character or spokesperson, typeface and style, visual element, or color combinations.
- The campaign has a visual/verbal identity that is clearly recognizable in all advertising and promotional devices.
- The concept direction creates a unique brand identity to set the product off from its competition.

Know what needs to be accomplished before you begin the design phase, exhaust the brainstorming and word list stages, and find the unique and discard the "been there, done that" ideas. It is key that any campaign include cohesiveness, consistency, and repetition.

Does your campaign idea have *all* of these key elements throughout the promotional mix? If not, what component(s) need to be adjusted to create the uniformity needed?

## The Concept Develops the Visual/Verbal Ties

A campaign's unifying nature brings a constant and reliable performance to each campaign piece. For a campaign to stand out from the competitive crowd and attract attention, it must have a visual/verbal look, tone, personality, and appearance all its own. The verbal elements include headlines, subheads, body copy, slogans or taglines, and jingles. Each element has a distinct job to do in order to tell the product or service's story. Sound can also unify a campaign through the use of jingles or music or the distinctive voice of a spokesperson. In order to define the brand's image, it will need a distinct, coordinated tone of voice that can express and identify the brand's personality.

Verbal elements should create a cohesive and consistent tone of voice throughout the campaign and across all media. A campaign's message should be so intertwined that the consumer gets the feeling of continuity of thought from one ad to the next.

Verbal elements include:

- *Headlines.* Headlines are most often used to announce the key benefit. Each headline's tone of voice should match the tone, approach, and appeal determined in the strategy and should give the brand an identity. The choice of headline style should complement the brand's image and bring the concept to life. For example, if you ask a question of the target in a newspaper ad, also ask one in magazine, outdoor, radio, and television ads.
- *Subheads.* A subhead should continue the thought concerning the key benefit began in the headline. The subhead's job is to keep the reader moving through the ad by offering tantalizing bits of information.
- *Body Copy.* The length and overall voice of the body copy is also a great way to tie ads together. Body copy tells the products story through its features and benefits, primary uses, and any additional or secondary uses that will help to demonstrate the product's importance in the target's life. The first paragraph should continue the discussion on the key benefit, the middle section should make the sale, and the closing paragraph should move the target to action.
- *Slogan or Tagline.* A slogan identifies a corporate or product philosophy; a tagline reflects the concept and key benefit used in a campaign. No matter which one is used, it should always appear just above or below the logo. If a slogan is spoken on radio and/or television, be sure it appears to be spoken in print by the character representative or spokesperson.
- *Jingle.* If you can sing the message in a catchy way, why bore the target by saying it? Jingles can get in a target's head and stay there; that's why jingles are described as "catchy."

Visual elements speak to the target in a different way; they help the target see or experience the product or service and the benefit it will bring to his life. Visual images can show the product in use or place the product in the hands of the target. The types of images chosen, as well as layout and typeface, can suggest the visual/verbal tone of voice to be used. Color choices can set a mood, and the purposeful placement of elements within an ad can help define the overall product image. Consistency and repetitiveness is key to binding campaign pieces together; nothing can be said or shown just once in any IMC campaign series.

Visual elements include:

- *Layout Style.* Layout style, or the overall way each component is laid out or placed within the ad, creates a consistent visual appearance across media. Use the same layout style for each printed piece. Layout styles can transfer to radio and television through tone of voice, with the character or spokesperson delivering the message.
- *Visual Images.* The choice of images depends on the concept. If using a nostalgia theme, think about using black-and-white photographs or a Norman Rockwell style of illustration that complements the concept. If the concept deals with making what is old new again, the use of spot color on a black-and-white photograph can highlight the product or logo by creating eye flow. Graphic images give a modern, stylish, or trendy feel to a product, while color photographs bring the product alive with rich colors, textures, and detail.
- *Typeface.* The same typeface, type style, and weight should be used in all ads in the campaign. Whenever possible, headlines, subheads, and body copy should be the same point size and length, as size creates a visual unity between ads.
- *Character or Spokesperson.* A representative, either animated or human, who can speak for and represent a product gives a personality or face to the product and should appear in all pieces. If possible, the image should be approximately the same size; at the very least, the same amount of image should appear in every ad. A repetitive head-and-shoulders shot, for example, can be used at different sizes.
- *Repetitive Border Treatments* can create a mood. Use of a decorative border, whether elaborate or simplistic, can isolate both the ad and the elements within the ad by pulling the viewer in, creating an air of exclusivity and elegance. Depending on the graphic images used, borders with images within them or as an extension of them, can create an illusion of playfulness or hominess, or give it a seasonal appeal.
- *Color.* Color, or the lack thereof, can make an ad unique in the same way a particular illustrative, graphic, or photographic style can. The choice of color should support the overall key benefit and strategy. Color choices can be used as design elements, to create specific emotions, or to set a mood or attract the eye. Color is also easier to remember than product names.
- *Logos, Slogans, or Taglines.* The logo, slogan, or tagline should appear in basically the same location on all pieces and should be the same size whenever possible.

To help determine whether your campaign is consistent across all media and has all the required elements, see the campaign checklist in figure 8.3.

**FIGURE 8.3**

Campaign Checklist

1. ____ Does each ad clearly state the key benefit?
2. ____ Does the campaign's message talk to the target audience in their language and in a way that holds their attention?
3. ____ Does the campaign's message address and answer each stated objective?
4. ____ Is the relationship clear between the key benefit, the headline, the body copy, and the visuals?
5. ____ Is this relationship reflected in the strategy?
6. ____ Does each ad or promotion's overall image match the tone, approach, and appeal stated in the strategy?
7. ____ Does the layout style chosen reflect the strategy?
8. ____ If you created a jingle, do the music and words reflect the strategy?
9. ____ Is the concept as strong visually as it is verbally, no matter what the medium it appears in?
10. ____ Is the concept unique to your product, and does it position itself away from the competition?
11. ____ Does the copy's tone of voice match that stated in the strategy?
12. ____ Does the first paragraph of the body copy continue the key benefit discussion began in the headline?
13. ____ Does the middle paragraph of the body copy give enough information about the product to understand what it is, what it does, and how it will affect the target's lifestyle?
14. ____ Does the copy close with a call to action?
15. ____ Did you remember to include the detail copy, to make shopping or ordering easier?
16. ____ Is the message clearly consumer focused?
17. ____ Do the visual components match the strategy?
18. ____ Do the visuals match the image created in the headline and copy?
19. ____ Is the logo clearly seen in every message?
20. ____ Does the slogan or tagline appear in every message?
21. ____ If you used specific color combinations in the ads, do they appear in every message and do they match the tone, approach, and appeal used in the strategy?
22. ____ Is the typeface and style consistent on every ad?
23. ____ Is the layout style evident and the tone apparent on every ad?
24. ____ Did you keep the headline size and body copy length as consistent as possible on every ad?
25. ____ If you are using a spokesperson or character representative, is he or she seen or heard in every ad?
26. ____ Is the cropping and image size as consistent as possible in every ad?
27. ____ Does the package's design match the brand's image?
28. ____ Does the campaign reflect a long-term focus, with enough time built in to build consumer loyalty?

29. ____ Are there interactive components built into the campaign?
30. ____ Does the promotional mix reflect the target's lifestyle and interests?
31. ____ Is the visual/verbal relationship so strong that if your campaign were thrown into a vat with a thousand other campaigns, the target would be able to pick out your series of ads?
32. ____ Does your IMC campaign have one clear benefit, a distinct appearance, and one tone of voice that is apparent across all media?

## Know Your Media

Know your promotional mix before finalizing concept direction. Knowing where the ads will be seen or heard will help determine the best way to show or tell the concept. For example, should the concept rely on a lengthy verbal message to get its point across, or will media restrictions allow only a few words to make the same point? Will visuals that show the product in use, in a setting, or through some kind of demonstration, say the key benefit better?

## Spokespersons and Character Representatives

When you have something you want to say visually, consider using a visual voice in the form of a spokesperson or animated character representative.

The spokesperson for a product is important. He or she must be likeable, with an appearance that fits the campaign's overall visual/verbal concept. To determine an appropriate spokesperson, ask yourself: Who does this product remind me of? Remember, it's your product's personality that sets if off from the competition, especially if there are no major differences between brands in the same category.

There are three basic types of spokespersons.

| | | |
|---|---|---|
| • Celebrities | • Specialists and CEOs | • Common Man |

### Celebrities

A celebrity's popularity with younger target audiences can be transferred to a product, and this popularity can actually build a product's brand equity. It is important that the celebrity's professional image be tied to the product's key benefit. This image translates to the product, so any character flaws that arise in a celebrity over time will reflect upon the product. Celebrity endorsements can be broken down into five different areas:

*Unpaid Onscreen Spokesperson.* Charities supported by a celebrity are the most common benefactors of an unpaid onscreen spokesperson.

*Paid Onscreen Spokesperson.* Paid onscreen spokespersons are one of the most common types of spokesperson. This is where a celebrity is paid to tie her image to a product and physically represent it in all advertising efforts.

*Celebrity Voiceover.* This type of spokesperson is used for radio and television. Voiceovers are less expensive spokespersons because they deliver the message offscreen and the celebrity is not identified or seen. Celebrity voiceovers are not a great choice for use in IMC campaigns since a visual image cannot be used on all media vehicles.

*Dead Person Endorsement.* A dead person can't speak, but his image can. The use of old interviews or movie clips can associate personality traits, political activism, and even nostalgia with a product. The use of this type of spokesperson is very controversial and often considered in bad taste.

*Animated Character Spokesperson.* Believe it or not, the Keebler Elves and the Pillsbury Doughboy are celebrities. We like them, we trust them, and they have been around so long we consider them friends. They might make us feel a little nostalgic, and we may even associate their image with a specific event.

## Specialists and CEOs

If something needs to be proven, use a specialist in the field, like doctors, scientists or engineers. If you want to develop a philosophy, create a friendship, or instill trust, use a CEO or owner of a small company or business.

## Common Man

The common man can be someone who uses the product and can talk about his or her experiences, or a paid actor representing the common man based on feedback from real consumers. Why use an actor when you can use a real common man? It has nothing to do with trying to deceive the public and everything to do with how the message is delivered. A trained actor will be able to deliver the message with less effort and with more believability. Any time a substitution is made, it must be stated in the ad. With that being said, common-man endorsements are becoming more common. It is thought that celebrities, with all their power and faults, have saturated the market and are becoming less believable. They also limit the length of time a campaign can run; star power rarely lasts as long as a product's does.

## Personality Traits for an Effective Spokesperson

In order to reach out and touch the target, the character or spokesperson must resonate with the target. If consumers don't like or respect the image or person delivering the message, they will tune out. We search for people like us, so personality traits should reflect the target's self-image and lifestyle. When developing a character or hiring a spokesperson, consider the following traits:

- Appearance
- Likeability
- Trustworthiness
- Expertise
- Credibility

Character representatives begin in an art director's imagination, much like a live spokesperson does. The choice to use a live person or to create a character spokesman will have a lot to do with concept and a little to do with budget.

There are times when a live actor can simply not be found that fits the client's direction or the art director's conceived personality for the product. When you can't find it, you create it. Budget can also affect whether a spokesperson will be local talent or a celebrity. But at any level, live talent is more expensive to maintain than a character on a page.

Character reps may come from word association, folklore, historical characters or events, or even from an art director's past experiences. Character reps are easy to work with; they have no demands, are never late, and never grow old. Their images can and often do last longer than a live representative spokesperson. Here are a few character representatives you may recognize:

- Aunt Jemima
- The GEICO Gecko
- The Energizer Bunny
- The Jolly Green Giant
- The Keebler Elves
- Charlie the Tuna
- Mr. Clean
- The Pillsbury Doughboy
- Tony the Tiger

It is important to remember you want your campaign to run for a long period of time, perhaps decades. If you keep in mind how the concept can grow and mature over time, you can almost guarantee the campaign will have staying power. This is one of the reasons to stay away from trends and current celebrities and create your own trends and your own celebrities through spokespersons or character representatives.

## Stand Up and Stand Out: It Pays to Be Different

Product categories with little or no product differentiation need a unique creative approach to set the product apart not by features, but by status, or image, or imagination. This is where the right strategic appeal creates difference among the masses. Targets will buy a created and creative image over the status quo; it just needs to fit their image and their needs. What will be the tie that binds—a character or spokesman, a jingle, or theme-related headline treatment, slogan, or layout style? The key to creative individualism lies in the research and the brainstorming stages. Create a trend, tie it to an existing trend, resurrect a trend, or create a voice or a statement that can be reinforced visually through photographs, illustrations, or graphic devices.

Campaigns and their creative imagery and messages allow you to continually remind the target what your product or service brings to them over the competition. See figure 8.4 for an additional campaign case study using guerilla marketing.

---

**FIGURE 8.4**

---

# GUERILLA MARKETING CASE STUDY: NIKE

## Background

Nike is a high-profile athletic apparel and footwear company. Rising into prominence during the late '70s and early '80s, Nike dominated its industry until the mid-'90s. In the past few years, however, Nike has experienced difficulties in positioning itself effectively with young consumers, who have purposely avoided overtly commercial brands. These consumers, particularly extreme and alternative sports enthusiasts, have instead pledged their allegiance to newer, younger brands like Volcom and/or "old-school" companies like Adidas who have staged recent comebacks.

## Challenge

To provide Nike with enhanced credibility and increased brand awareness within the alternative and extreme sports demographic.

## Solution

To achieve this goal, a youth-focused skate- and bike-jumping contest was conceived. The contest was to be promoted primarily through unconventional marketing techniques, rather than mainstream advertising. It was decided that this strategy would best drive action and awareness within the Southern California alternative and extreme sports market.

Video footage was first collected, with highlights taken of the best skaters and bike jumpers in the local areas. The footage was posted on the Nike website, along with information about the upcoming contest. The contest was then heavily promoted on a street level basis throughout specific target markets, driving further buzz and excitement. The contest was held in Venice Beach, in order to maximize awareness and exposure. Many of the entrants came from neighboring areas, which helped to enroll community support and interest.

In addition, Nike branded materials such as bracelets and Frisbees were distributed at local skate parks/shops, BMX stores, sports competitions, and many other venues that consistently draw members of Nike's target market. Thousands of Nike stencils were chalked on areas outside of popular local hangouts, and a "picketing" campaign was executed with street marketers using bullhorns outside of urban music concerts to promote the contest.

## Results

The contest was heavily attended and Nike was able to significantly increase its brand awareness/ image within the highly influential Southern California alternative sports market.

*Case study courtesy of OnPoint Marketing.*

# Public Relations

## The Strategic Use of Public Relations in IMC

Public relations is a mostly nonpaid form of communication that builds relationships with both internal and external audiences through communication efforts that reinforce, defend, or rebuild a corporation's or product's image. External audiences are a company or organization's "publics" or target. Internal audiences are referred to as stakeholders or those who have a stake or vested interest in the company's success and reputation. See figure 9.1 for an integrated marketing communication (IMC) public relations case study.

## Marketing Public Relations

When IMC uses public relations to promote a brand, it's known as marketing public relations (MPR). MPR uses nonpaid media vehicles in either print or broadcast to inform the public about a product, service, or corporation.

MPR deals with the "selling" of a corporate or brand image to a specifically defined target audience. Traditional corporate public relations deals with many different publics, both internal, such as shareholders and employees, and external, such as consumers and organizations. This is different from traditional public relations, which is most often utilized as a promotional or informational outlet. Public relations in the past has been relegated to a support role, responding more to what the client wanted than what the advertising message required. This disconnect often generated unplanned, mistimed, incompatible messages that

---

**FIGURE 9.1**

---

# IMC PUBLIC RELATIONS CASE STUDY: PBB GLOBAL LOGISTICS

## The Client: PBB Global Logistics

- Worldwide Integrated Logistics Company
- 900 employees, 70 offices
- Diverse service offerings
- Tri-Media is PBB's outsourced marketing department (1996-2002)

## The Challenge

To create an Integrated Marketing Communications strategy including a wide range of collateral materials for a 50-year-old company transforming itself from a customs broker into a worldwide logistics leader. The company needed a new global approach for its marketing strategy, better ways to reach its expanding target audiences and more efficient means of communication with existing customers and suppliers worldwide.

## The Solution

The Integrated Marketing Communications strategy started with solid research. The team spent considerable time studying the company and its competitors, becoming knowledgeable in the logistics industry.

Tri-Media developed an Integrated Marketing Communications plan, which outlined a number of strategies and tactics to achieve the company's objectives in the most effective and efficient way possible.

The first tactic was to revitalize the corporate identity. Founded as Peace Bridge Brokerage in 1946, the company had grown to offer much more than just customs brokerage. The PBB corporate identity was repositioned to reflect the worldwide focus of the company and its new name.

By creating targeted marketing materials that reflect the drastically changing landscape of global trade, PBB Global Logistics increased awareness of its integrated services, introduced its new brand name and image, and built revenues and sales. The following is a description of the printed materials that Tri-Media developed for PBB Global Logistics that were used to revamp its corporate image.

## I. The Print Materials

### 1. Corporate Brochure

**The Challenge** To integrate nine distinct service offerings into one seamless print piece, positioning the company as a global leader in logistics management while underscoring the brand image.

**The Result**  A 12-page brochure with cover (English and French) that allows PBB's sales team to educate prospects and introduce services.

## 2. Solutions Newsletter (External—Produced Quarterly)

**The Challenge**  To position PBB as a knowledgeable global logistics company, spotlight upcoming trends and industry news, promote new services and personnel, while increasing top-of-mind awareness within its target audience.

**The Result**  An 8-page full color newsletter (English and French)—direct mailed to a database of clients, prospects and subscribers. Accountability was tracked through reader response mechanisms and online surveys.

## 3. Teamwork Talks Newsletter (Internal—Produced Quarterly)

**The Challenge**  To create an informative and useful platform to educate and inform PBB's team of employees and facilitate internal communication.

**The Result**  An 8-page newsletter—distributed to each employee around the world. Accountability was tracked through staff feedback surveys and questionnaires.

## 3. Service Sales Sheets (Produced as Required)

**The Challenge**  To create service specific information sales sheets for each of PBB's integrated services within the creative framework and brand image of the company.

**The Result**  A series of English and French sales sheets indicating key features, benefits and locations for each service.

## 4. Introductory Brochure

**The Challenge**  To create a conveniently sized brochure for widespread distribution that introduces targets to PBB and its diverse integrated services while including a response mechanism.

**The Result**  A 5-panel brochure, folding to 3.75" x 8.5" with perforated reader reply card—two mail-back versions—U.S. and Canada. The brochure reflects and reinforces the PBB brand image.

# II. Advertising Program

## The Challenge

To develop an advertising campaign including advertising print and digital programs across North America. To use several mediums to create a multilayered message that ultimately produces synergy.

*(Continued)*

---

**FIGURE 9.1**

---

## The Result

A continent-wide media plan was researched and implemented. The goal was to inform essential business target markets of PBB's full complement of logistics services while introducing the company in newer markets.

Implementation occurs after market and media research is done. Various media sources are used to review each medium. These include but are not exclusive to CARD, CARD online, Bowdens, Ulrich's and the Internet. Various steps are taken to ensure that only the right publications are used. These steps include communication with PBB (listen to feedback on the previous year's experiences) review and chart editorial and researching related articles to products offered by PBB.

Tri-Media places over 100 ads each year in national publications (both Canadian and U.S.) and in regional publications (in Canada: British Columbia, Alberta, the Prairies, Ontario, Quebec and Atlantic Canada; in the U.S.: Northeast and Western New York, Atlanta, Chicago and the Pacific Coast).

## III. Digital Media

### Web Site

http://www.pbb.com
PBB's Website is an important part of the IMC Plan. The informative and interactive site features a full catalogue of PBB services and innovative customs ProDoc software. It includes customs information as well as forms to expedite shipping and border crossing. The site features an Intranet and Extranet that helps to streamline information processes and result in efficiencies.

### Power Point Presentation

Tri-Media has developed a Power Point presentation template that is used as a base for sales, trade shows and other corporate presentations.

## IV. Promotions—Trade Show Materials

PBB participates in many trade shows across North America, involving a range of logistics services and industry sectors. Tri-Media developed a trade show booth that integrated PBB's corporate feel and look. The creative was designed to draw traffic to PBB's booth and heighten the professional image of PBB. Trade shows help to effectively reach new prospects that are not already in the company's database, and provide the opportunity to interact with existing clients.

## V. Public Relations Program

Tri-Media has developed public relations programs for PBB Global Logistics. We use news releases, feature articles, and print supplements to generate publicity.

News releases are sent to major trade media to solicit coverage of new services and announcements for PBB, projecting an unbiased message via editorial content, and establishing credibility.

Feature articles in trade magazines and other print media contain background information to promote and add credibility to all of PBB's services as well as help to position PBB as an expert in the field of logistics and as the leading provider of logistic solutions.

An internal communications plan, which is a vital component for stakeholders and employees, was developed. The purpose of the program was to encourage constant communication between different departments and different offices and to build a high level of awareness of corporate goals and objectives. The "Teamwork Talks" internal newsletter is a key component of the public relations program.

*Case study courtesy of www.tri-media.com.*

---

often confused the target and eroded a brand's identity. Today, timing is controlled and all communication efforts coming from public relations representatives use the same tone of voice and appearance as other IMC messages. It is not unusual for public relations to be called upon from time to time to create or promote media events to strengthen or maintain interest in the product or service. Because of its access to the press, and their ability to reach the target, and its credible reputation, public relations is able to grease the way for the rest of the promotional mix both internally and externally.

Tactics used in marketing public relations might include:

- Print News Releases
- Media kits
- Video News Releases (VNRs)
- News Conferences
- Celebrity Spokesperson Interviews or Personal Appearances
- Sponsored Events

## Reinforcement

Public relations comes into the IMC process with experience in creating opportunities for two-way communication between the company, product, or service, and the target, making it a vital player in determining and managing the relationship between buyer and seller.

Because of this, public relations is excellent at initiating communication efforts through interactive exchanges between the consumer or technical assistance representatives and the consumer. This dissemination of information gives symmetrical information to all interested parties, bridging the communication gap between word-of-mouth gossip and factual information.

## Defense

Ideally, public relations practitioners will find themselves in an offensive position when introducing or maintaining image, but if any kind of negative publicity does arise, they will need to take a defensive position. These actions can play a huge role in creating and maintaining brand equity and brand loyalty. In a crisis or negative situation, the way in which the corporation's view or position is proactively handled can eliminate any negative or lingering effects concerning the corporation, product, or service.

## Rebuilding

If the public is not given the satisfaction of hearing from the corporation or organization, word of mouth takes over and affects equity and loyalty. Once consumer confidence is lost, it is very time consuming and costly to gain back. Continual informative messages countering opinions, hearsay, or investigative inquiries are critical to a product or services continued success.

## The Diversity of the Public Relations Voice

Public relations defines action. Its job is to get the word out about what a corporation or organization is doing locally, nationally, or internationally, how it affects their product or service, and/or their relationship with the target. This action becomes usable information to the public. Externally, its most traditional action-oriented tactics include news articles; televised events or interviews with company spokesmen, executives, or CEOs; news releases to local or national newspapers, or radio and television stations; and news conferences, to name just a few.

Communication inside a corporation is just as important as the message sent to the consumer. Devices such as newsletters deliver information on company events, insurance, investments, promotions, and retirements. Additionally, public relations representatives may act as a go-between for the corporation and the media, setting up interviews, writing speeches, and arranging sponsorships in order to arouse public interest or attract attention.

Additional responsibilities include planning any necessary restructuring for internal adjustments to any new company policies or philosophies associated with an IMC message, the development of corporate or community sponsorships, and the development of celebrity endorsements or the arrangement of appearances at an event.

When used as a marketing tool, public relations can launch products, build or enhance images, and inform consumers for very little money. Costs associated with public relations most often deal with salaries and development of printed materials.

A public relations representative's ability to build relationships and interact with consumers creates an interactive dialogue that makes the customer a part of the product's success and future development. An ongoing relationship with the press gives public relations media options not available with any of the other communication approaches. This ability to garner media coverage through events, news releases, press conferences, and interviews makes public relations especially suited to:

- Launching a new product or service
- Positioning or repositioning a product or service
- Generating "buzz" about a product or service
- Affecting and reaching specific target groups
- Handling scandal or negative publicity for a product, service, or corporation
- Building or maintaining the image of a product, service, or brand

## New Products

With a new product launch, public relations can create excitement or anticipation with facts rather than through creative execution. Because of its relationship with the press, public relations is considered more reliable than straight advertising.

## Positioning

The way a brand is positioned or repositioned will have everything to do with the target and/or parent company or corporation. If the product is positioned as safe and the corporation that manufactures that product is currently under investigation by a federal agency for safety violations, the product's position will be hurt by corporate actions. Once the consumer loses faith in a product or service, both brand loyalty and brand equity are affected. It can be very expensive and time consuming to rebuild a product's image. If the consumer dislikes or is distrustful of the corporation, extensive media coverage can enhance these feelings of distrust, successfully dooming any communication efforts.

## Generating Buzz

Public relations is a great source for creating a "buzz" or hype for a new product launch. Perfectly timed leaks to the press can create a perceived need for a product or service before it even hits the market. Because the information is coming from a credible source, the news media, a product can hit the market ahead of its competitors based on little information and a lot of excitement. However, the product or service must deliver on what is promised or implied to reinforce credibility and trust. Public relations representatives have many options available to them in order to create and build brand awareness that have nothing to do with the use of traditional advertising methods. Consider the following options when "buzz" is needed:

- *Sponsorships.* A sponsorship is when a corporation or brand commits its name and money to an event such as a golf tournament, concert, or charity event.
- *Talk shows.* If you can get a talk show host like Oprah or Howard Stern to talk about a product they use and like or a company that sponsored an event they were involved in, their popularity and credibility transfers to the product or service.
- *Product placement in movies or television programs.* If you remember the Reese's Pieces trail in the movie *ET*, you understand the importance of product placement. A product's success is usually associated with a character, but it can, if repeated often enough, become associated with a movie or television show. The sheer number of loyal viewers or moviegoers for popular features can boost sales and create or reinvent a brand's image.
- *Celebrity endorsements.* As discussed in chapter 8, celebrities can represent a product based on their success or reputation.
- *On-the-spot promotions.* In an on-the-spot promotion, a corporation takes the product to the people in order for them to try or see the product in use. These types of events are often set up on busy street corners, in malls, or anywhere a large number of people will be available to participate.
- *Inadvertent celebrity spokespersons.* An inadvertent celebrity spokesperson happens by accident when a spokesperson's persona is so well liked by the target, he or she becomes something of a celebrity. Often they appear on talk shows and in the news, creating a nonpaid form of advertising for the product or service.

## Reaching Specific Targets

The ability to create a dialogue with both internal and external audiences allows public relations to coordinate messages between its "publics" and its stakeholders. Public relations works from the inside out to reach the target with a product they trust, from a credible source, that has earned a reputation based on a products repeat performance and quality.

## Handling Scandal

A brand cannot survive if the corporation is under fire or its public or stakeholders are unhappy or disgruntled. Positive relationships, built from the inside out, are as important as the message. Public relations representatives orchestrate much of a corporation's image. How the media, consumers, government agencies, community, and employee affairs view the corporation is determined by public relations.

## Building or Maintaining Image

Any negative publicity is damaging to a brand's image. Corporations who do nothing often face intense scrutiny from the media, forcing a corporation to face up to, and act upon, the charges or allegations. Corporations who respond immediately to damaging allegations can kill the momentum of any kind of investigation quickly, often with little or no damage to image or equity.

Public relations brings a reputation built on trust and credibility with both the media and the target to the IMC promotional mix. As longtime practitioners of consumer-focused information, public relations representatives are used to building and retaining a rapport between a corporation, brand, or service and its public and other stakeholders.

## How Does Public Relations Help IMC Be Consumer Focused?

The emergence of public relations from a supportive role to an essential member of the promotional mix is the result of its compatibility with IMC tactics such as:

- *Relationship Building.* IMC concentrates on tightly defining a specific target audience. Products and messages are developed with this target audience and their specific needs in mind. Public relations can take this definition a step further by including internal stakeholders in the planning and execution of the IMC message. By segmenting these various targets into smaller, more manageable groups, a key benefit can be adapted to address each consumer or stakeholder's needs and wants more specifically. Consumer-focused marketing, or relationship marketing, has always been a priority for public relations. The move from traditional sales-based advertising to relationship marketing, or the building of long-term relationships with the target or other stakeholders, is critical to building brand loyalty and creating a dialogue, or two-way communication between buyer and seller.
- *Tone of Voice.* IMC focuses on messages delivered with one tone of voice and one image. Public relations can reflect the key benefit, the strategy, and the visual/verbal message on all communication, both internal and external. This consistent and repetitive use helps to maintain that voice and image not only with the press, but through contact with customer service representatives, operators, sales personnel, delivery drivers, and consumers. This coordination of ideals and attitude are as important to brand loyalty as they are to a brand's image.

- *Databases.* IMC employs the use of databases to personally reach individuals within the target audience. Public relations uses databases as informational and educational devices to develop a relationship by interacting one-on-one with the target.
- *Brand Management.* IMC focuses on creating and maintaining the image of a product, service, brand, or corporation and developing brand-loyal consumers. Disgruntled employees, negative word of mouth, government investigations, and recalls can affect a brand's image. The job of public relations is to manage this image from the inside out before it can affect a target's attitude or mindset toward a product or service.
- *Two-Way Communication.* IMC focuses on ways to develop an interactive dialogue between the buyer and the seller. Public relations is the first to understand that what happens inside a company affects the product and the consumer. Interactive opportunities allow the consumer to be an internal stakeholder by offering feedback on products and/or customer or technical services.

## Salvations and Disasters of Public Relations

In order to decide whether public relations is right for your IMC campaign, let's look at some of the salvations and disasters associated with it.

## What Makes Public Relations So Great?

The more notable salvations associated with public relations include:

- *Elevated corporate or brand image.* Public relations determines what the target thinks about a product or service, or the corporation that produces the product, by maintaining its positive position in the consumers mind through customer service contact or the proper and swift handling of any negative publicity.
- *A well-developed interactive relationship with the target.* Public relations can reach, talk, or bring the product or service directly to members of the target or target groups through news conferences, sponsored events, infomercials, or public service announcements, to name just a few.
- *More communication outlets.* Able to communicate at length with both internal and external targets, public relations can tailor a message to an external target individual or on a larger scale to internal groups such as union workers.
- *Low cost.* Public relations can get the message out through free media sources such as newspapers, magazine feature articles, or broadcast news sources.
- *The ability to present believable technical or scientific evidence through a credible news source.* Because of public relations' association with the press, both

print and broadcast news departments choose to report on studies presented through public relations sources because it can be, and most often is, backed up by research.

## Is There Anything Wrong with Public Relations?

The more notable disasters associated with public relations include:

- *Short shelf life of news items.* Nothing presented in newspapers or through broadcast channels last longer than twenty-four hours.
- *Difficult to modify behavior.* In order to build loyalty and equity the target needs to be repeatedly reminded about the product and its benefits to the target. Public relations cannot get this done without the help of other media sources.
- *Inability to measure results.* Determining if your objectives were successful requires a way to measure results such as how many units were sold, or the number of people who attended an event or saw a news conference. Since public relations rarely asks the target to do something like purchase, and is often paired with other mass media or promotional vehicles that do, there is no immediate way to tell if the message got to the intended audience.

## Public Relations and Advertising

The tension between advertising and public relations has always been about timing. The question of who should lead and who should follow should be based on the objectives outlined in the creative brief. If the objective is to build brand awareness or maintain a brand's image, then advertising is the best communications approach and should lead the way via print or broadcast. Any time a product or service has news value, is reinventing its image, launching a new product, or makes claims that need to be substantiated to give them credibility, public relations should lead with news articles, press conferences, or even exclusive press events.

What makes public relations and advertising a good communications and media mix?

- Advertising focuses on the consumers in the form of a monologue or one-way communication. Public relations turns the communication into a dialogue or two-way communication.
- Advertising and marketing concentrate on one product for one consumer group. Public relations concentrates on building relationships with many groups to accomplish varied objectives on many levels.
- Public relations and advertising make an excellent team for creating brand awareness, building brand equity, and maintaining brand loyalty.

## Putting Public Relations to Work

Before implementing the public relations portion of an IMC campaign, several decisions must be made, such as:

- What tools need to be used: news releases, news conferences, brochures, and so on?
- What public relations tactics and/or approaches will be used to execute the key benefit and strategy determined in the creative brief?
- What media will be used to deliver the message, and when will the message be delivered?

Public relations and advertising are two opposing forces both trying to get the right message out to the right people. Each uses slightly different techniques to achieve the same results; the only major difference is that one is often free and the other is not.

## The Strategy behind Public Relations Begins with Planning

The strategy behind using public relations has everything to do with the key benefit, the target audience to be reached, the message, and what promotional mix will accomplish the stated objectives.

When you talk about strategy, the first thing that needs to be determined is who will be at the planning table. What role will advertising, public relations, sales promotion, and/or direct marketing play? Or will some other, less traditional form of promotion be used to reach the target? The answers will depend on what the IMC campaign needs to accomplish and the best way to reach the target.

Planning looks at the target, the objectives that need to be met, the strategy that will be employed to accomplish the objectives, timing, and what assembly of media vehicles can be used to strategically accomplish the objectives.

IMC planning is not just about message development but also the development of a holistic message for change throughout an organization. Change must take place everywhere for an IMC campaign to be successful. Strategically, IMC must execute an internal plan that reflects the external message. This inside-out examination of the varied target groups helps coordinate communication between these very specialized groups. Whether you're talking to the consumer, the media, retailers, or any other quantifiable target, each audience must receive the message behind the key benefit in their own language and with their specific benefit clearly defined. The ability to define each group and its needs is exclusive to public relations and invaluable when defining the best member of the promotional mix to meet those needs.

Objectives need to be examined to determine the best promotional vehicle to strategically accomplish the stated objectives. Public relations is in a perfect position to manage word of mouth, maintain customer service, manage brand issues, and oversee any unplanned events such as media inquiries or recalls, all of which affect image and strategy.

The strategy determines how the objectives will be accomplished. It is the voice and style that must be carried across the promotional mix. An IMC's message can be related through press relations, sponsored events, internal and external communication, and reaction to both internal and external feedback to make the message stronger. Its credibility and virtually no-cost way of doing business makes public relations a critical mouthpiece to get and keep the word out about a product, service, or corporation through varied media vehicles.

Strategically any approach, appeal, or tone can be adapted to public relation's tone of voice. Choices made will ultimately depend on the make-up of the campaigns promotional and media mix. For public relations to hold its own at the planning table, its practitioners will have to see the product or service through the eyes of the marketer and understand that sales and customer relations are intertwined. In order to accomplish the stated objectives, public relations needs to be able to speak the language of marketers, initiate the strategy, and understand the diversity of the promotional mix. This will require adopting an attitude of planned action based on research as opposed to reaction to events and information from corporate executives.

Today, public relations practitioners need to be more than media liaisons, relationship managers, and designated watchdogs for a brand or service's image; they need to be strategic market planners.

On the downside, public relations does not offer the power of the other communication approaches to effectively remind the target about the message. Because of this, it is difficult to change consumer attitudes using public relations alone. Being able to evaluate the effectiveness of each of the communication efforts is a priority for any IMC campaign. The implementation of an IMC campaign requires each member of the promotional mix to understand what marketers need and want to accomplish, and be able to define how public relations can strategically be used to accomplish objectives, and determine the estimated return on investment (ROI).

When public relations is attached to marketing and sales, in order to receive its share of the marketing budget it must be able to show measurable and quantifiable results associated with its efforts. ROI very simply refers to the amount of profit left after advertising and other costs have been deducted. Many believe public relations, as a member of the marketing team cannot show a measurable ROI unless it is the sole member of the marketing team, as might be found in business-to-business marketing. Others believe it is measurable or quantifiable based only on the amount of media placement predicted during planning as opposed to the actual placement earned. The question that has to be answered is: Do certain media outlets carry more weight than others? The answer is yes. Just like the other members of the promotional mix, the final media mix should be determined based on whether the target is exposed to the media vehicle in order to see the article or hear the interview.

How does the public relations representative communicate with the media and/or their publics? Let's take a look at some of the techniques involved. Remember, public relations will also be working off the creative brief, so the message will be coordinated with all other IMC messages.

## The Many Documents That Make Up Public Relations

There are many ways public relations talks to its publics and/or stakeholders. Most creative executed by public relations consists of large, copy-heavy pieces such as annual reports, educational materials, infomercials, press conference copy, or public service announcements. The choice of vehicle does not depend on length but rather on who is being spoken to, the promotional mix employed, the message to be communicated, and the desired outcome. Let's take a look here at some of the more commonly used message vehicles: news releases, fact sheets, media advisories, pitch letters, press kits, newsletters, brochures, and publicity.

### News Releases

A news release contains the latest news and information about the product or service in the form of a finished news article. A news release is sent unsolicited to an editor and, if published, will be a form of nonpaid advertising.

News releases need to be both well written and newsworthy enough for editors from print or broadcast media to consider it for publication or broadcast. Writing should be clear, concise, and factual. Leave the creative writing to the advertising creative team; news releases are meant to inform, not entertain.

The ultimate goal for all news releases is to be noticed. An editor may receive hundreds of releases on any given day. Finally, assuming the information is interesting and valuable to readers, listeners, or viewers, it must also appear in the proper format.

**The Look of a News Release**  A typical news release should follow a very specific format. Figure 9.2 shows an approximation of this format. It should be typed, double-spaced, on an 8½ x 11 sheet of paper, with 1-inch margins on all four sides.

The preparer's information should appear in the upper left corner:

- The preparer's name or contact name
- The corporation or organizations name
- The corporation or organizations address
- The preparer's daytime phone number
- The preparer's evening phone or cell phone number
- The preparer's fax number or e-mail address (optional)

Beneath the preparer's information and to the far right, type in all caps and underline FOR IMMEDIATE RELEASE. If this is an advanced release, state the time and date to be

Your Name
Client's Company Name
Client's Address
Your Phone Number (Day)
Your Phone Number (Evening)

## **FOR IMMEDIATE RELEASE**

Knoxville, TN. June 24—Three-time mountain biking world champion Tinker Juerez will be signing cans of Kroger yogurt on Friday, June 28, 2006, at the Knoxville Kroger.

Tinker Juerez, the new spokesperson for Kroger yogurt, will be arriving at the Knoxville Kroger at approximately 10:00 a.m. and will be signing autographs and discussing the importance of a well-balanced diet until 1:00 p.m. Following the autograph session Tinker will perform an assortment of mountain bike maneuvers.

Tinker will be making appearances around the country to promote Kroger yogurt's "Fit for Life" campaign. "I feel Kroger yogurt should be an essential part of every persons diet. Not only is Kroger yogurt healthy, it's delicious," Juerez said. "With the variety of flavors Kroger yogurt is offering, there is a flavor for everyone. If you're not eating Kroger yogurt you're missing out."

"We feel Tinker Juerez is the perfect spokesperson for the job," stated Barber Williamson, Executive Vice President of Sales. "The purpose of this campaign is to show the public all of the health benefits Kroger yogurt offers. Choosing a well-conditioned athlete fits the image of Kroger yogurt. We feel this new campaign will draw much attention to our product."

-more-

The goal is to have Kroger yogurt stand out from the rest of the yogurts on the market.

Kroger will be releasing its new yogurt design at the beginning of next month. This design will be an entirely new look for the company, one that top executives at Kroger yogurt feel will give the company the edge it needs in the yogurt market.

Kroger yogurt will also begin handing out many new promotional items. These items will include free cans of Kroger yogurt, water bottles and coupons.

Kroger wants to stress not only how important it is to eat its yogurt, but also the importance of a well-balanced diet. If all goes well this summer, Kroger yogurt will truly stand alone in the high-profile yogurt industry.

- # # # -

**FIGURE 9.2**
Sample Press Release

released, for example, FOR RELEASE ON SEPT. 26 EST AT 8:00 AM. Advanced releases are known as embargos. The media is under no obligation to honor embargoed material until the date stated on the release, but the release date is generally observed as a courtesy.

Open the first paragraph with the city and state from which the release or news originated, or where the event will be taking place. Next to that, add the month and day of the release or event. The opening paragraph will deal with the key benefit, and the body of the release should ideally use at least two quotes from a reliable, relevant source.

Most news releases should not be longer than one page, but if you do have more to say you can break an article into two pages by adding the word -more- centered at the bottom of the first page. This signals that there is more than one page and is useful should a page be misplaced.

On the second page in the upper right, place the page number and then an identifier or slug. This can be the preparer's last name or the name of the product or service. The copy should continue on the next line. When finished, add the symbol -###- to the bottom of the last page, centered, to signify that no pages follow.

Be sure to edit your release before sending it out. Did you spell all names correctly? How is the grammar? Did you double-check your facts? Now is the time to proof your work; don't wait for very public errors to crop up.

**What Should Be Said**  Here are a few crucial guidelines for writing a news release:

1. *Headline.* Announce the key benefit. It is just as important in a news or magazine article as it is on any creative piece. This is also a great way to tie to any communication efforts to come to existing efforts.
2. *Opening.* The opening paragraph should list the most important facts. MPR, as used in an IMC campaign, focuses attention on the key benefit and answers the questions who, what, when, where, why, and how. Do not make the opening paragraph longer than three to five lines.
3. *Facts.* The second paragraph should deal with backing up your facts, perhaps with a quote or a scientific study.
4. *Get to the point.* Don't waste words. Give the facts in a concise and relevant way.
5. *Avoid hype.* Hype does not lend itself well to a news format. Leave the superlatives to the advertising creative team.
6. *Avoid Jargon.* If you're writing to the general public, use a language they can understand. News is no different than advertising copy when it comes to boredom or confusion; if the text is boring or confusing, the target stops reading or listening.
7. *Action.* The final paragraph should close with what you want the target to do or know about: locations, informational websites, dates, or times.

As with any copy, it is a good idea to have the client read over and sign off on the brief before it is sent to the press.

Because the competition to be noticed is so fierce for any news release, help yourself out by addressing your release to the appropriate editor. We all like to be called by name rather than "Sir" or "To Whom It May Concern," so start building a rapport with the arrival of the envelope, the e-mail, or the fax.

A news release doesn't just happen. Extensive research has defined your target and determined the key benefit to push and the objectives to be accomplished. Use this information to make your release something of interest and value to your target.

## Fact Sheets

Fact sheets are basically an outline of the news release. It highlights the strategic information gained from addressing the six basic questions: who, what, when, where, why, and how, in essence creating a cheat sheet for the media.

## Media Advisories

A media advisory, or media alert, is sent to the media to entice coverage. It briefly lists the specifics about an event as well as information about interviews, news conferences, or photo opportunities.

## Pitch Letters

The purpose of a pitch letter is to entice media coverage. The difference between a pitch letter and a news release is that pitch letters are just that—letters. A pitch letter is addressed to a specific editor and should be creatively written; its role is to get attention. This is a good time to get some feedback from the advertising creative team to make sure the letter is written in the same tone of voice that is used in other communication pieces in the IMC campaign.

## Press Kits

Press kits are most often used to promote special events or announce new product launches. The purpose of a press kit is to inform and educate the media as well as entice a little media coverage.

The press kit consists of a large pocketed folder, usually attractively designed. Again, the appearance should match that of other advertising and promotional pieces that make up the IMC campaign. Inside the folder is a news release, a fact sheet, backgrounders or background articles, black-and-white publicity photographs, and maybe even a promotional item or two. Press kits tell the story of the event.

## Newsletters

Newsletters are an informal way to reach your target. They educate, entertain, and inform. Newsletters are most commonly distributed to employees or stakeholders of a corporation or to volunteers and supporters of nonprofit or specialty organizations.

The standard newsletter is four to six pages in length and is printed on 11 x 17-inch sheets, folded and stapled to 8½ x 11. Although they are often informal in style and appearance, newsletters should continue the tone and appearance of the IMC campaign for which it is associated. By adjusting type size, placing important points in boxes and double-dosing the use of white space, a newsletter can be attractively designed and easy to read. If the campaign uses unique graphics or a spokesperson or character representative in the campaign, use them along with logos or slogans and representative corporate or product typefaces on the newsletter. Informal does not mean ugly or poorly written. The image developed for the other advertising and promotional pieces must carry through in the newsletter.

### Newsletter Topics of the Day

No matter who the newsletter is intended to reach, the goal is to provide information of interest to their job, their membership, or their association with the organization, and any internal or external factors that could affect them or the business or organization. Use this forum to preview upcoming events and new product launches, solicit donations, or announce new hires, promotions, and retirements.

Stories of a more complicated or serious nature should not be tackled here. However, information should be supplied to tell the reader where to go, write, or call to find more information.

A newsletter should be an eclectic grab bag of surprises and human-interest quips varied enough to reach a diverse audience. In writing it, you should use short sentences and multiple paragraphs to enhance white space. Do not waste words; a newsletter is not something the reader will linger over.

## Brochures

Brochures are informational documents the public wants to read and will spend time reading. They are frequently technical in nature, explaining detailed procedures, so the writing style must get to the point, avoiding any hype or jargon and aiming instead for clarity.

As a part of the IMC campaign, brochures should maintain the corporate or product image delivered in the advertising and other promotional efforts. Color and good-quality images make a brochure an attractive communication device.

Even the simplest brochures are fairly expensive to produce. Diversity in appearance can range anywhere from a simple fold to multiple folds; a brochure may also include inserts or have holes or shapes, known as die cuts, cut out of them.

As style pieces in an IMC campaign, brochures are attractive and informative. Best of all, the target is interested in and will spend time reading the brochure. Here are some simple writing and design tips to keep in mind.

- Photographs, graphics, diagrams, and charts are essential for a brochure to tell its story.
- Multiple subheads will help to move the reader from important point to important point.
- Short sentences and multiple paragraphs make reading easier.
- Type size should be a little larger here, 10 to 12 point, to tell the story or to explain technical information. Charts and graphs can go as small as 8 point; anything smaller affects readability and legibility.
- Vary the weight of your text to visually break up the page.
- Brochures consist of multiple folded panels. The size of these panels varies, but they are most often $3\frac{1}{2}$ to $3\frac{3}{4}$ inches wide by 8 inches tall. A standard brochure has six total panels, front and back, when opened flat.
- Headlines can be used on the outside or inside of the brochure. Inside headlines can be confined to a folded panel or cross over multiple panels.
- The front cover should cover the key benefit, either visually or verbally. It is not as important to hit your target over the head with your key benefit in a brochure, since the reader elects to read the piece.
- Copy inside the brochure can elaborate on the key benefit.
- The back cover should feature the logo, slogan, or tagline and contact information. Additional items might include a map or decision- or action-oriented information such as seating charts or price lists.

More elaborate brochures may have pockets to hold additional information such as business cards or free passes. Elaborate or diverse folds are also an option, as are large fold-out brochures measuring 11 x 17 inches flat, $8\frac{1}{2}$ x 11 inches folded, that may show a detailed map or floor plan. If you have the budget, brochures are a creative open door.

## Publicity

Publicity is the strategic use of public relations. It is through the use of publicity that a product is made newsworthy to the media. Articles placed in the newspaper, if possible in the section most likely to be read by the target, provide the target with information about the product. Other media options include magazine feature stories, radio or television talk shows, and even advertising during programming.

In an article appearing in the *Public Relations Journal*, Joan Aho Ryan and George H. Lemmond sum up the need for product publicity this way: "[C]ynical consumers, zapping commercials and ignoring print ads, are more receptive to the editorial message. The third party endorsement allows advertisers to sell a new product while enveloping the commercial message in a credible environment." That is the essence of marketing public relations.

The first stage of the campaign was the public relation's news release and internal and external management of information and image; the next step determines how the other promotional mix media will be used, if at all. These will be discussed in the chapters that follow.

# 10

# Newspaper Advertising

## The Strategic Use of Newspaper in IMC

Advertising is a paid form of nonpersonal mass media in which the sponsor of the advertised message is clearly identified. Advertising uses persuasion to sell, inform, educate, remind, and/or entertain the target about a product or service.

Considered a mass medium because it can reach large numbers of consumers, advertising is most often considered a media option for new product launches or more homogenized and inexpensive products such as ketchup, toilet tissue, and cleaning products, to name just a few. Mass-advertised products appeal to large numbers of indistinct consumers and can be purchased across the United States.

Probably the best-known member of the promotional mix, the term "advertising" is often used to describe all forms of marketing-based communication. Although that is not technically incorrect, advertising actually refers to the media mix that makes up mass media advertising, including print (newspaper and magazine) and broadcast (radio and television). Each of these mass media vehicles will be examined separately over the next several chapters. Let's begin the discussion with a look at newspaper advertising. See figure 10.1 for an integrated marketing communication (IMC) advertising case study.

## What Is Newspaper Advertising?

Newspaper advertising, also known as retail advertising, must accomplish two things. The first is to sell a product or service, and the second is to entice the reader into a response. This is a tough job. The reader has to wade through an enormous amount of written information

---

**FIGURE 10.1**

---

# IMC ADVERTISING CASE STUDY:
# TOSHIBA AMERICA CONSUMER PRODUCTS

Toshiba America Consumer Products, L.L.C., better known as just Toshiba to Americans, created and successfully used an IMC campaign that focuses on "lifestyle" and the idea of "Image is Everything™."

## Toshiba

Toshiba America Consumer Products, L.L.C., is located in Wayne, New Jersey, and is owned by a subsidiary (Toshiba America, Inc.) of one of the biggest names in high-end technology worldwide, Toshiba Corporation. Toshiba has been an innovator of technology related to DVD and DVD recorders and is a leading manufacturer of such products as projection and flat panel televisions, portable devices, and home theater projectors.

## Discussion

Toshiba has a reputation of working closely with consumers in order to bring them the best and most technologically advanced products on the market. The company effectively uses data collection not only to target the right audience, but also to construct messages that are sure to resonate with the target's interests and lifestyle. Using client input is a great interactive tool in an IMC campaign. Consumers can actively participate in a product's launch or growth, for instance, or comment on a corporate issue such as customer or technical services. This creates a feeling of empowerment for them, knowing that their input can make a difference as well as creating a team spirit of "we are all in this together."

Using research that focuses on consumer needs allows Toshiba to focus media choices to those vehicles most likely to be seen by the targeted audience. This focus is not only external, (advertising) but internally as well through sales teams, product trainers, and customer service representatives who represent Toshiba's advertised message to authorized dealers nationwide. The ability to develop a message strategy that can consistently be delivered between internal and external sources is one of the ways Toshiba is able to continually promote a strong brand image and build brand equity within its product categories.

## What's the Message?

In this particular campaign, Toshiba promoted its "lifestyle" appeal in its advertising efforts. The campaign focused on the brand, highlighting Toshiba's extensive television and digital audio/video lines as well as product ease of use, convenience, and even size.

## Media Mix

Toshiba's IMC media mix included public relations, news related items, direct mail, product placement, trade show events, catalogs, and the Internet. Internally, Toshiba made its training and dealer support available in cities throughout the United States. Although this team mainly focused on answering dealer questions and concerns, it served an additional role as customer and technological service representative to Toshiba's targeted consumers without ever actually coming in contact with them. By working behind the scenes, they made sure the dealers represented the brand from an informed perspective. This internal/external helping hand not only built Toshiba's reputation with the dealer but also was an extension of its image to the consumer, to make customer contact a positive experience. All marketing materials supplied to aid dealer training promoted Toshiba's ongoing "lifestyle" theme. Toshiba used all available channels to bring a viable visual/verbal message to the target through a diverse media mix, concept consistency, and one-on-one dealer support.

Each medium's message, along with the customer service initiatives, promoted and unified the "lifestyle" themes used throughout the campaign. In a press release featured on the Toshiba website at www.tacp.toshiba.com, Tina Tuccillo, Toshiba's Vice President of Marketing Communications, points out that "by incorporating lifestyle imagery throughout our catalogs, advertising, on the website, and bringing them to life at press events like Toshiba in Your Life and at trade shows, we are able to communicate an overall Toshiba brand feeling and cognition to consumers."

## How Was the Media Used?

For public relations purposes, the "lifestyle" focus referred to how the electronics affected consumers' lifestyles, such as what benefits or specific features could enhance their daily lives. Public relations efforts also highlighted various consumer experiences with products. Product feedback from consumers was collected for future use in advancing the brand and continuing to bring the best most technologically advanced products to Toshiba's customers.

Toshiba used both public relations and advertising as educational tools to promote new and existing products and to show the target audience the lifestyle-enhancing qualities of cutting-edge technology. Some of the strongest external educational tools included catalogs and collateral material, such as brochures reporting on product performance, attributes, and extensions. This type of promotional material can be designed to educate, entice, or address specific target needs by providing detailed information on products, warrantees, or user guides, to name just a few.

To make fact-finding and product ordering easy and convenient, Toshiba redesigned its website (www.tacp.toshiba.com). Featuring the "lifestyle" theme, the site offered owner's manuals and customer service information, product registration capabilities, and, of course, the ability to order products or accessories conveniently from the target's home or office.

## IMC, the Media, and a New Product Launch

The Web was also a major player in launching Toshiba's new audio/video player, called gigabeat®. A special website, www.gigabeat.com, announced gigabeat and outlined its features. The target consumer could go to the site to access music links, get product information or updates, and find information on available accessory items.

*(Continued)*

**FIGURE 10.1**
Continued

The gigabeat product launch featured an overall them of "Music in Color®" and was promoted through public relations, advertising, the Web, and point-of-purchase. Visually, the campaign used music personalities such as Joan Jett and the Blackhearts and Blues Traveler to promote the product, including through live events. The tagline "Because Music is Just Better in Color" represented the campaign's visual/verbal voice. The media mix included both print and broadcast, as well as a strong online presence. Gigabeat's introduction was helped by retailers such as Circuit City who touted it as "a virtual portable party" in its advertising.

### From Brand Loyalty to Brand Equity

Toshiba fully integrated this IMC campaign into the target's lifestyle. Because of this, and Toshiba's ongoing reputation for producing quality products, the company successfully contributed to developing a strong brand-loyal following and a piece of the coveted brand equity pie. Maintaining this position will require continued product advances and performance.

*Sources*: Toshiba Press Release, "Integrated Marketing Communications Program Helps Toshiba Maintain Competitive Edge in Consumer Electronics Market," May 19, 2005, www.tacp.toshiba.com/news/newsarticle.asp?newsid=77, accessed January 23, 2007; Circuit City website, www.circuitcity.com/ssm/Toshiba-Gigabeat-30GB-Audio-Video-Player-MES30VW/sem/rpsm/oid/153084/catOid/-12952/rpem/ccd/productDetail.do, accessed January 23, 2007.

before noticing your client's ad amid the mass of indistinguishable gray that characteristically makes up an average newspaper page.

Newspaper advertising must engage the reader with new and improved claims and juicy got-to-have sales by using bold headlines. Action-oriented claims such as "Buy Now," "50% Off," or "While Quantities Last" are commonly used attention getters in retail advertising.

Advertising appearing in newspaper falls into two distinct categories: local (including classified and display) and national.

## Local Advertising

The term "local advertising" has two meanings: The first is that the advertising is of a local nature and tells readers where in their area they can find the product; the second is that the advertising was initiated locally.

**Classified Advertising**  Local newspapers do classified advertising, dealing with consumers buying and selling, in-house. Categories feature garage sales, auctions, job opportunities, and real estate opportunities, to name just a few.

**Display Ads**  Display ads can be either local or national. The term "display" refers to the complete list of components appearing within an ad such as headlines, visuals, body copy, or logos.

## National or Brand-Name Advertising

National advertising features brand-name products that can be found at local establishments or acquired through toll-free phone numbers or on the Internet. Carried in newspapers throughout the country, national advertising requires few modifications from city to city outside of personalizing phone numbers and/or addresses.

## The Diversity of the Newspaper Voice

Newspaper advertising reaches a lot of people, is effective, offers flexible deadlines, and is relatively inexpensive. Since ads normally arrive at the newspaper complete, deadlines of twenty-four hours or less can still make the next day's edition.

Newspapers are read not only for news value, but for the news of advertising; it's where people look for information about sales. It should inspire the consumer to want and/or need the product or service being advertised right now. To do this, price and product description play a prominent role. Retail advertising's primary job is to make a sale. One way to accomplish this is by instilling a sense of urgency through such devices as limited-time offers, limited quantities, two-for-one offers, special sale hours, preferred customer sales, and coupons.

## Sales

Newspapers are the place consumers go for sales. Everybody loves a sale. They are abundant in retail, and they promote predictable themes. The key is to decide how your client's sale will be unique, and then grab the reader—preferably by the throat. To do this, the creative team must first do a little brainstorming. What is unique, fun, or unusual about the sale? How will the strategy promote the key benefit? Headlines, subheads, visuals, and typeface choices all need to reflect the IMC concept or strategy.

Sales should not seem routine. The personality of the sale should reflect that of the target, the key benefit, strategy, and the product or store. Sales create traffic within a store, and traffic promotes additional purchases. Most sales events are associated with holidays, special events, and overstocks, but why limit yourself? Take an approach the competition would never think of and be creative with your sales. Why not have a sale called "It's Tuesday—Let's Shop Till We Drop Together"?

## Coupons

Coupons are the IMC bridge between newspaper advertising and sales promotion. Coupons offer the target an incentive to buy.

All consumers like to get a break, and coupons are a way to offer something in return for their patronage or loyalty, or as an introduction to the product or service. A coupon is an effective, temporary sales device. It should be easy to remove from the ad, should clearly point out the offer, and be easy to redeem. Incentives often include two-for-one offers or percentage- or cents-off deals.

One of the more attractively designed coupons is known as a freestanding insert (FSI). FSIs are one-page, full-color coupon ads that are nationally produced and inserted into Sunday newspapers.

### How Much Does It Cost?

Every consumer wants to know how much something costs before making a final buying decision. This not only determines value but also facilitates brand comparison. However, ads for known high-dollar products often eliminate price and entice the reader through copy promoting benefits, image, and a special sale or financing to make purchasing easier.

As a rule, you should not shy away from displaying price. Make it big, make it bold, and give it class. Let it stand alone or tie it to a copy point. It doesn't matter where it appears, as long as it's there.

## How Does Newspaper Advertising Help IMC Be Consumer Focused?

One thing newspaper *isn't* is consumer focused. It does not build a relationship with the target, and it isn't interactive in any significant way. So why use it at all in an IMC campaign?

The answer lies in its relationship with the other members of the promotional mix and the advertising media mix. Newspaper is a great follow-up to news releases, press conferences, or interviews, helping to raise awareness or build an image for an existing product or a new product launch. Other options supporting public relations might include the promotion of a corporate cause by asking the target to bring in a canned good or donate clothing to receive free movie passes or a free entree.

By including a coupon, newspaper can work with sales promotion by promoting "try me" offers. T-shirts, cups, toy characters, and even watches promoting a current movie might be given out in local fast-food restaurants when the consumer gives the correct password or repeats a slogan printed in the newspaper.

When a website address is featured, newspaper advertising can refer the target to the Internet in order to request additional information, or it can feature a toll-free number to call in order to speak to a customer service representative and/or place an order.

# The Salvations and Disasters of Newspaper Advertising

In order to decide whether newspaper is right for your IMC campaign, lets look at some of the salvations and disasters associated with it.

## What Makes Newspaper Advertising So Great?

The more notable salvations of newspaper advertising include:

- *Getting It There*. Newspapers have very short deadlines. This allows for last-minute ads, or a second chance to make changes to an existing ad, up until twenty-four hours prior to printing.
- *Sized to Fit*. Because of the low cost of newspaper advertising, ads can be sized up or down to accommodate both budget and/or information needs.
- *Believability*. Advertising takes on more credibility because it appears alongside editorial material. The difference here from public relations is that public relations *is* the editorial material.
- *Loyal Readers*. Consumers buy a newspaper because they want to read the news of the day and the sales of the week.
- *Cost*. The uncoated paper stock, or newsprint, newspaper is printed on is inexpensive. It can be bought in large quantities, used, and then thrown out. Because of this, newspaper space can be purchased fairly inexpensively. It can reach a mass audience on a daily basis, making it a very attractive medium.
- *Geographic Concentration*. Newspaper ads are seen only by those in the same geographic location as the product or service, minimizing media waste.
- *Frequency*. The number of times an ad can be viewed is affected by how often the newspaper is printed. A newspaper can be published weekly in smaller markets, or daily in larger ones. An ad appearing in a daily for one week is six times more likely to be seen than one appearing just one time in a weekly.
- *Coupons*. The use of coupons in newspaper advertising creates an interactive opportunity by giving the target more than information. Coupons must be torn from the ad and carried to the product location to be redeemed.

### Where Should the Coupons Go?

Deciding where coupons should go is another one of those great questions. Although there's no rule, you'll want to consider how easily the coupon can be removed. Coupons can appear aligned at the top of an ad, vertically down either side, or, most often, at the bottom of the ad.

## Is There Anything Wrong with Newspaper Advertising?

The more notable disasters associated with newspaper advertising include:

- *Mass Media*. It is difficult to ensure that your ad will reach the intended target. Newspaper advertising is the least targetable of all the media vehicles we will look at.
- *Creative Disadvantage*. The worst problem is the paper stock. The uncoated, inexpensive newsprint causes the ink to bleed, affecting type quality and causing poor photo reproduction. The virtual lack of color can also affect both visual and verbal stimulation.
- *Clutter*. The gray page of a newspaper has a lot going on. An ad could be missed if it is not designed to stand up and stand out.
- *Life Span*. Newspapers and the advertising within them are old news within twenty-four hours.
- *Declining Readership*. Readership by younger adults is steadily declining, as they instead rely on news television such as CNN or MSNBC for up-to-date news.
- *Limited Viewing*. Special sections, such as the sports or financial pages and the comics, allow readers to bypass the rest of the newspaper.
- *Passive Medium*. Newspaper advertising does not involve the reader in the message.
- *Price Based*. Newspaper advertising announces sales. Unfortunately, there is nothing classy or image-oriented about pushing price.

## The Strategy behind Newspaper Advertising

Understanding the capabilities and limitations of print advertising as opposed to other media options, such as broadcast, outdoor advertising, or direct mail, is crucial for the success of an IMC strategy. Not all ideas can transfer between media. Knowing this in advance will save the identity of the campaign and ensure the message will reach the target. Strategically, your key benefit must be able to be delivered both visually and verbally in the combined media outlets, most used by your target.

Mass media advertising alone does not look to build a relationship with individual consumers or create dialogue, but instead works to inform and build awareness. Newspaper advertising cannot guarantee the target will see the message. It is possible, however, by placing the ad in a newspaper section of particular interest to your target, to increase the odds the target will be exposed to the message.

Like all other components of the media mix, advertising selection depends on the target and the overall objectives. If the target is eighteen- to twenty-five-year-olds, newspaper advertising would be a poor choice, since few people in this age group read the paper on a regular basis, and few, if any, read the paper from cover to cover. Objectives that might benefit from newspaper advertising include creating brand awareness, maintaining or retaining brand loyalty, building and maintaining brand image, creating sales or generating interest, announcing product changes or additions, and increasing store traffic. Key benefits that lend themselves to the use of newspaper advertising include a USP giving the product or service a competitive advantage over the competition, a unique price, a strong consumer benefit, or incentive-based coupons.

Don't lose the strategy you laid out in your creative brief. Newspaper advertising features the same key benefit, layout style, approach, tone of voice, and images as other pieces within the IMC campaign.

Strategically, newspaper is better suited to a product-based approach, such as generic or product feature. Newspaper's poor reproduction capabilities make a consumer-based approach or use of an emotional appeal difficult to adequately portray both visually and verbally. Rational appeals such as straight fact, testimonial, or news can best hammer home a products features and benefits.

It is important before making any final strategic decisions to look at the salvations and deterrents associated with the product or service and the media mix to be employed, as well as the overall objectives to be accomplished.

## The Look of Newspaper Advertising

It is up to the client to decide whether to use an advertising agency or the corporation's own in-house art department to fulfill its communication needs. In-house design is most often used for small jobs that need to be done right away or that don't happen on a regular basis. Most clients working with IMC have large advertising budgets and choose to use the expertise found in an advertising agency to develop and retain a consistent visual/verbal message.

When you pick up any newspaper it is often easy to tell the difference between in-house advertising and that done by an advertising agency. Most large in-house advertising departments are staffed with good creative teams, but often ads originating from small in-house art departments (usually composed of one or two people) lack the necessary components to build and maintain a brand image and create memorable advertising that is cohesive with other advertising materials. Most often ads lack a consumer benefit headline and a subhead that further educates and entices the target to read on. Prices are often too small to be a viable selling point. Price should always be a benefit in newspaper advertising. It doesn't matter if price does not reflect the key benefit; it is an important consumer benefit. Finally, the layout is often chaotic. The lack of eye flow and white space causes a junky, cheap look. Agency ads are clean and have a distinct movement from top to bottom and left to right. Everything is seen and read in the exact order that the designer intended.

A good ad exploits the page, using one dominant image (verbal or visual) on the page to create a solid, black-looking area that stands out from the grey clutter of the page. Strong contrasts in newspaper are very effective. Line art drawings are very effective because of the strong black and white contrasts. Alternately, lots of white space can also make an ad stand out and can create an aura of elegance.

A successful newspaper strategy requires you to put yourself in the consumer's place. What catches your eye? What do you need to know? How do you use it? Where can you find it? Why can't you live without it? The answers can be found through meticulous message construction and the use of a few simple layout techniques.

Advertising is basically a relationship between words and imagery. You should seek to create a match between what you say and what you show. The key elements of print are divided between copy and art. As previously discussed, the copy or verbal elements include headlines, subheads, body copy, slogans/taglines. Art or visual elements include illustrations, photography, charts/graphs, or graphic design as well as type style and the overall layout.

Designing for newspaper isn't difficult, but does take strategy, and a good design plan needs specific tactics. Be sure you have a strong concept developed from the strategy and a headline that informs the target about the key benefit. The ad must feature the product and promote its price. Each layout should develop or maintain a visual/verbal identity that reflects both the brand and the target and is consistent with the other visual/verbal messages in the IMC campaign. Be sure to create strong black-and-white contrasts, feature one dominant element, promote price or availability, and use white space effectively. Body copy should develop the key benefit, and include a call to action. Type should be easy to read and be brand image specific. The ad should flow easily from element to element, closing with the logo, slogan, or tagline and detail copy to make shopping easier. The simple, inexpensive, yet informative nature of newspaper advertising makes it one of the leading advertising vehicles.

## Clutter

Retail ads have a lot to say and show in a small space. Clutter and chaos are not the designer's ultimate goal. A good newspaper ad organizes elements to control the structure of the ad. To create elegance and order, and to stress quality over price, use white space liberally. Stay away from bold or bulky typefaces. Consider using serif typefaces, which are more sophisticated. For a more disciplined look, consider lightweight sans serif faces.

## Size Specifications

Newspaper space is measured from side to side in column inches, or the width of a column of typeset copy plus the gutter. Column width is measured in $2\frac{1}{16}$-inch increments from $2\frac{1}{16}$ inches to 13 inches. The depth of an ad is measured in $\frac{1}{4}$-inch increments up to 21 inches. While the newspaper works within predetermined widths, the depth of an ad is determined by design and budget constraints. A full-page ad measures 13 column inches wide by 21 inches deep.

## The Effect of Newsprint on Design

Newsprint is not an optimal printing surface. The coarse, uncoated, highly bleedable stock affects print quality and color reproduction. Photographs can look flat and delicate illustrations and typefaces can literally disappear off the newsprint's surface during printing. Good design choices can help to alleviate these problems. Make sure your type is not too dainty; keep it big and sturdy. Large type creates large, rectangular blocks of black on the page. Just the opposite happens when headlines and subheads are smaller; they create an excess of white space. Either option can produce positive results.

Body copy should be kept to a minimum. Highlight only what you want the target to do, and include enough about the product to seduce the reader into action. Remember, you want your target to act, to get up and visit the store, surf to the website, or make a toll-free call and place an order. Newspaper advertising is not meant to educate through the use of large blocks of copy; instead, it entices.

## Co-op Advertising

Co-op or cooperative advertising means that two individual but compatible clients have paired up to share the cost of the advertising and encourage consumers to use their products together. It is not unusual, however, for there to be more than two members of the advertising media or promotional mix to participate in co-op opportunities. There are two types of co-op advertising: vertical and horizontal. Vertical cooperatives are where one sponsor pays more and plays a larger or more prominent role in the ad. Horizontal cooperatives have budgets that are equally distributed giving each sponsor equal exposure.

These highly successful partnerships might team an airline with a hotel chain to promote air and hotel packages to a destination accessed by both. Other co-op ventures might include name-brand coffees served at national restaurant chains, or even computers that feature "Intel Inside."

## Evaluation

Evaluating results is critical to determining the success of any IMC campaign. Success or failure is determined by whether the objectives were met or not. Advertising will rely on other media within the promotional mix to determine if brand awareness and increased sales were achieved, the two most important objectives associated with both print and broadcast advertising.

Newspaper advertising is believable, simple to design, inexpensive to place, and informative. Although it is not highly targetable, loyal readers seek out newspaper advertising for unbelievably low price points, to-die-for sales, limited-time offers, and coupons. Consider making it a part of the media mix for your campaign to localize a national product, create traffic within a store, or announce a new product launch.

# Magazine Advertising

## The Strategic Use of Magazines in IMC

Magazine advertising concentrates on the creation of an image or mood through visual and verbal relationships. In order to entice the reader, magazine ads need to create a conceptual environment that the reader can both relate to and experience through the words and visuals. The show-and-tell nature of magazine advertising allows products to speak for themselves and demonstrate results. Although diverse in nature, many products appearing in magazines are often exclusive or unique and expensive to own. Other products are more mainstream, and their features may be indiscernible from the features of their competitors' products.

Products boasting higher price tags are less likely to be purchased on impulse. Before buying, discerning consumers will research a product's benefits and features, identify where the product fits into their own lives, and determine which problems it can solve. Integrated marketing communication (IMC) magazine advertising should make information readily available to assist the consumer in making an informed buying decision.

The opposite of the discerning consumer is the trendy shopper who uses magazine advertising to look at all the competing products within a category. With little to differentiate one brand of sneakers from another, product features take a backseat to how consumers are affected by the advertised message and are convinced to purchase by how they will look, feel, or be perceived in the sneakers.

When image and product features are prominent, price plays a more subordinate role in the design; the focus is placed instead on the benefits of owning or using a product or service. Because of this, visuals tend to play a more dominant role, as does lengthy, fact-based copy. By creating a strong visual/verbal relationship, you can tap into a reader's left- and right-brain tendencies by allowing him to see the product being worn or used, to learn what colors and sizes are available, and to review safety information and warranties.

## The Diversity of the Magazine Advertising Voice

Unlike publicity and newspapers, a magazine's message has a long life span. Because of the highly individualized content of magazines, consumers tend to hold onto them longer, often trading with other enthusiasts or friends. This gives advertising a second chance to make a first impression and reach out to a larger portion of the target audience.

A magazine's editorial content plays an important role in the advertising that appears between its covers. For example, advertising found in a home decorating magazine will promote products such as barbecue grills, paint and wallpaper products, and furniture and carpeting as well as patio and pool items.

### The Variety of Magazines

There are three basic categories of magazines: consumer, business or trade, and farming. Each of these three categories is broken down significantly further into special interests such as fashion, sports, cars, hobbies, advertising, marketing, public relations, and so forth.

**Consumer Magazines** Consumer magazines are an eclectic group of publications comprised of articles and advertising either loosely targeted to a broad audience or specifically targeted based on the target's special interests or hobbies. Let's take a closer look at each category by breaking it down further into two distinct types: general interest, including local and regional editions, and special interest publications.

*General Interest Magazines* General interest magazines such as *People, Time,* and *TV Guide* enjoy national coverage and large, indistinct target audiences. This type of magazine supports advertising with a more generalized appeal such as cars, food and beverages, cold and flu medications, and so on, that can be sold across geographic and demographic boundaries.

Metropolitan editions of magazines are edited for consumers in a particular city. Titles most often reference the city in which they are published and editorial content reflects topics and advertising of local interest. This type of magazine allows local advertisers to reach those targeted consumers in the local community only, eliminating advertising waste.

Geographical editions of national magazines are published for specific regions of the country or for individual single states or cities, rather than nationally. This allows clients to appear in a national magazine for a regional price, again narrowing the target and eliminating advertising waste.

*Special Interest Magazines* Special interest magazines feature editorial material directed specifically to a targeted group having a specific interest in the magazine's featured topic. Because of this, advertising that appears in these publications generally matches the editorial content, guaranteeing to reach those members of the target most likely to use the product or service.

The more specialized the magazine, the more the advertising creative team knows about the consumer who will see their client's advertising. Dog lovers read dog magazines, car lovers read car magazines, and clothing lovers read fashion magazines. This kind of specialized readership challenges the creative team to create an environment that allows readers to participate in the advertising based on personal experience; this specialized interest produces readers who are loyal and who regularly subscribe to or pick up these magazines at the local newsstand.

The target's special interest in the magazines editorial material allows for advertising with longer, more fact-based copy that can educate and encourage product trial. Full-color photographs and informative copy can be intimately tied to the self-image of the target audience, creating need and inducing loyalty.

## Business or Trade Magazines

When selling products to businesses, the best way to reach this conscientious market, other than expensive personal-selling tactics, is to advertise in business-specific or trade publications. Those in charge of purchasing actively seek out both editorial content and advertising for the newest innovations in their specialization, making advertising in business publications advantageous. Business consumers not only need to buy, they want to buy the newest product or business-related equipment that will increase productivity and profit. The relatively small size of almost all business markets makes targeting easier than in consumer magazines.

In order to more precisely determine which business magazine(s) will reach your audience, business magazines can be broken down into two distinct types: general business and specialized business.

**General Business** If you are trying to reach upper-level managers or those in executive positions, business magazines such as *Forbes*, *Business Week*, or *Fortune* are some of the best bets. Editorial material as well as advertising content in these publications covers industry on a broad and generic scale.

**Specialized Business Magazines** Just like special interest consumer magazines, specialized business publications deal with specific industries, such as industrial including manufacturing and research and development, trade including retail or wholesaling and advertising, and professional, including medial, engineering, and computers, and so on.

## Farming Magazines

This very diverse and highly targeted type of magazine deals with both consumer and business issues. Most are technically based and deal with the newest innovations in farming, and they are often published regionally in order to deal with the diverse planting, soil, and weather conditions across the country.

## How Does Magazine Advertising Help IMC Be Consumer Focused?

Magazine advertising does a little better than newspaper advertising at being consumer focused. Because of their highly targetable nature, it could be argued that magazines are both interactive and educational. Advertising efforts can talk directly to the target's special interests by tapping into the target's self-image. The ability of magazine advertising to build a relationship, and thus brand loyalty, with the target is the result of the product image transferring to the target's self-image, creating a bond.

What advertising cannot do is develop a dialogue with the consumer. The advertised message is a one-way monologue with an often passive and distracted audience. In order to create a two-way dialogue, advertising must be used to move the target to the next step: to actively seek out more information by calling a toll-free number or visiting a website to order or obtain additional information. A small degree of interactivity can be introduced through the use of coupons, samples, folds, pop-ups, and website addresses by involving the target in the reading or viewing of the ad.

If you need to selectively target and have a substantial budget, consider a media mix comprised of magazine, cable television, and radio. Mainstream or major television networks such as ABC, CBS, NBC, and FOX along with magazine advertising provide a good combination for more generalized products or services that need to look attractive or be demonstrated. Because magazines are printed so infrequently, it is important to consider transferring the brand's image to television, where identity can be frequently reinforced.

Magazines are a good choice if you want to inform with long copy or dazzle with color. They are also great at promoting trial by associating the product or service with an activity the target enjoys, or developing image or brand identity. Magazines bring elegance, prestige, and beauty to the product—and thus, the target's image.

Image-based products are often referred to as high-involvement products. The target's wallet and self-image are tied to the brand's identity. If magazine advertising is used for a new product launch introducing any type of sales promotion at this early stage, it could affect a brand's perceived exclusivity in the mind of the target. However, sales promotion might be used to promote trial or create initial interest through contests or sweepstakes.

Direct marketing can utilize magazine advertising by offering an order form within the ad that the consumer can use to place an order or request additional information.

Other direct-marketing devices used for ordering or making inquiries might include a bound-in postal reply card or a freestanding postal insert, also known as a blow in.

By placing a web address within the magazine copy, consumers can be directed to use the Internet to acquire additional information or for advanced purchase, another way of making the sale personal, interactive, and exclusive.

Magazines are a bad choice to use with any type of current publicity unless it is planned or manufactured because of limited printing schedules and long lead times associated with publication. New, old, and reinvented products with messages based on image or innovation are ideal for magazine use. However, unlike a new or reinvented product, the image of a more mature product will not be affected by the sale mentality of pairing newspaper with magazine advertising in the promotional mix.

Design for magazine advertising, like the other members of the promotional and media mix, will work with the same objectives: strategy, key benefit, and visual/verbal message. It will speak with the same tone of voice and use the same imagery as other communication efforts used in the IMC campaign such as type, color, spokesperson, and/or layout style, for ease of recognition by the target.

## Salvations and Disasters of Magazine Advertising

In order to decide whether magazine advertising is right for your IMC campaign, let's look at some of the salvations and disasters associated with it.

### What Makes Magazine Advertising So Great?

The more notable salvations associated with magazine advertising include:

- *Select Target Market.* The highly targeted and specialized nature of magazines allows copy to talk directly to the person most likely to purchase the product or use the service.
- *Printing Capabilities.* Better paper, better print quality, the addition of color and detailed visuals allow targets to imagine themselves using the product. Printing capabilities allow for both large and small photographs to hold detail.
- *Life Span.* Due to the highly individualized content of magazines, consumers tend to hold onto them longer, often trading with other enthusiasts or friends, extending the life of the advertising.
- *Image.* Since magazines reflect readers' lifestyles and interests directly, visuals and concept directions that address lifestyle directly address image (see figure 11.1). Full-color visuals and detailed copy work in tandem to build or retain a product's image.
- *Informative Copy.* Copy can be longer since readers selectively spend more time reading a magazine.

#### CHAPTER 11

**FIGURE 11.1**

The Fruit & Walnut Salad four-page insert was created by DDB for McDonald's. This insert appeared mainly in women's consumer magazines in spring 2005 as part of the Fruit & Walnut Salad launch. Images courtesy of McDonald's.

- *Creative Options.* About the only restrictions creatively in magazine design are the ability to actively demonstrate a product or service—and budget.
- *Geographic Selectivity.* Local or regional advertising efforts can reach those most likely to use the product or service without waste.

## Is There Anything Wrong with Magazine Advertising?

The more notable disasters associated with magazine advertising include:

- *Lengthy Deadlines.* Advance deadlines often require designers to work months ahead of a publication date. These advance deadlines need to be watched closely in order to coincide with other IMC publication or print dates.
- *Cost.* Magazine advertising is indeed more expensive to produce than most other forms of print advertising. The better paper stock and printing capabilities do, however, improve quality and influence design.
- *Clutter.* Unlike newspaper advertising, which has to deal with clutter on the page, magazine advertising has to compete with the enormous clutter of ads that appear in any one magazine.
- *Publication Deadlines.* Magazines have fewer publication dates—ranging from weekly to quarterly—making timely material almost impossible.

## The Strategy behind Magazine Advertising

Magazines are a time capsule, capturing lifestyles and values and immortalizing trends. Magazines can offer up your key benefit in brilliant color, and, if necessary, with detailed copy points. The more you know about the target's interests, lifestyles, and general demographics, the better. Strategy development designed to meet the special interests of the reader makes isolating a key benefit more individualistic and can accomplish the stated objectives more precisely.

Strategically, magazine is not a good choice if your product or service is not image based or your budget is tight. Other options in these cases might include sales promotion or direct-marketing techniques, where the target can be addressed as an individual.

The strategy behind creative determines the tone of voice and images that will represent the product or service's message and identity. The decision to use magazines as a part of the promotional mix will depend on the objectives. Magazines are best used for consumer-based strategies where brand image, lifestyle, or brand attitude can be specifically addressed through the visual/verbal message.

Product-based strategies should not be entirely ruled out if a new product needs to be positioned in the mind of the consumer or if the product or service truly has a unique selling proposition; in these cases magazines are an ideal media vehicle.

Before determining whether magazine advertising is right for your IMC campaign, here are some additional questions to ask yourself: Do you need color? Can you afford to use magazines? Are you selling an image to a specific target audiece that can be reached through magazines? Where is the relationship being developed? How will advertising in magazines help reach the target audience? Will magazines be used as a part of the campaign launch or as a support vehicle? What is the life cycle stage of the product or service? Do you need to create a dialogue or just reinforce image? How will you create interactivity? Is it important to direct the target to customer service or a website? Do all IMC communication efforts work toward building both loyalty and equity?

## Transforming Monologue to Dialogue

How can you take a passive, one-way communication and develop a two-way dialogue? As previously discussed, interactivity begins by asking the target to do something: call, log on, sign up for a contest or sweepstakes, come into the showroom, call for an appointment, or take a test drive. Interactivity builds the relationship that will develop brand-loyal consumers and build brand equity.

Objectives that benefit from magazine advertising might include generating interest in a new or reinvented product or reinforcing the decision to purchase an expensive product or service by showing benefits of ownership. Additional objectives might include creating awareness, positioning, or building or maintaining a brand attitude.

Key benefits that lend themselves to magazine advertising include the promotion of a unique selling feature, exclusivity, image, prestige, or elegance.

Carrying the strategy through each of the media or promotional mix options in your IMC campaign will require a strong sense of how the target thinks. Strategically, the objectives, key benefit, and visual/verbal message will dominate each media vehicle. A strong tone of voice and equally strong visual imagery must resonate with the target's self-image.

## What to Avoid and What to Include in Magazine Advertising

Since magazines sell an idea or an image of affluence, beauty, and even intellect, prices should not be prominent in magazine advertising. Often these ads have no price at all, and they generally include little copy; they let the image sell the product. Consumers should be able to experience the benefits associated with the product or service through the visual/verbal message and be encouraged to call, log on to a website, or visit their nearest retailer for more information.

Depending on the product, this is also an opportunity to develop a storyline or plot that ties the benefits and image of the product or service to the target's needs and lifestyle. When creatively written, longer copy can sustain a reader's interest long enough to educate and inform. However, the printing surface of magazines is ideal for detailed photographs to show the product's benefits and/or attributes without the need for lengthy copy. The ability to use a broad range of color, to set a mood, or to re-create a time period is second only to the use of visual discussions through photographs, illustrations, or graphics that can show a product in use, assist with image development, and create a trend or an air of exclusivity or fun.

The highly targeted and educated nature of magazine readers allows copy to talk directly to the person most likely to purchase the product, the person who clearly understands its benefits. This is one of the few instances in which "been there, done that" works, as consumers relate their experiences to those the product can solve.

Magazines should be avoided if message frequency is required or if deadlines are an issue. Where most newspapers are printed daily, magazines have fewer publication dates—ranging from weekly to biweekly, from monthly to bimonthly or even quarterly—making the publication of timely material almost impossible. Unlike the twenty-four-hour turnaround of most newspapers, magazine deadlines or submission dates range anywhere from a few weeks to a couple of months before the magazine appears on newsstands.

## The Look of Magazine Design

Everything about designing for magazines is sexier and more exciting than designing for almost any other medium. Elite products allow the designer's fantasy world to come alive. The numerous products without independent identities present a design challenge. Product individualism, or what sets your client's product apart from the competition, is achieved through strategy development, layout styles, and/or type choices.

Magazines reflect personal image. Image portrayal means that it's the creative team's job to make targets see themselves driving this car or using this perfume, or understand the envy friends will feel when they're seen in this piece of Tiffany jewelry. It is the goal of magazine advertising to assist consumers with their buying decision by making them feel, see, taste, and imagine the product in their life.

Before designing, take the time to study the special-interest direction of the magazines your ads will appear in. Look at competitors' ads and do the opposite—or do something similar, but with more individualistic or targeted appeal.

Advertising that appears in the pages of a magazine should provide a visually stimulating and informative experience for readers. Visual images should develop an identity and create a visual personality for the product or service. Copy should take the reader on a fact-finding adventure. Product image and user image should be woven throughout this personalized visual/verbal relationship. The magazine's relationship with the consumer allows the advertising to talk directly to the people who will be buying and using the product.

Concepts that address lifestyle directly address image. Full-color visuals and dynamite copy work in tandem to create the appropriate consumer response.

Photographs bring the product or service alive with enhanced details by offering an exclusive viewing opportunity. Textures are magnified, emotions are highlighted, and colors pop off the page. Copy can be longer since readers selectively spend more time reading a magazine than they do a newspaper. Storylines or plots can be developed to promote uses, scientific studies, demonstrations, purchase options, and trends.

Graphic designs or colorful illustrations attract attention by showcasing interesting shapes and brilliant color variations. Design styles and color usage can re-create time periods and suggest liberal or conservative views. Bold, colorful graphics suggest youth and energy, while subdued colors reflect relaxation and stability.

## What to Consider When Designing for Magazines

### The Importance of Headlines and Subheads

Headlines highlighting strong consumer benefits seduce the target by relating product benefits to image. By touching an emotional chord in your target, advertising can suggest uses and promote new-age fads or renaissance revivals.

Unlike those in newspaper ads, headlines should not overpower the ad but should be designed into the product's personality or around the ambiance created within the design. Garish is out; structure and informative class are always in. Sizes for headlines vary in magazine ads; however, they are never so loud as to decrease the brand's image or insult the educational or social level of the reader.

In magazines you can hold a reader's attention for a longer period of time, so headlines as well as body copy can be longer and more informative or instructive. Because of this, subheads are often not needed. However, if you have a great deal of body copy, you can use multiple subheads to break the ad into more pleasing and readable blocks. Like headlines, subheads should not overpower but should blend within the copy block.

### The Story of Body Copy

Copy should let the consumer know what the experience will be like when using or interacting with the product or service. Be descriptive; write to the senses and the emotions. In magazines, there is no "buy now while supplies last" mentality, as there is in newspaper advertising. Magazine advertising makes you feel, taste, and smell the product.

Body copy can be virtually nonexistent, short, medium, or long, depending on the message being explained or introduced. The average ad has copy of medium length, just enough to continue the discussion about the key benefit and describe any additional yet relevant attributes. Good descriptive copy should spell out how the product works, what it sounds like, what it feels or smells like, and how much it weighs; it should include a complete examination of benefits and uses. The consumer should experience the product through your words.

## The Image of Photographs

Magazines often use visuals to do the talking. Photographs offer an exclusive viewing opportunity. Because of the high-quality printing used in magazines, the consumer can very clearly see what the product looks like and/or how it is used.

Photographs bring reality home. As readers, we can see patterns, textures, quality, and color as if the product were sitting before us. The idea of visual variety offers designers the option to include background or to isolate the product or image by eliminating background clutter.

Photographs can be small or large; they can show the product alone or in use, placed in a relevant setting, or being compared to a similar product.

The main thing to avoid in magazine design is clutter. The blending of type and photographs should create an elegant or classy, informative, playful, or imaginative appearance. Abundant white space or even black-and-white photographs will set your ad apart from most others in the magazine.

## The Appeal of Illustrations

Illustrations create an image of youth and vibrancy as well as a clean way to display charted information. Their colorful interpretations of the product in use or in a setting can reveal a product's personality.

## It's All in the Size

Ad sizes depend on the overall size of the magazine. The most common full-size ad is around 8½ x 11. Ad sizes range from a one-third of a page to a full page. Available sizes vary by magazine, and they can be found by consulting the Standard Rate and Data Service (SRDS), which lists specific size guidelines for individual magazines as well as closing dates and print-related specifications.

## Visually and Verbally Involving the Target

The varied concept approaches used in magazines must accomplish an action or promote the quest for additional research on the part of the consumer. Good interactive or educational devices might include encouraging test drives, using some novel design option such as folds or pop-ups, or interactive options such as samples or order forms.

Testimonials also successfully create consumer involvement by evoking curiosity. Informational ads are great educational vehicles, as are recipes accompanying a food product. Emotional appeals, how-to ads, and product demonstrations all work well in magazine advertising.

## Cooperative Advertising and Magazine

As with newspaper advertising, it is not unusual for magazines to participate in co-op opportunities with other members of the advertising media or promotional mix to sell compatible products or support a special event.

The benefit co-op advertising brings to the target is the ability to combine two viable products into a package saving deal. Product pairing, when done consistently, makes the target think package rather than separate products when considering repurchase.

Magazines may be used to support public relations, direct mail, sales promotion, or newspaper, in promoting special events such as the Special Olympics, breast cancer awareness, or AIDS-related events. Since magazines influence image and promote prestige, the visual/verbal message will influence all other design associated with the event, from publicity to the design of the direct mail packages, any accompanying outdoor boards, donation and/or thank-you cards, posters, and banners, to name just a few. Sales promotion items such as T-shirts and cups or water bottles will also project the same image and overall design.

The choice to use the visually stimulating pages of a magazine to bring prestige to a product and reflect the target's interests, self-image, and lifestyle is a design journey into the study of human nature. Magazine advertising can be fun, sexy, serious, colorful, imaginative, and visually/verbally informative. It is perfect for developing a new product's image, maintaining an established image, or rebuilding or repairing the image of a reinvented product.

# Radio Advertising

## The Strategic Use of Radio Advertising in IMC

Radio permeates our world. We are exposed to it everywhere: in the car, at work, while on hold on the phone, in the doctor's office, and while shopping. Because of this, radio has the distinction of being one of the few media vehicles that can be used to reach the targeted audience close to the time of purchase.

As a verbal medium, radio is often considered handicapped when compared to other media vehicles within the promotional mix. Limited by its sound-only format, radio is nonetheless burdened with delivering both the visual and verbal message. Looked at another way, radio could be considered the ultimate integrated marketing communication (IMC) strategic vehicle. Creative teams that try to make radio advertising conform to the same visual/verbal or show-and-tell standards as print and television inhibit targets from truly imagining "themselves," without the assistance of a predetermined visual stimulant, using the product or service. Radio is the ultimate strategic use of the targets imagination.

Radio ads must create a sense of visual stimulation for the listener. A radio ad should attack the listener's visual imagination with a verbal narration that outlines the features and benefits associated with the key benefit. To make listeners create a personalized visual picture, the verbal message must be colorful, informative, and tied to their personal experiences in order to entice them to place the product in their visual perspective.

Great for building awareness, radio can be used as a primary advertising vehicle for local advertising or as a support or secondary vehicle for regional and national advertisers.

As a support vehicle, radio is an effective way to entice the target to action and/or reinforce other communication efforts within the promotional mix.

## The Diversity of the Radio Advertising Voice

Delivering simple, low-cost messages to a small but specialized group of consumers is radio's specialty. Radio spots can be written, produced, and aired in as little as a few days. Changes and/or updates to existing spots are easy and relatively inexpensive to make, keeping material timely and making the medium adaptable to changing market conditions.

Radio's very personalized nature builds relationships with the target, especially if you can get a popular radio personality to read the spot on air, giving the product or service credibility and effectively tying the product identity and/or image to that of the DJ.

One way to maximize brand awareness is to tie the product or service to an ongoing sponsorship such as the news, the weather, or a special feature. Sponsorships highlight the product's name and are guaranteed to run at the same time every day, adding extra emphasis to the product's name and image beyond the advertised message.

As one of the most inexpensive media vehicles available, radio allows more advertising to reach the right target. Cost is determined by the length of the spot—fifteen, thirty, or sixty seconds—and the time of day the ad will air. The two most popular and expensive advertising slots, known as "drive times," include mornings from six to ten and afternoons from three to seven. Midday and evening hours are less expensive, as listenership drops off when listeners begin and end their workday. Other costs associated with radio include production-related costs such as the hiring of talent, the inclusion of sound effects or music, and the frequency with which the ad airs.

Since people are often distracted by other things while listening to the radio, spots must be aired repeatedly in order to catch the listener's attention. It is also important to remember that the target will probably not listen to only one station, so multiple buys on multiple stations will be required to reach the intended target.

Airtime can be purchased on either AM or FM radio stations. Determining what stations will best reach the targeted audience depends on the stations' programming format. The two most basic types of radio formatting include talk or music. A station's format defines the listening audience; because of this, radio advertising can talk directly to the target's special interests.

Because radio is sound only, it's important that what is said or read in other media used in your IMC campaign be repeated on the radio. This might include a jingle, sound effects, or the distinct voice of a spokesperson or character representative from television, or a slogan, tagline, or headline style from print.

Radio is not considered interactive or a great image-building option. Although radio is a one-way monologue, it need not be passive. Consider jingles, especially if they can be turned into participatory singalongs in the old-fashioned but well-loved "Hokey Pokey" style. Remote broadcasts, or broadcasts that take place from a location other than the radio station, are another way to get the target involved and the best way to use radio to encourage two-way communication between buyer and seller.

In radio, image is created verbally. But radio can be visually stimulating if an ad is written to support the target's self-image. If targets can see themselves using the product, their image will be much stronger than one manufactured by the creative team. This is especially true if the image was first introduced elsewhere in the promotional mix and radio is being used as a support medium.

When radio is a part of the promotional mix, the advertiser will need to decide if the message will run nationally, with the same generic message in all markets, or locally, with the message adapted for each market. The generic form of radio advertising is known as national network advertising, while the more geographically tailored messages are known as local or spot advertising.

The national generic message is not used very often. It goes against everything that radio is: a highly targetable, highly specialized, and highly personable medium. Local or spot radio is where most advertising is placed. This relatively inexpensive medium offers small local business owners and national advertisers the same opportunity to tailor their message to a specific demographic based on a station's musical format, psychographically based on lifestyle, and geographically based on location.

## How Does Radio Advertising Help IMC Be Consumer Focused?

This very verbal medium must imprint the product's benefits on an inattentive mind, and one of the best ways to do this is to make radio as interactive as possible. Radio ads should give the target an activity—let them sing, hum, or clap along to a catchy jingle, the kind that intrudes upon the unconscious mind whether the ad is airing at the time or not. Radio also offers promotional opportunities through contests or sweepstakes such as trivia games, where a listener calls in with the answer in order to win a prize, such as a gift certificate or product sample. Remote broadcasts can encourage listeners to stop in to a particular location and take a test drive, pick up giveaways like T-shirts or CDs, or meet a celebrity or local DJ. Another method is to take a page out of an old radio script and create an ongoing visual slice-of-life vignette. If you use intrigue, humor, or some other curiosity-building device to tell a compelling story, the target will tune in to get the next piece of the puzzle or learn how the next episode turns out.

Radio is often used in public relations to promote events such as blood drives or collection drives, or even for new product launches.

Unlike print, where it is easy to ignore advertising by turning the page, the radio audience is captive to the message unless they switch stations or turn the radio off. This is less likely when listeners are involved in other activities while listening.

Radio and newspaper advertising can be a powerful combination when adapting to changes in the marketplace, since messages can reach the public quickly and inexpensively.

Like magazines, radio is able to deliver a specialized message to a small niche market. However, unlike magazines, radio is as not useful for big-ticket merchandise or detailed copy. Radio, like newspaper, is meant not to educate but to excite the target to action. If price plays a major role in your communication efforts, radio's fleeting message makes remembering price points difficult.

Radio can also be used to reinforce and localize messages seen on television. The verbal message from television can be used on radio, keeping the cohesive IMC message going. Listeners who have been repeatedly exposed to the televised commercial will be familiar enough with the message that they will be able to replay the visual message or video from the television commercial in their minds.

## Salvations and Disasters of Radio Advertising

In order to decide whether radio advertising is right for your IMC campaign, let's look at some of the salvations and disasters associated with it.

### What Makes Radio Advertising So Great?

The more notable salvations associated with radio advertising include:

- *Cost.* Radio is very inexpensive to use when compared to other media vehicles in the promotional mix.
- *Targetability.* The varied music formats of radio stations make targeting a specific audience easier.
- *Portability.* Radio can easily be taken by the target anywhere.
- *Quick Turnaround.* Messages can be quickly developed and be heard on-air within a matter of days, sometimes even within hours.
- *Interactivity.* Listeners can become involved in the message by calling in to receive a free sample or stopping by a remote broadcast location for free gifts.
- *Imaginative Impact.* Radio is an imaginative stimulus. It is a verbal message visualized in the mind of the consumer.
- *Local and National Adaptability.* Radio spots can be easily adapted for airing in any location.
- *Frequency.* Radio's relatively low cost allows messages to be aired more often to ensure they reach the targeted audience.

### Is There Anything Wrong with Radio Advertising?

The more notable disasters associated with radio advertising include:

- *Background Noise.* Radio gets little direct attention, so advertising must be cleaver in order to catch and hold the attention of a target who is doing something else while listening.
- *Sound Only.* Radio is the imagination of the message. Messages must be written in a visually stimulating way since the target can only hear the message.
- *Fleeting Message.* Lengthy informational messages are impossible, the message is gone in fifteen, thirty, or sixty seconds. Listeners cannot spend time going back over the message.
- *Fragmented Audiences.* In larger markets, radio ads need to be aired on multiple stations since the target has many options with the same or similar formats from which to choose.
- *Clutter.* Radio stations run a lot of ads between songs or talk programming. Radio is a cluttered medium, airing anywhere between fifteen and twenty minutes' worth of advertising in an hour, with the bulk of the advertising being local.

## The Strategy behind Radio Advertising

Nobody "listens" to the radio any more: It has been relegated to background noise that keeps us company while we work, drive, shop, or get our teeth cleaned. For radio to work, it must do one of two things: have a catchy tune or jingle associated with the message—or just be downright intrusive.

Whether radio is strategically right for your IMC campaign will, of course, depend on the key benefit, the objectives, and the strategic approach. Anything that can be told in story form will work on radio. It is an excellent media vehicle for bringing character representatives or spokespersons to life, and it gives immediacy to your message. Anything that has to be spelled out through lengthy copy in order to educate or be demonstrated will not work on radio.

Effective communication objectives might include immediate sales, loyalty programs, increased store traffic, product or service inquiries, encouraging test drives, or developing brand awareness.

Strategically, radio is better suited to a product-based approach, such as generic or product feature. The use of a consumer-based approach requires image to be substantiated in other areas of the promotional mix before it can be discussed on radio. The type of strategy used to deliver the message can be either emotional or rational in nature, but the rational appeal does offer more imagination-based options. The best rational execution techniques include straight fact, product as the star, testimonials, or news. Remember, the best emotional appeals include fear, humor, dramatization, sex, fantasy, and slice-of-life. The choice of tone, approach, or appeal is affected not only by the stated objectives and target audience but by a product or service's salvations and deterrents.

Radio is not a good choice if your strategy is based on a unique selling proposition (USP), since this often must be visualized to be understood, especially if it involves some kind of new technology, look, or use.

# The Sound of Radio Design

Radio stations can air prerecorded spots or present the material live by an on-air personality. Since DJs are as much apart of the listening pleasure as the music or talk format, the product gets an added boost of credibility. On-air personalities are not provided a script from which to read, but instead are given a list of the product's features and benefits to present for thirty to sixty seconds in their own words.

Radio ads need not only employ the use of a spokesperson or on-air personality to deliver the message; they can also use music and sound effects to activate a listener's imagination.

If it's true that nobody's actively listening, then it's the creative team's job to find a way to get the listener "tuned in" to the message—and this must be done within the first three seconds. This can be done through the use of specialized voices or voices that are unique to the ear, sound effects, or music.

A number of different execution techniques can be used to deliver your radio message.

---

- Music and Jingles
- Narrative Drama
- Straight Announcement
- Celebrity Delivery
- Live Donut
- Single Voice

- Dialogue
- Multivoice
- Sound Effects
- Vignette
- Interview

---

## Music and Jingles

If your message can best be delivered attached to music, then use it. If you want to create ambiance or evoke certain emotions, use music from popular culture or a golden oldie. Music, especially oldies, attract our attention by dredging up memories and feelings from the back of our minds. These imaginative musings will enhance and enrich the current message.

Jingles are intrusive. They creep up on our unsuspecting consciousness when we least expect it: in the shower, a meeting, or while at a movie. If you want to create a theme song that ties to your tagline or slogan, then develop a jingle. Jingles are interactive, memorable, and a great way to prolong or extend the life of your message.

## Narrative Drama

If you have a story to tell, use a narrative approach. Narrative dramas take a little slice out of life and deliver it to the listeners as dialogue between characters.

## Straight Announcement

A straight announcement is just that—an announcement, most often delivered by an on-air personality. This is not a story or an imaginative stroll down memory lane; it's the facts delivered in a straightforward manner. The commercial usually starts out with the key benefit (USP or big idea) and ends with the announcer asking the listener to try the product.

## Celebrity Delivery

If your IMC campaign has a character representative or spokesperson, he or she should speak on behalf of the product in the radio spot. If the product has no recognized spokesperson and a celebrity voice is used, be sure the celebrity and the brand's image are a match.

## Live Donut

A donut uses a prerecorded opening and closing message. The center, or "donut hole," is filled in live by an on-air personality. This keeps the message moving and does not allow room for the DJ to ad lib.

## Single Voice

Use one specific voice when you have a recognizable spokesperson or character representative who can deliver your message and is known through use on other IMC pieces.

## Dialogue

Dialogue is a good way to let characters talk about the product and its uses, benefits, and features. These characters will be more credible if you add an announcer to your spot to actually make the pitch.

## Multivoice

In a multivoice approach, multiple characters carry the message not by talking to each other, but by talking directly to the listener.

## Sound Effects

If you have a repeatable sound, like the drum-banging Energizer Bunny, use it to bring a visual image to your verbal message. Sounds can also be used to make a point, as with a grumbling stomach to signify that the product can relieve acid indigestion. Music can also be used to set a scene or mood, the same way it might in a movie or television show.

## Vignette

A vignette is an ongoing storyline. The varied storylines are tied together by some repeated device such as music, a jingle, a slogan or tagline, or a spokesperson. The first vignette is used to set up the key benefit within the concept, with the following commercials used to expand the storyline or as reminder advertising.

## Interview

The interview approach is a good way to use testimonials. In this approach, DJ's or product spokespersons solicit interviews with users of the product or service. Often displays are set up at grocery stores, malls, sporting events, or street corners to encourage trial and feedback.

The creative team can use a combination of techniques to get their message across on the radio. The approach you chose should be the best one to reach the target.

## What to Consider When Designing for Radio

It is important that radio ads continue the IMC campaign theme. Be sure to carry over music, character representative, or spokesperson from print or broadcast ads. If you created any representative sounds or theme music or wrote a jingle, reuse them in radio. This will help with early recognition of the brand name. Be sure within the first three seconds to attract the listener's attention and then open with your key benefit. Radio advertising must accomplish the following:

- Your message must tune the listener in. Get the listener's attention quickly, but be sure to use the tone of voice used throughout the IMC campaign.
- Let the listener know right away the product name and key benefit.
- If the product is hard to spell or pronounce, find a way to help the listener remember it. One way is with a mnemonic, such as a word association or rhyming scheme, to make it easier to remember.
- Write your copy the way a person speaks. Proper grammar is great in print but does not transfer well into broadcast. Use short sentences to make copy points easier to remember.
- If there is a way to control the visual in the listener's mind, do it. If the product's packaging is distinct, perhaps in color or shape, let the listener know.

- Don't be afraid to repeat the product name and its key benefit often; in fact, the more often, the better. As long as the repeated devices are delivered creatively and diversely, a listener will not be annoyed or tune out.
- Talk to the listener in real time. Since the overwhelming majority of radio spots are local, deal with local issues, localities, and personalities.
- Don't lose your listener with a list of facts. Radio is great for building brand awareness, but leave any repositioning or the building of brand image to other mediums better suited for that task.
- It is important to use the ongoing message of the IMC campaign to bind the campaign together. For radio, you could use the slogan or tagline from print, the personality from television and print, or the music or jingle from television. Radio rarely leads off an IMC campaign, so use what you can to continue the campaign's tone of voice in radio spots.
- Be careful with sound effects. They are great for getting attention, but they can be annoying and sometimes can even scare a driving listener. It's important to make sure the noises you use are easily recognizable to the listener.

The copy sheet used in radio advertising is known as a script. The script can be prerecorded by talent hired by the agency or read live by an on-air personality. A radio spot can be of almost any length, but the most common are thirty- or sixty-second spots. The script must be able to be read in its entirety without sounding rushed in the time allotted. A thirty-second spot is approximately 60 to 70 words long, and a sixty-second spot is approximately 150 to 180 words long. How many words used will depend on who is reading the script, how fast he or she has to read, and if the ad contains any complicated word combinations or technical jargon. Two speakers in conversation will take up more time. See table 12.1 for additional word counts.

## Choosing Talent

The person chosen to speak the dialogue for your ad should represent the product's image and the target demographics. If the product is lawnmowers, a young person speaking the

**TABLE 12.1**
Radio Copy Word Counts

| | |
|---|---|
| 10 seconds | 20-25 words |
| 15 seconds | 30-35 words |
| 20 seconds | 40-45 words |
| 30 seconds | 60-70 words |
| 60 seconds | 150-180 words |

copy can talk about how easy it makes their summer job. But if the message is relaxation time at the end of the day or price, an older speaker will be required. It is also important to be sure every word is spoken clearly so the message can be understood.

Radio commercials should feel like one person talking to another. Keep the tone of the ad either light and upbeat or laid-back and friendly. It is important to make sure the tone is continued throughout the ad to avoid a choppy or disjointed feel.

When deciding whether to use talent or an announcer, look to your IMC concept for the right tone of voice. The choice of an announcer should speak with authority, representing the client's voice and personality. Characters should replicate real members of the target audience.

## How Should the Message Be Delivered?

Radio spots most often arrive at the radio station in a prerecorded digital format that is ready to be aired. But there are other options available, such as sending a script to be either read live or prerecorded by a member of the station, or sending a fact sheet and allowing on-air personalities to ad lib on the air. How do you know which one will work best for your product or service? First, look to your strategy and the delivery used on other IMC pieces. Additionally, consider the following:

- A script read live on the air works only if no additional sound is required and only one person will be speaking, as with a straight announcement approach.
- Fact sheets allow the on-air personality the opportunity to chat openly about the product or service. If the personality has had an opportunity before the spot airs to test drive, taste, or wear the product, she can add that experience to the discussion. The fact sheet should place the features and accompanying benefits in their order of importance, with your key benefit being first. Often, if the personality is familiar with the product you will get more than your thirty to sixty seconds of airtime. But there is a danger that the radio personality will go too far and deliver the information in a negative or cynical way. Consider this approach only when the personality is reliable or if last-minute changes are required to an existing ad, for example, with fare changes for airline travel.
- Copy that needs to be routinely updated might benefit from a live donut. Here, an advertiser prerecords a musical opening, and closing. Often the music will fade under, or be reduced in volume, creating a musical bridge that ties the opening and closing together. The hole between the opening and closing is then filled in with scripted copy that is read live on the air. The music is the constant that ties the ads together as copy is regularly changed out.
- A commercial that is prerecorded in its entirety is the safest and most professional way to go. If your script requires the use of sound effects, music, or multiple speak-

ers in any combination you will need the structure, timing, and assurance of a pre-recorded commercial.

## The Sound We Hear and Its Effects

Sound effects (SFX) are the noises we hear in ads: doors slamming, dogs barking, babies crying. They should be used to capture attention and move the copy forward. In other words, they should not be used to create noise alone, they must have a point.

SFX should aid the listener's imagination by creating a visual image in his or her mind. Music can also be used as an attention getter. It is important to note that although music is a sound, it can be used to get attention or to create a mood or set a tone.

A good copywriter tries to paint a picture with words and uses sound to back them up, create excitement, or gain attention. The spoken voice alone is not enough to hold a listener's attention, so SFX are a great way to break up the tedium of the spoken message. There are a multitude of SFX available to the creative team. As with all other creative elements, the

### Things That Help to Tie Your Product to Sound

- *Spokesperson.* If the product or service can be tied to a specific country, such as teas from the Orient or perfumes from France, then consider the use of a speaker with that accent. Be careful though; this can become very clichéd.
- *Music.* If you're working with a product or service that has little pizzazz, like insurance or investment brokers, then create pizzazz by using music familiar to the target. Musical associations help listeners remember your client's product or service.
- *Authoritative Voice.* Authoritative or expert spokespersons attract attention and bring credibility to a product or service.
- *Interviews.* Testimonials by current users of a product or service bring credibility; testimonials delivered from an on-site location bring immediacy.
- *Humor.* Be sure your commercial is funny to your target or avoid it like the plague. Humor can do more harm than good if not done well or is offensive to listeners. When done well, the listener looks forward to the commercial rather than switching the station until it's over.
- *Sound Effects.* Use sound effects to make a point and move the message forward. If there is any doubt the sound could be misinterpreted, tell listeners what they are hearing.
- *Diversity.* Alternate commercials regularly. Once a message becomes repetitive, the listener tunes it out. Keep interest high by delivering your key benefit in different ways.
- *Sponsorships.* If your product or service sponsors the news or traffic report, its name will automatically pop into a listener's mind before paid advertising airs.

choice of sounds must be carefully considered. If a sound doesn't move the message forward or have a point, leave it out.

## The Creation of a Radio Script

For the copywriter, a script is like an artist's canvas; descriptive words and visually constructed sentences are used like paint to create a picture in the mind of the consumer.

The key to any script is to make the copy flow in a conversational manner and give the talent or person reading the script visual copy cues as to what is coming, such as music or sound effects. Let's take a look at how to set up a script and what type of visual cues make reading a script easy.

All radio scripts are typed on 8½ x 11 paper and are double-spaced. Double-spaced copy adds white space to the page, making it easier to see and read the copy. Use 1-inch margins on all four sides, with 1 inch of space between columns.

A script is broken into two columns. The left side of the script is devoted to labels and the specific audio effects, such as SFX, MUSIC, ANNOUNCER, TALENT, and so on, and should appear in all caps. This makes the instructions stand out from the readable copy.

The right column, directly across from the appropriate label, is devoted to the music and/or SFX we will hear and any spoken dialogue. Any special instructions or suggestions for emphasis should be shown in (ALL CAPS AND PLACED IN PARENTHESES). All spoken copy or dialogue should appear in caps/lowercase and be enclosed in quotes.

SFX, or the noises or sounds that will be heard in the ad, are typed in all caps and placed in the right-hand column. Directly under these instructions should appear a dashed line. This is a visual cue to the talent reading the copy that a sound is coming up. It also flags those responsible for the SFX as to when they are coming up and where they belong. SFX may be done live, but most often they are prerecorded to ensure accuracy.

Music instructions are also placed in the right-hand column and also appear in all caps. Directly under these instructions should appear a solid line. This is another visual cue for those responsible for the music as well as the talent. See the example in figure 12.2.

If you are introducing a reoccurring character, give the character a name and use it in the copy. If you are not using a reoccurring character, use the label ANNOUNCER to indicate the speaker.

Remember, don't be afraid to intersperse the spot with ear-catching sound effects or mood-setting music. It will help to hold the listener's attention.

Be sure to close your spot with the product name and a call to action. Tell listeners where they can find the product, including landmarks, or a phone number or website address if it is easy to remember. Be sure to mention the product's name, key benefit, and where it can be purchased at least three times in a sixty-second spot and twice in a thirty-second spot. See figure 12.3 for a sample radio script template.

**FIGURE 12.2**

Sample Radio Script Showing Solid- and Dashed-Line Divisions

| | |
|---|---|
| SFX: | SOUND EFFECTS ARE TYPED IN ALL CAPS AND SHOULD BE UNDERLINED WITH A DASHED LINE. Any special instructions or suggestions for emphasis should be shown in (ALL CAPS AND PLACED IN PARENTHESES). |
| | ------------------------------------------------------------- |
| MUSIC: | MUSIC IS TYPED IN ALL CAPS AND UNDERLINED WITH A SOLID LINE. Why the different line work? Remember, this is being read aloud. The lines easily show the reader or talent what is coming up or going to happen. This is particularly helpful when the script is read live. |
| | ------------------------------------------------------------- |

**FIGURE 12.3**

Radio Script Template

| | |
|---|---|
| Advertiser: | Target: |
| Run Date: | Strategy: |
| Length: | USP or Big Idea: |
| | |
| SFX: | TERRIBLE COUGHING FIT. |
| | ------------------------------------------------------------- |
| ANNOUNCER: | "Feeling a little under the weather, Mr. Billy Bob?" Straight dialogue should be typed in caps/lowercase and should include quotes around any spoken dialogue. If you are not using a reoccurring character, label the speaker as ANNOUNCER. |
| BIILY BOB: | "Ah (COUGH) Ha." If you need a quick sound, place it within the dialogue. If you are introducing a reoccurring character, give him or her a name. |
| ANNOUNCER: | "Then you need Cough Reliever; it will fix you right up and get you back in the swing of things." |
| SFX: | DO NOT BE AFRAID TO INTERSPERSE THE SPOT WITH EAR-CATCHING SOUND EFFECTS. IT WILL HELP TO HOLD THE LISTENER'S ATTENTION. |
| | ------------------------------------------------------------- |
| BILLY BOB: | "Cough Reliever?" |
| MUSIC: | PITY MUSIC PLAYS IN THE BACKGROUND. |
| | ------------------------------------------------------------- |
| SFX: | TERRIBLE COUGHING CONTINUES. |
| | ------------------------------------------------------------- |
| ANNOUNCER: | "When you're this sick, be sure to pick up Cough Reliever. Available at your nearest Walgreen's Drug or CVS." Be sure to close with the product name and, if applicable, the location where the product can be found, including landmarks, or a phone number or website address if it is easy to remember. |

When using radio, be sure the copy will both visually and verbally stimulate the listener's imagination and incite action. The fact that it is low cost, portable, and highly targetable make radio advertising an attractive and inexpensive media option. Although most often used as a support vehicle for other media in the IMC promotional mix because it does not build image or promote a two-way dialogue, radio is still a great choice when you need to build and maintain brand awareness and localize the product's message.

# Television Advertising

## The Strategic Use of Television in IMC

Television advertising influences what we wear, drive, use domestically, and aspire to own. Its show-and-tell style can bring the product or service's story to life, set a mood, demonstrate a use, create a memory, initiate a fad or trend, or define a style.

Despite its cluttered environment and overall expense, television is still one of the best mass media vehicles available to reach the target audience, build awareness, and develop an image.

Through the use of sight, sound, and motion, television can attract and retain the target's attention, giving the ad the opportunity to entertain and inform. Its ability to reach the target through very specialized programming allows the product's story to be personalized to match the target's lifestyle, interests, and needs.

When used as a primary media outlet, television is ideally suited for use with new product launches, reminder advertising for mature products, and repositioning an old product in the mind of the consumer. However, it is too expensive to use if the product or service is not unique in any significant way or does not possess an inherent drama that only sight, sound, and motion can dramatize.

Television as a source of entertainment keeps television sets turned on and viewers tuned in. Millions of consumers watch television programming and are exposed to a lot of commercials, but that does not mean they actually watch the commercials. Today's television environment is cluttered with back-to-back commercials, further fractionalizing consumer interest. Getting the attention of any consumer who wields a remote control or owns a fast-forwarding VCR, DVD player, or DVR requires that advertising be not only entertaining but also useful.

Finding ways to avoid commercials is a new American pastime known as zipping, zapping, and grazing. According to Dean M. Krugman, Leonard N. Reid, S. Watson Dunn, and Arnold M. Barban in their book *Advertising: Its Role in Modern Marketing*, zipping, zapping, and grazing is one of the most serious concerns advertisers have to contend with. The fact that television commercials are considered a nuisance is nothing new; however, it's only recently that viewers can do something about them. Commercials considered uninteresting or irrelevant can be zapped with a channel change. Commercials recorded along with television programs can be zipped over with just a push of the fast-forward button. Viewers who once channel surfed can now lovingly caress their remotes while grazing through channels.

So what's an advertiser to do? First, you must get more creative and target your audience with more accuracy than ever before. Second, consider weaving some form of interactive response into the commercial. Television advertising often asks the target to visit a showroom, log on or call for additional information, or make a purchase. Third, consider creating a contest or sweepstakes where the target can be the first to own the product or use the service, or use added-price incentives or free gifts as motivators to order now.

## Traditional Advertising versus Interactive Advertising

Research for an integrated marketing communication (IMC) campaign identifies the target audience, the programs they are watching, and how they view family, fun, health, and leisure time. IMC works to create an interactive, two-way dialogue between buyer and seller. Traditional advertising methods talk *at* the target. Creative teams take great pains to ensure their message entertains and informs in the hope of enticing the intended target to read, listen, or view their message. This traditional interaction between buyer and seller is known as a passive monologue.

Interactive television, also known as direct response, involves the target in the message process by asking them to call, log in, or stop by for further information or to make a purchase. If so inclined, the target can order immediately without the inconvenience of leaving his home or office. Interaction requires contact, so each commercial should display a toll-free number or website where the target can find additional information, technical assistance, or help in placing an order. This interaction is active and takes place in the form of a dialogue, or two-way communication. The target identifies the message, digests the information, and can get a direct response from the advertised source with just the click of a mouse or push of a few buttons. Advertising clutter is reduced because the target chooses what he wants to see and when he wants to see it.

Traditional advertising delivers an uninvited message to a distracted target and can take weeks or even months to build brand awareness and motivate the target to purchase.

Direct response advertising is immediate, allowing the consumer to buy while the commercial is still running. There is often a bonus offering if the consumer buys in the next few minutes or is one of the first one hundred callers. Active involvement shortens the amount of time needed to build awareness because consumers pursue additional information on their own time.

Most direct response products, on the other hand, have little or no competition and thus make the decision to purchase generally easier and faster. Writing for direct response is simple: grab the listener's attention within the first three to five seconds; make your offer simple, especially ordering information; use experts, testimonials, or studies to validate the product; demonstrate how the product works or what it sounds like; make ordering easy; and repeat the most important information frequently.

Writing a direct response ad may be simple, but to say it all takes a little longer than traditional advertising, requiring around 90 to 120 seconds. This extra time is needed to lay out the specific selling points and allows the viewer to hear and/or see the product in use. Direct response commercials are basically a shorter version of the infomercial.

## Infomercials and Home Shopping Channels

Most direct response commercials are found on cable stations, which are less expensive than the networks and have a more specialized programming format. The two most commonly seen forms of direct response advertising are infomercials and home shopping channels.

Infomercials are simply long commercials, usually about thirty to sixty minutes long. This extended commercial message allows time for a demonstration of how the product works; testimonials from satisfied customers; perhaps a professional endorsement or two by an engineer, health professional, or scientist; and finally the payment and ordering options. The basic premise of these long commercials is no different from that of their smaller fifteen- to thirty-second cousins: entertain and inform the viewer while making a sale. Infomercials are growing in popularity and effectiveness due to their use of toll-free numbers, the availability of credit cards, and ease of return.

Home shopping channels allow the consumer to purchase anything from jewelry to mattresses from the comfort of their own recliners by dialing a toll-free number or logging on to a website. Special prices or payment options are prevalent, and returns are easy. Unlike infomercials, home shopping channels do not concentrate on selling one item from one manufacturer, but offer multiple items, often from multiple manufacturers. The channel's designated host most often presents products, but a product representative, designer, or inventor may also represent the product's attributes to the viewer. A one-hour program may include anything from pots and pans to hair products and each product will receive anywhere from six to ten minutes of presentation time.

# The Diversity of the Television Advertising Voice

## How Television Breaks Down

Television can be categorized into five separate areas: network, spot, cable, syndication, and public.

**Network Television**  Network television is home to the big four networks: ABC, CBS, FOX, and NBC, with each receiving a sizable share of the available advertising revenue and viewing audience.

Network affiliates, local television stations located across the country, are paid to air network programming at a predetermined time. When network programming is not filling the schedule, local stations fill airtime with local broadcasts or nationally syndicated programs.

**Spot Television**  Spot television gives advertisers the opportunity to run their ads in individual markets rather than on a national basis. These commercials air between programs, while network advertising airs during programming. Most local advertising revenue is generated from these spots.

**Cable Television**  Viewers can receive the big four networks in their homes for free, but cable television is a subscription service. Because of this, cable receives revenue from both subscription rates and advertising revenue. Cable advertising is less expensive than nationally placed advertising, and the highly selective and special interest programming on many channels makes reaching a specific target audience easier. Unlike network programming that offers a more generic schedule of shows, different cable channels offer very specialized lineups, including news, movies, documentaries, history, sports, and children's programming, with most running twenty-four hours a day, every day.

**Broadcast Syndication**  Programs that are in syndication are produced independently, and then sold to individual local stations, with no consideration being given to any one-network affiliation. Syndicated programs can also include reruns of older programs. Local stations are granted some of the commercial airtime, while the syndicate sells its portion to national advertisers.

## Sponsor Public Television

Public television is largely noncommercial and supported by individual viewers, and in part by nonprofit organizations and state and local governments. Corporate sponsors often underwrite certain programs, but the use of traditional advertising methods on public television is rare. While some sponsored announcements have evolved into a shorter, less aggressive versions of commercial advertising, most sponsorships are understated and use only a logo, tagline or slogan, address, and/or phone number.

## How Does Television Advertising Help IMC Be Consumer Focused?

Television involves the viewer through sight, sound sets the tone or mood, and motion allows the target to see the product in action. Used together, sight, sound, and motion place the product in the target's imagination and life. Television is a very expensive mass media vehicle. It is important when using television to be sure your target is watching. The hit-and-miss mentality of years gone by has been replaced with a high degree of selective targeting. Cable allows advertisers to select specific channels and programming that can reach the intended target in the same way magazines and radio can.

In an IMC campaign it is important that every time the target is exposed to the message, no matter the vehicle, it reinforces the key benefit and project strategy. Look to what visuals are being used in other materials and be sure your dialogue matches the tone of voice. Beyond that, consider color, spokespersons or character representatives, headline styles, or the execution techniques used elsewhere in the promotional mix to bind the IMC pieces together.

Each of advertising's media vehicles, with the exception of newspaper, takes advantage of audience fragmentation and focuses on reaching the consumer through selective targeting, based on special interests making advertising a great place to build brand awareness or brand image. Public relations can be used to toot a corporation's own horn. Newspaper offers time-sensitive offers and low price. Magazines offer tradition, status, prestige, and class. Television can entertain us with sight, sound, and motion, and demonstrate the product in use.

When used in conjunction with television, public relations can be used to sponsor or promote local charity events or to acknowledge a corporation's local or national contribution to important ecological or safety issues.

Magazines and television can be a powerful combination if the objective is building or projecting a product's image. Used together, these two vehicles can deliver unique, unusual, and creative solutions to an image based strategy.

Magazines, cable television, and radio advertising are all great vehicles for selective and specific targeting. Reaching and affecting the target is made easier because special interest magazines and programming allow advertising to talk directly to the target's interests.

When used as a support vehicle to television or other media within the promotional mix, radio allows listeners to take part in the message by imagining themselves using, wearing, or tasting the product, and purchase can take place quickly by encouraging the target to drop by and test drive, pick up a sample, or set up an appointment.

By including an interactive component, television can draw the target to a website or to customer service representatives. Information found there can be used to build a relationship between the buyer and seller and contribute to building brand loyalty and equity. Television may be a one-way monologue, but the information presented can encourage interaction through additional research or even trial.

## Salvations and Disasters of Television Advertising

In order to decide whether television advertising is right for your IMC campaign, let's look at some of the salvations and disasters associated with it.

### What Makes Television Advertising So Great?

The more notable salvations associated with television advertising include:

- *Impact.* Television delivers sight, sound, and motion, allowing the target to view the product, see it in action or in the proper setting, and hear the message all at the same time.
- *Selectivity.* Between the networks and cable, television offers enough diverse programming to selectively choose the exact program the target will be watching, eliminating hit-and-miss placement and cutting down on advertising waste.
- *Audience Size.* Television is a mass media vehicle that reaches a lot of people. Although network television does not reach the numbers of viewers it used to in the past, it is still one of the best ways to reach a target. Network television's national reach allows advertising to introduce, maintain, or reposition a brand's image.
- *Trends and Fads.* Television sets trends and influences the way we look and talk; we believe what we see on the screen. We are influenced by what we watch and adapt it to our vernacular or wardrobe. Programming and advertising often rolls over into our personal and work environments as we talk about what we saw on television the night before.

### Is There Anything Wrong with Television Advertising?

The more notable disasters associated with television advertising include:

- *Cost.* Television advertising is expensive. The length of the commercial, the program airing, and the time the commercial will run all determine cost. It is important to know where your target audience will be and what they will be watching when considering television as a viable media option.
- *Clutter.* There are a lot of commercials running in any given time slot, some running back-to-back. In order to fight consumer apathy and remote control rampages, an ad must stand out visually and verbally by specifically addressing the target audience and their needs.

- *Fleeting Message.* Television commercials are fleeting; the creative team has only fifteen or possibly thirty seconds to make a point to a group of people who need a sandwich or a bathroom break. Develop your concept to repeat major points and use music to flag the target to stop, look, and listen; if they missed the ad the first time around, the music can announce a repeat performance.

## The Strategy behind Television Advertising

Writing for television is not an easy task. Copywriters must balance their words with the video portion of the commercial. They must also ensure that the proper information is included to strategically promote the key benefit and ultimately accomplish the stated objectives. All copy decisions will be based on strategy decisions stated in the creative brief.

How do you tell a story in only fifteen to thirty seconds and still accomplish the objectives set up in the creative brief? What will make the key benefit standout strategically? Consider some of the following:

- Let your research guide you.
- Make your key benefit relevant to the target.
- Talk to your target audience in words and about situations they can relate too.
- Open with the key benefit.
- Be sure the commercial stays on strategy and on target. Be sure it reflects the same visual aspects and tone of voice as the other pieces in the IMC campaign.
- Choose a tone or execution technique that complements and highlights your key benefit and accomplishes the stated objectives.
- If you can show it in television better than you can say it, then do so.
- Get to the point and hammer it home, frame after frame.
- Make sure the audio and video work together as a cohesive unit.
- Write to your target. Have your announcer or voiceover talk directly to the target or have your talent deal with situations the target can relate to.
- Mention the product's name and show its packaging repeatedly, so the target will remember it.
- Make your key benefit the star of the commercial, and make sure it is clearly pointed out to the target.
- Involve your target in the commercial. Show her how she will look in the product, or how it will keep her kids safe, or make her clothes whiter; tell her about the benefits the product or service delivers. Give the target an interactive activity such as a website to visit or toll-free number to call for more information.
- Make sure the commercial is the right length. The announcer or talent should be able to speak and move at a natural pace, without rushing. Fill any holes where there is no action taking place.

- Be sure the last frame in your storyboard has either the logo or a final shot of the product with the logo showing. To assist with recall, especially for a new or reinvented product, both are preferred.

It is important to remember that the key benefit must be sold in every frame. It cannot be mentioned or shown only once. Television's short life span, fleeting messages, and inattentive audience requires the key benefit to scream out for fifteen or thirty seconds.

Objectives best suited for television advertising include product demonstrations, and concepts that entertain, excite, or have a social or personal impact.

Strategically, there is no approach, appeal, or execution technique that does not work for television. The creative team is armed with a toolbox of creative opportunities to show and tell, demonstrate, and activate the target's imagination.

## The Sight, Sound, and Motion of Television Design

Television is more than just the random use of sight, sound, and motion. It is about determining the most appropriate setting for the product, the correct choice of talent to deliver the message, the right lighting to set the scene, and the appropriate use of props and music to set the mood or make a point. Finally, the pace or delivery of the message must be in keeping with the overall look and tone of the message. Television is the coordination of sight, sound, and motion.

A television commercial begins as a storyboard. This storyboard consists of two parts: the visual aspects, or scenes, and the script, or what will be said and heard. Television scripts are much more detailed than radio scripts; because television requires a lot more people to produce a spot, the storyboard and accompanying script must talk not only to the client but to talent, directors, camera operators, lighting and sound people, producers, editors, composers, food stylists, and computer animators, to name just a few.

### The Ins and Outs of a Television Shoot

Designing, planning, and shooting a television commercial is a complicated and lengthy process. Very little is done on a whim or at the last minute. Most commercial shoots can take anywhere from several days to several weeks to complete. Before any actual footage is shot, the creative team, along with the director, must walk through the shoot and go over any changes; hold auditions; look at possible locations; gather up the product, props, or costumes; and go over the various technical aspects of the shoot, such as lighting and sound, with the production crew.

Additional decisions, such as whether the television commercial should be produced on film, videotape, or computer, are made at this point, as are decisions about media placement. Most all decisions will be made during the preproduction, production, and postproduction phases. Preproduction includes the development of the script and storyboard, budget, and the hiring of on-air talent, a director, and a production crew. The production stage includes the actual shoot, and postproduction includes the editing process.

## Big, Small, and Elaborate Productions

How and where a commercial is shot depends on the product, the budget, and the strategy. Commercials can be done relatively inexpensively when shot and produced locally. This type of shoot is relatively simple and contains few bells or whistles. The goal is to get the message out as quickly and effectively as possible.

Nationally produced commercials, on the other hand, use all the bells and whistles necessary to attract the targeted audience. These spots are usually produced and often shot in the major advertising markets and then delivered to the major affiliates or cable television stations.

Many national spots are produced right in the studio, employing use of expensive computer graphics. Real or animated talent may be developed in order to attract attention, or create a specialized atmosphere or some type of special effect.

Another, often equally expensive option is to shoot away from a production studio or "on location," where a remote location is used for the background of the commercial. Locations may be exotic or mundane, and are determined by the commercial's overall strategy or concept. Being shot on location gives a dose of reality to the commercial, allowing consumers to see the product in the setting in which it might be used.

## Scripts and Storyboards

A television commercial is made up of a script and accompanying storyboard.

**Television Scripts** A television script is a very detailed document. Not only does it include everything that will be heard, such as dialogue, music, jingles, and sound effects, but it also contains details and any special instructions to talent, camera, and sound and editing people, and any information concerning scene changes.

**Storyboards** Storyboards show the visual portion of the commercial and the timing sequence between what is heard and what is seen, one frame at a time. See figure 13.2 for a sample blank storyboard.

The visual aspects of a television commercial are known as scenes. Each scene is confined in a frame, or the shape of a television screen, on the storyboard. Each individual scene depicts a major piece of action or location change. Any given scene may require additional shots from a variety of angles, but there is no need to show them all. A fifteen- to thirty-second spot usually consists of four to six frames; a longer, less common sixty-second spot will need six to eight frames.

Under each frame appears the accompanying dialogue, sound effects, and music, or the audio portion of the commercial (or the portion of the script that corresponds to that

**FIGURE 13.2**
Sample Blank Storyboard

Student Name: _____    Name of Television Spot: _____

15   or   30   second spot (Circle One)          Grade: _____

scene). This is an exact reproduction of the script combined with the visual action. A storyboard is how the commercial will be presented to the client and any other major production players. The script alone will be used almost exclusively by the talent, although members of the production team may also consult it.

The storyboard lays out the action. Since you cannot realistically show every scene, choose just the most important ones: those that move the commercial forward and that show concept direction. Don't worry about your artistic skills on the storyboard; the message is more important.

The actual television shoot is exhausting and stressful; two or three seconds of actual footage can take several hours to shoot. It is important to have a detailed script, to keep the enormous number of people it takes to shoot one thirty-second spot on the same page. Copies should be distributed to the talent, the director, the client, and the varied production staff, to name just a few. If everybody is on the same page when shooting begins, the commercial will be much more likely to stay on budget and shoot on schedule.

The cost of shooting and producing a television spot is huge. Television airtime needs to be bought, which is a major chunk of the budget; the spot must be designed, the script written, and the talent and production crew hired. If you plan to go on location or use a celebrity, the cost skyrockets even higher. A detailed storyboard is imperative. It must be very tight and very detailed; the schedule and budget can be significantly affected if the storyboard is incomplete or requires changes of any kind once shooting begins. A good storyboard lets the entire production team know in advance where they need to be and what needs to be done.

## How to Deliver Your Message

Before choosing an execution technique for your commercial, look to your strategy to help determine the best approach or combination of approaches needed to deliver your USP or big idea. Each appeal will be effective no matter whether an emotional or rational style is used.

### Commercial Tones and Execution Techniques

Consider one or a combination of the following commercial execution techniques to deliver the commercial's tone of voice.

- Slice-of-life
- Spokesperson
- Testimonials
- Demonstration
- Torture Tests
- Visual Images
- Metaphors
- Creative Comparisons
- Vignette
- Expert Presenters

**Slice-of-life** Slice-of-life refers to the dramatization of a little slice of the target market's everyday life. This type of approach presents the product as a problem solver. The standard format introduces the viewer to the product, the characters, and the problem. Next, it shows the viewer how the product can solve one or more of the problems, perhaps in a series of vignettes, or short stories. The closing tells viewers that the next time they have a similar problem, the product can make their lives better, easier, or healthier.

**Spokesperson** The choice of a spokesperson or animated character representative will define the personality and overall image of your client's product or service. You will have to decide if this visual representative should be real or animated; a celebrity, the CEO or company president, or an unknown person whose image will be synonymous with the product or service. When choosing the representative, be sure to choose an image that matches that of the product and the target. Important considerations might include age, gender, and appearance, such as height, weight, and demeanor. How should your character or spokesperson sound? Should his voice be average or distinctive, or perhaps a deep baritone or a Southern drawl is appropriate? All these decisions will affect how the product or service will be viewed—and, hopefully, remembered. The perfect spokesperson should represent, or add to, the product's inherent drama. You don't have to settle for only one speaker. Whether the spokesperson(s) or character representative(s) appear on screen or as off-screen speakers who are heard but not seen, additional personalities give life to a concept and to dialogue.

**Testimonials** Getting a current user to talk about his or her experiences with the product or service is priceless. Real people have credibility and are often quite colorful. It can be difficult to work with people not trained to perform on cue, however, so depending on the approach you are going for, the budget, and/or the time frame, it may prove easier to use real experiences from the public delivered by trained actors. This approach does require the acknowledgment that trained actors are used in lieu of the actual consumer.

**Demonstration** Television is great for this show-and-tell approach, which offers several options:

- *Side by Side*. If there are distinct differences between your client's product and the competition, consider placing the products side by side and pointing out the differentiating or unique features.
- *Before and After*. This demonstration technique proves there are times when it is better to show how a product solves a problem rather than talk about it. Here, the product is challenged by a problem it quickly solves.
- *Product in Use*. This technique shows the product in action while discussing the relevant features and benefits.

- *New and Innovative Uses.* This type of demonstration is great for reinvented products that have undergone a transformation from one use to another.

Demonstrations must be based on proven results to be credible. If there have been any scientific results or government stamps of approval, or if your product is simply unique, consider showing viewers, rather than telling them, about the product or results.

**Torture Tests**  If durability is an important product feature, rip it, tear it, and beat it to a pulp. Do not hesitate to show how the product performs under adverse conditions.

**Visual Images**  Images are windows to opening up the viewer's imagination. If your strategy is to develop an image campaign for your product, consider using visuals to set the scene. What kinds of images, real or imagined, does your product bring to mind? Can you combine some of these visual solutions together, or perhaps create new associations or ideas? Images should present the message both visually and verbally.

**Metaphors**  If the product can be compared to something not usually associated with it, like sandpaper to dry skin, showing it can attract attention and prove a point more quickly than thirty seconds of copy.

**Creative Comparisons**  Comparing the product to a great work of art or a famous piece of music creates status and indicates quality.

**Vignette**  A vignette is a series of short stories that are tied together to highlight the product's key benefit. These stories may have a repeated character or feature a variety of characters who routinely use the product to solve a problem.

**Expert Presenters**  An expert in a relevant field—such as a scientist, engineer, or CEO— lends credibility to product claims. You can also use a celebrity here to lend status or class, or just define the essence of cool by using or wearing the product.

## The Length of a Commercial Message

Length depends on budget, but the most common is thirty seconds. It is not uncommon for advertisers to purchase a thirty-second spot and then break the commercial time in half, producing two related commercials. This allows the advertised message to deliver two separate points in succession, building awareness one feature/benefit at a time. If the dual messages are mutually dependent, this technique is called piggybacking. If your budget allows, a sixty-second spot offers more time to drive your point home.

### Who Is Going to Talk the Talk and React to the Sounds We Hear?

There are many sounds in a television commercial, whether spoken, created, or musically based. Let's take a short look at each one.

**Talent** Talent refers to the individuals who will be seen on camera reading the copy or dialogue; it also includes any off-screen announcers who will be heard delivering the copy. It is important that the talent visually and/or verbally represent the product and target image.

**Voiceover** When an announcer is heard reading the dialogue but is not seen on camera, this is known as a voiceover. A voiceover can be used to deliver all the dialogue or just the closing. This is often a good time to consider using a recognizable celebrity voice. Using a celebrity in a television commercial is less expensive when the celebrity is only heard and not seen.

**Announcer** An announcer is both seen and heard on camera delivering the dialogue. This is a great way to associate, introduce, or use a character representative or spokesperson as the voice and face of the product.

### Music

Music is used to set a mood. Imagine a movie without the soundtrack: We wouldn't know how to react or what to expect when the action finally takes place. Music can be used to replace words, represent an emotion, or assist in placing the viewer in the proper emotional state. Volume can also be used to set a mood. Music should be used in the same way talent and dialogue is used to tell the story.

### Sound Effects

SFX replicate reality. We can relate to the headache of a slamming door, the tension associated with screaming babies, or the calming sound of the ocean. SFX should support the message, not get in the way of it.

### The Preparation of Television Scripts and Storyboards

A script is laid out in three columns. Column one is used to label the frames, column two is for labeling instructions, and column three is for dialogue, music, SFX, and any special instructions. Be sure each label lines up to the corresponding information. Labels must be set in all caps; instructions should be enclosed in parentheses. All dialogue should be typed in caps/lowercase and enclosed in quotes. Be sure to double-space the script, place ½ inch to 1 inch of space between columns, and use 1-inch margins on all four sides.

There are many ways to lay out or set up a script; the following is just one possible solution. Let's take a look at each item that is needed on the script in the order in which it should appear. Depending on the action happening in your script, placement of SFX, music, or dialogue can be altered. Any information concerning camera instructions, camera shots, or frame transitions must be consistent from script to script no matter the content or concept. When preparing copy for a television shoot, nothing can be assumed or taken for granted. Television is expensive, and there are too many people involved to safely use generalities. When in doubt about an instruction, write it out.

**Opening Frame**  Each storyboard must be opened. The opening frame must tell us what we will be seeing when the commercial begins. OPEN: (on grocery store checkout), followed immediately by the camera shot. OPEN is used only in frame one. All additional frames will use the frame transition, or the last instruction in the frame, to tell us what we will see next in each additional frame.

**Camera Shots**  Camera shots are the first thing to appear in each and every frame besides frame one, where an opening description of the scene appears. Camera shots tell the cameraperson how close or how far away to be from an image or scene. Refer to the human figure example 13.4 to see what the camera is focusing on. Adapt this example to your product; the visual cue would be the same if you were shooting an apple, a car, or a dirty dish.

The following is a list of possible camera shots for use in your script. Refer to figure 13.3 for examples used in each of the following sections.

- ECU (Extreme Close-up): Chin to top of the head would appear in the shot
- MCU (Medium Close-up): Throat to top of the head
- FCU (Full Close-up): Neck to top of the head
- WCU (Wide Close-up): Collar bone area to the top of the head
- CU (Close Up): Chest area to the top of the head
- MCS (Medium Close Shot): Waist to the top of the head
- MS (Medium Shot): Stomach to top of the head
- MFS (Medium Full Shot): Knees to the top of the head
- FS (Full Shot): Bottom of the feet to the top of the head

There are no instructions that appear beside a camera shot. The camera shot tells only the position of the camera, not what the camera will be looking at. When writing your script, there is no need to spell any of the camera shots out; use only the abbreviations and place in all caps.

**FIGURE 13.3**

Camera Shot Examples

| Frame 1 | OPEN: | (Open onto a grocery store checkout line full of people). |
|---|---|---|
| | MCS: | |
| | CAMERA: | STILL. |
| | SFX IN and UNDER: | SFX IN (A lot of people complaining and mumbling in background) UNDER. |
| | WOMAN 1: | "Why don't they get some more help around here?" |
| | SFX OUT: | SFX (Of people complaining and mumbling in background) OUT. |
| | CUT TO: | (Another grocery store where another woman is checking out her own groceries). |
| Frame 2: | MFS: | |
| | CAMERA: | PAN (grocery store, notice all the available check-out lanes) LEFT AND RIGHT. |
| | CAMERA: | STILL. |
| | WOMAN 1: | "Grocery shopping is always fast and easy." |
| | MUSIC IN and UNDER: | MUSIC IN (It's a Hot Time In the Old Town Tonight) UNDER |
| | ANN: | "At So So Bees, you will never have to stand in line. Open 24 hours, for your convenience." |
| | SFX OUT: | SFX (It's a Hot Time in The Old Town Tonight) OUT |
| | SUPER: | (Logo on parking lot, with grocery store in the background). |

**Camera Instructions** Camera instructions tell the camera what to do or how to move in a shot. Camera instructions can appear anywhere in a frame, depending on when the camera needs to move. If each shot will be a stationary or STILL shot, you need to mention the camera instruction in frame one only, following the camera shot. If the camera instruction begins as a STILL shot, but moves to a PAN in frame three, for instance, you must state that camera instruction in frame three. If you don't, the camera will not be there, set up and ready to go when needed. If the camera goes back to a STILL in frame four, you must state that in frame four. Camera instructions follow camera shots in a frame.

The following is a list of possible camera instructions for use in your script.

- STILL SHOT: Instruction for camera to hold on the shot, no movement at all.
- PAN SHOT: This instruction tells the camera to move horizontally left or right from a fixed point. You must tell the camera which way the pan should go, PAN LEFT or PAN RIGHT.
- TILT SHOT: This instruction tells the camera to move up or down from a fixed point. Again, you must tell the camera which way to go, TILT UP or TILT DOWN.
- ZOOM SHOT: This instruction tells the camera to move in for a rapid close-up or away to a distance shot. Again, you must tell the camera which way to go, ZOOM IN or ZOOM OUT.

- DOLLY SHOT: This instruction tells the entire camera to move forward or backward more slowly than a zoom shot, DOLLY BACK or DOLLY FORWARD.
- BOOM SHOT: This instruction tells the camera you need the shot to come from above, from either a boom or a crane. Used for overhead views.
- TRUCK SHOT: This instruction tells the camera to shoot alongside a moving subject. Again, you must tell the camera where to be and what to do, TRUCK SHOT (along the right side and slightly to the back of the runner).

**Audio Instructions**  Audio instructions can appear before or after a character speaks in a frame. The placement depends on when you want the listener to hear the noise or music. The following is a list of possible audio instructions for use in your script.

- SFX: Use SFX alone when a noise is brief and immediately over, SFX (one hand clap)
- SFX IN: This instruction signals the sound to begin and continue, SFX (the clattering of pots and pans) IN
- SFX OUT: Instruction to end the sound effect, SFX (the clattering of pots and pans) OUT
- SFX UP: This instruction asks for the volume to increase, SFX (of clapping hands) UP
- SFX DOWN: This instruction asks for the volume to decrease, SFX (of clapping hands) DOWN
- SFX UNDER: This instruction asks for the volume to go under or to decrease in volume enough that dialog can be spoken over it, SFX IN (of clapping hands) UNDER
- MUSIC UP: This instruction asks for the volume to increase, MUSIC (Old MacDonald Had a Farm) UP
- MUSIC DOWN: This instruction asks for the volume to decrease, MUSIC (Old MacDonald Had a Farm) DOWN
- MUSIC UNDER: This instruction asks for the volume to go under or to decrease in volume enough that dialogue can be spoken over it, MUSIC IN (Old MacDonald Had a Farm) UNDER
- SEGUE: This instruction signals there is more than one piece of music being used. A segue is a musical transition from one song to another often used to indicate a change in time, place or mood, SEGUE (Old MacDonald Had a Farm to Row, Row, Row Your Boat).
- FADE: This instruction indicates that the noise or music needs to fade out or away.

It is important to note that both SFX and music can continue from frame to frame or go in, out, or under from frame to frame as needed. Use music to set a mood or pace and use SFX only if they move the commercial along and help make a point. Too many noises can be annoying and can distract from the message.

**Dialogue** Dialogue includes anything spoken by your talent, on or off screen, and can appear before or after SFX or camera instructions. All dialogue should be typed in caps/lower case and enclosed in quotes.

- VO (Voiceover): This instruction indicates that the speaker will be heard but not seen on-air.
- ANN (Announcer): This instruction indicates that the speaker will be seen and heard on-air.
- BILL: If you are creating a recurring character whose name will be used within the commercial, label the part appropriately.
- WOMAN or MAN: If more than one person will be speaking in the commercial, label their parts separately. If they are not recurring characters and no names are used in the dialogue, there is no reason to assign specific names.

**Frame Transitions** Frame transitions tell the director and postproduction editors how you want to get out of one frame and into the next. They also indicate what will be seen in the next frame.

Frame transitions appear in the bottom of every frame except the last one. The final frame does not need a transition because the network or cable station will control the move from one commercial to another or from commercial back to programming.

The following is a list of possible frame transitions for use in your script.

- CUT: This instruction indicates that the picture will change instantly or in the blink of an eye, CUT: (To CU of victim).
- DISSOLVE: This instruction indicates the transition will fade out of one picture and into another. A good way to show the passage of time. Dissolves do take a lot of time to evolve, so use them sparingly, DISSOLVE: (Show aging from youth to adult).
- WIPE: This instruction indicates the transition will physically push one picture off the screen in order to reveal another. Great for showing a rapid transition from one activity or one location to another, WIPE: (CU of wound to CU of a healed wound).
- SUPER: Use this instruction when one image will sit on top of another image, color or pattern. The top image is then superimposed on top of the bottom image. Often, the top visual is reversed out (prints white) over the background image. Supers usually appear in the last frame, and are used most often when the logo is placed on top of a background image, SUPER: (Note logo placed on top of the lake).

Figure 13.5 shows a sample script and matching storyboard.

**FIGURE 13.4**

# Camera Shot Frames

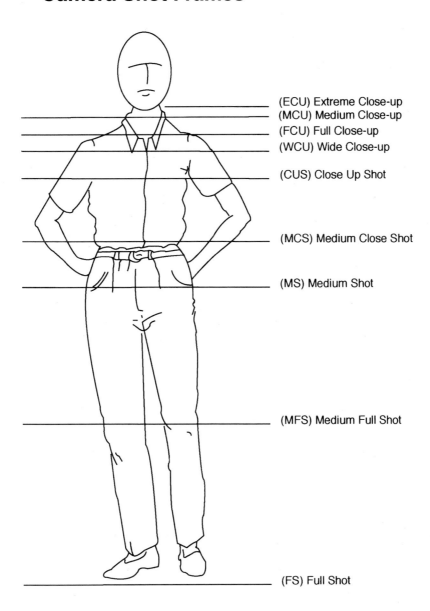

(ECU) Extreme Close-up
(MCU) Medium Close-up
(FCU) Full Close-up
(WCU) Wide Close-up

(CUS) Close Up Shot

(MCS) Medium Close Shot

(MS) Medium Shot

(MFS) Medium Full Shot

(FS) Full Shot

**FIGURE 13.5**

Script Template and Example Storyboard: Viravac. Viravac storyboard and script by T. J. Bonner, West Virginia University.

A script is laid out in three columns. Column one is used to label the frames, column two is for labeling instructions, and column three is for dialogue, music and sound effects, or any special instructions. Be sure each label lines up to the corresponding information. All labels must be set in all caps; any instructions should be enclosed in parentheses. All dialogue should be typed in caps/lower case and enclosed in quotes. Be sure to double-space the script. Place $\frac{1}{2}$ inch to 1 inch of space between columns, and use 1-inch margins on all four sides.

| Frame 1: | OPEN:<br>MS: | OPEN (on soybean field ravaged by weeds and grasses). |
|---|---|---|
| | CAMERA: | STILL |
| | VO: | "You don't need a field choked with unwanted weeds." |
| | CUT TO: | (Shot of 50-lb. bags of Viravac). |
| Frame 2: | CU: | |
| | VO: | "What you do need is Viravac." |
| | CUT TO: | (Farmer pouring bag into a field cultivator). |
| Frame 3: | MS: | |
| | SFX IN and<br>UNDER: | SFX IN (Sound of contents of bag being poured into the field cultivator) UNDER |
| | VO: | "Simply add the correct amount of Viravac to your field cultivator or disc and let the machine do the work." |
| | SFX OUT: | SFX (Sound of contents of bag being poured into the field cultivator) OUT |
| | CUT TO: | (Diagram of soil, weed, and Viravac pellets). |
| Frame 4: | MS: | |
| | VO: | "The Viravac Pellets are mixed into the top 2-3 inches of soil where they go to work immediately to kill germinating grasses and weeds." |
| | CUT TO: | (Soybean field thriving without weeds or grasses). |
| Frame 5: | LS: | |
| | CAMERA: | PAN (soybean field) LEFT AND RIGHT. |
| | VO: | "The results are, cleaner fields, a faster more efficient harvest and happy farmers." |
| | CUT TO: | SUPER (White Viravac logo on a black screen). |
| Frame 6: | CU: | |
| | CAMERA: | STILL |
| | VO: | "Call your agricultural chemical dealer today and ask for Viravac Herbicide by name or visit our website at www.viravac.com." |

**FIGURE 13.5**
Continued

Television has a great amount of influence on who we are as both individuals and consumers. We watch a lot of television, making it a great choice when launching a new product, maintaining or reinventing an existing product, building or maintaining awareness, or developing both a product and a consumer image. Although expensive to use, television advertising can be highly targeted, and with the right message the use of sight, sound, and motion can attract and hold the target's attention long enough to make a message or image impact. If television is appropriate as a member of your media mix, make it entertaining and be sure to make it interactive by asking the target to do something.

# Direct Marketing

## The Strategic Use of Direct Marketing in IMC

Direct marketing is the first of the three promotional devices we will look at. You may be wondering what the difference is between advertising and promotion? Advertising is all about educating the consumer on a products feature and benefits, to encourage purchase. Promotion on the other hand, makes a proposition by offering packaged deals to induce immediate purchase.

When you know exactly who your target audience is and you want to talk to them one-on-one, consider direct marketing as an alternative to traditional advertising vehicles.

Direct marketing is all about creating a dialogue between buyer and seller. Communication is coordinated and individualized through the use of multiple media vehicles and databases. The information collected in databases allows direct marketing to reach targets based on their past buying history, demographics, psychographics, behavioristics, and geodemographics.

Knowledge about the consumer allows you to create a more personalized message, eliminating the more generic mass media messages delivered through traditional advertising methods. This more intimate environment makes reaching and talking to the target in a language they can relate to, and about a topic they are interested in, easier and more successful. The result is the development of an interpersonal relationship between the client or marketer, the product or service, and the target. This relationship is one of

FIGURE 14.1

## DIRECT MARKETING CASE STUDY: NOTRE DAME FEDERAL CREDIT UNION

### Product/Field

Full-service provider of consumer financial products.

### Marketing Opportunity

As successful in the community as Notre Dame Federal Credit Union has been, it had not, until recently, enjoyed a significant breakthrough in marketing first mortgages to its members. The credit union wanted to develop an aggressive campaign to build its mortgage portfolio.

### Strategy

Villing & Company made use of the credit union's extensive database, which enabled the creation of a mortgage campaign targeted to the audience most likely to respond. The data suggested that direct mail should be the key promotional medium. Our experience has shown that direct mail works best when supported by other media—the essence of what's known as Integrated Marketing Communications (IMC) strategy. So we also used radio, newspaper and point-of-purchase displays to reach our target audience. The creative approach was simply to tout the credit union's low-interest-rate mortgages and how easy it is to apply for one. The image of a small boy on a tricycle "bringing home" a low mortgage rate in a little red wagon was used to reinforce the theme and copy.

### Result

Phones in the credit union's mortgage office began ringing as soon as the campaign kicked off. The Notre Dame Federal Credit Union website received over 800 "hits" on its mortgage page in the first month alone. Mortgage applications rose to an all-time high and continue to rise. And mortgage volume increased each month during the promotion.

*Case study courtesy of Villing & Company, Inc.*

the foundations needed to build and maintain brand loyalty. The availability of toll-free numbers and access to the Internet carry this interpersonal relationship a step further by allowing the target to communicate directly with the advertiser.

Traditional advertising is where advertisers and their agencies have historically turned to build brand awareness, accomplish repositioning, and eventually build brand loyalty. Today, the cost of advertising—especially on television—and the fractionalization of media are changing the way consumers receive messages. Advertising simply doesn't reach the target as well as it used to. The interactive and more personalized nature of direct marketing makes it a better alternative to build a brand's image.

Direct marketing is everything traditional advertising efforts are not. As a mass media vehicle, advertising delivers a message to thousands—often millions—of readers, listeners, or viewers, most of whom are not a part of the targeted audience. Direct marketing can personalize its message on an individual basis, addressing the target by name.

Traditional advertising requires more time to entice the target to action. Its impersonal format requires more frequent messages to reach, educate, and then remind consumers to purchase the next time they are at the grocery store or the mall. Direct marketing eliminates the middleman and makes purchase or additional inquires as easy as the click of a mouse or push of a few buttons. To receive a quick response, direct marketing often employs the use of sales promotion devices such as coupons, contests and sweepstakes, samples, giveaways, and rebates, to name just a few.

Because traditional advertising offers few interactive opportunities before purchase, the target remains anonymous, and it is difficult, if not impossible, to know where his exposure to the message took place. The highly targetable and interactive nature of direct marketing makes sales efforts easier to measure, especially if advertising efforts use an identifying marketing code, often a combination of letters and/or numbers, that pinpoints the medium in which the order or inquiry originated. Most importantly, since direct marketing is sent to a specific person, it is easy to track who responded to the message and who did not. Ultimately, this information will be used to help determine whether the proper media mix was employed.

Because it is so individualized, reaching the target audience through direct marketing is much more expensive than advertising. As a mass medium, advertising is seen and/or heard by a large number of people who may or may not be interested in the product or service advertised. Direct marketing, on the other hand, targets one individual that research has deemed most likely to buy the product or use the service advertised, increasing the overall interest and purchase rate.

Trust in direct marketing has grown steadily over the years, mainly because advertisers have delivered reliable products, included guarantees, and made purchases and returns easy. Additional perks promoted in direct-marketing efforts might include some of the lowest prices anywhere, the opportunity to be the first to own, exposure to limited-time offers, and additional incentives, such as free gifts or rebates and/or refunds, just for buying from the televised or direct mail message.

The goal of both advertising and promotion is to elicit a sale. However, when direct marketing is a part of the IMC promotional mix, its role may not be to generate an immediate sale. Sometimes it is used to generate interest or to encourage information gathering through requests for more information. Additional prepurchase research on the target's part may require an appointment with a salesperson, a trip to the retailer or brick-and-mortar location, or a test drive. See figure 14.1 for a direct marketing case study.

Before looking at the diverse list of media voices direct marketing employs, its important to look at why it can personalize a sales message, what makes it a relationship-building tool, and what makes it a successful alternative to mass media advertising. The answers lie in direct marketing's use of database information.

Databases begin life as a short, internally or corporately created list of names, addresses, and phone numbers. Database marketing as an IMC tool requires several years of data collection. Individual customer data is culled from previous interactions with a company, such as purchases or requests for more information. By developing their own database, marketers can save money and aid in customizing future communications while continuing to build customer loyalty. More extensive lists can be purchased from external sources based on the target's demographic or psychographic information.

Where do these names from databases come from? Companies the target has done business with in the past generate many names, and many from existing databases that are purchased from outside sources. Others might come from telephone directories, the U.S. Census, warranty cards, UPC scanners at the grocery store, credit cards, and professional organizations.

Database information ultimately helps marketers develop messages that are tailor-made for the target audience based on their likes, needs, and lifestyles.

Privacy is an ongoing concern for consumers, and the ease with which marketers can gather and sell private information without their knowledge or permission is becoming an unacceptable and avoidable way of doing business. Many corporations and services are refusing to sell their customer lists in order to protect their targets' privacy.

## The Diversity of the Direct Marketing Voice

Direct marketing uses a diverse array of contact vehicles, including mass media, the mail, the telephone, and personal contact.

| | |
|---|---|
| • Catalogs | • Direct Response |
| • Direct Mail | • Telemarketing |
| • Infomercials | • The Internet |
| • E-mail | |

### Catalogs

Catalogs, whether they arrive unsolicited or not, are often opened, read, and lingered over. Like magazines, catalogs are often saved for later use or shared with friends or colleagues, extending the catalog's life and reach. Ordering is made easy using toll-free numbers, the mail, or the Internet; guarantees allow most, if not all, items to be returned for a full refund if the consumer is not entirely satisfied.

Many of the larger catalog companies create what are known as specialty catalogs. These are smaller versions of a larger catalog, and the specialized content reflects those products targets are most likely to buy based on their past purchase history.

## Direct Mail

Direct mail pieces are like bills: they find their way into consumers' mailboxes unsolicited and eventually into their hands unwanted. Direct mail isn't actually as hated as most people would think. Consumers respond to the personalized messages because such messages specifically address their interests and lifestyles.

Direct mail, also known as database marketing, is a highly targetable, personal, and measurable form of direct response. The consumer can respond to an advertised message by sending in an order form or logging on to a website to place an order, receive more information, or give feedback about the product or service. A toll-free number can also be used to speak directly to a customer service representative about colors or sizes, shipping, and guarantees, or to place an order. A typical direct mail kit can arrive in almost any shape or in any form, but basic pieces include an outside envelope, a personalized pitch letter, an informational brochure, an order form or business reply card for ordering, and a return envelope for mail orders.

As an informational tool, direct mail can be used as an announcement device, a brand-building tool, or an incentive to entice nonusers to switch or try a new or existing product or service, or to reward loyal long-term users.

As an involvement tool, a multipiece mailer requires the target's attention to sort through and read through the various pieces, play with the movable parts, or scratch off a game piece. The more time the consumer has to spend with the piece, the more memorable and involving it will be.

A good direct mail response rate is around 2 percent of the total mailings. For direct mail to succeed, it is important that it be mailed to the right audience and present the right message. Too often, names are duplicated, wasting money and annoying targets.

As a media option, direct mail is very diverse. It can be used as a sales or promotional device or as a primary or secondary media vehicle for almost any product or service. Currently, the heaviest users of direct mail are insurance, financial service firms, and department stores.

Direct mail needs time to work, so don't make the mistake of thinking your first mailing will be your only mailing. A few gentle nudges may be needed to get your target moving.

It is interesting to note that currently most direct mail is sent to white households. The average consumer in the untapped Hispanic market, according to Kenneth A. Clow and Donald Baack in their book *Integrated Advertising: Promotion and Marketing Communications*, receives an average of only ten pieces of direct mail a month. An average of 72 percent of Hispanics actually read direct mail, and 66 percent place an order. Messages designed for any minority group need to be customized to meet that target's special needs.

## General Tips for Working with Direct Mail

- If you can give something away do it. The word "free" is an attention getter, but it doesn't get much tackier or enticing if that's all you have to offer.
- If your direct mail piece is for charity, be sure to use black-and-white photography and a lower grade of paper so as not to appear wasteful.
- All additional pieces that appear with your direct mail letter should be of different sizes and, if possible, varied colors. It is helpful to reuse the graphics or colors from the envelope on the inside pieces.
- Guarantees, limited-time offers, quantity limits, coupons, free gifts, and other offers will increase the number of responses or orders.
- The tone of the message should match the image of the product or service. Personalize the letter, but remember that as a business document it must make a sale.
- A creative tone works well, but humor belongs in another media.
- Stick to what your product can do and/or offer; stay away from comparisons with competitors.
- You have a lot of room to make your point; use it wisely.
- Back up facts and benefits with testimonials whenever possible.
- Make the piece appealing and surprise the target with diverse inserts or copy.

One lesser-known form of direct mail is the statement stuffer, also known as a piggy-back because it hitches a ride with a credit card bill, financial notice, or anything else a consumer might receive on a regular or monthly basis.

Direct mail also includes magalogs and polypaks. A magalog deals with a single product, but instead of using a letter, brochure, or circular it features a layout more like a magazine and presents information in the form of articles. Purchase options and order forms are identical to those used in a direct mail kit.

A polypak is a series of small index cards, often 3 x 5, used to advertise a variety of products, which are bundled together and delivered through the mail. Often in color and double-sided, each card has about enough room for a picture and headline on one side and the order form on the other. These are often used to generate interest in a product, asking the consumer to call, mail in, or log on to receive additional information.

## Infomercials

Infomercials are thirty- to sixty-minute-long television commercials that allow the consumer to order immediately using information provided on the television screen. Infomercials use the sight, sound, and motion of television to demonstrate a product, to educate, and to entice a consumer to buy. Infomercials take the time to create interest in a product through the use of testimonials from current users and/or endorsements from celebrity users, or technical advisers. Consumers are offered purchasing options with varied guarantees or return policies. A successful infomercial should:

- Place facts into a storyline that speaks to the target's special interests.
- Break down potentially complicated information into easy, demonstrable steps.
- Use a celebrity or expert to talk about uses or key features and benefits.
- Summarize key features and benefits and then repeat them regularly throughout the program.
- Repeatedly tell the target what you want them to do.
- Make ordering easy by showing a toll-free number and credit cards accepted.
- Outline the guarantee or return policy.

## E-mail

Direct-marketing messages delivered by e-mail are the newest version of direct mail. Personalized messages can be delivered to a target's e-mail address more quickly, more often, and for a lot less money than traditional direct mail. It won't be long before we see direct marketers hooking up with the Internet using e-mail in lieu of or as a supplement to current direct mail use.

## Direct Response

Direct marketing often employs the use of mass media vehicles such as newspapers, magazines, radio, and television, where the consumer can directly respond to the message via the telephone, the mail, or the Internet.

**Newspapers**  Newspapers bring news value to direct-marketing efforts and can be used to target specific geographic areas. Audience size suggests that products with a more generic appeal should be placed in newspapers. However, audiences can be targeted to some degree by placing the advertising in the appropriate special section. If you're not interested in a standard ad, consider using newspaper inserts, which are often full-color and can range from a one-page FSI with perforated coupons to a multipage booklet.

**Magazines**  Magazines, like radio and cable television, have very specialized formats for a very select target market. Magazines should use the opportunity to show the product in color and in a setting the target can relate to, reinforcing the product or services image.

Additional options include multipage inserts bound into the magazine or a bound-in reply card appearing beside the ad that can be torn out and used to order.

**Radio**  Radio, like magazines and cable television, has a highly selective programming schedule with highly definable listeners. Often used as a support medium for other direct marketing or IMC campaign messages, radio can speak directly to the target through the use of a celebrity or a locally or nationally known spokesperson to ensure trust and credibility.

Direct response radio is a less expensive alternative to television. Radio can be aired quickly, and messages read live by on-air personalities can be updated or changed at the last minute. However, before electing to use radio, remember that listeners are doing everything but concentrating solely on the advertised message, which makes remembering phone numbers or elaborate messages difficult.

**Television** Because television allows the consumer to see the product in use, it is an ideal medium for direct-marketing efforts. Direct marketing uses television to make a sale, create leads, or build awareness, and it also works well as a support vehicle or companion piece for direct response advertising appearing in other media.

In the near future, interactive television will allow the target to order a product directly from the television screen. Although the technology is already available, public acceptance has been slow to take off. Additional technology options include text messaging where messages can be received and orders sent directly from your cell phone without ever talking to anyone.

## Telemarketing

Companies that engage in telemarketing use the telephone as a media device and a salesperson to deliver the message personally to select members of the target audience. This is known as outbound telemarketing. Databases are used to identify and contact members of the target who have a known interest in the product or service, or who are seen as potential buyers based on past purchase history. When a customer initiates contact with a company for any reason, usually through the use of a toll-free telephone number, this is known as inbound telemarketing.

## The Internet

The Internet is an important player in direct marketing. Full of information, the Internet allows consumers to search out the answers to questions and compare products, in order to make an educated buying decision. A web page can highlight sale products or suggest accompanying purchases without sales pressure, making purchasing fast and hassle free.

Businesses that take advantage of the Internet for sales and ordering might also find it profitable to offer a catalog or create a direct mail kit, initiating additional contact points and offering customers a choice of shopping venues.

As this list illustrates, direct marketing has grown beyond just direct mail. Some of the biggest changes, like the use of the Internet, text messaging, and infomercials, have come about because of product reliability and quality, the availability of credit cards and toll-free phone numbers, and guarantees or easy return policies that lower the risk of buying what you can't touch or smell.

## How Does Direct Marketing Help IMC Be Consumer Focused?

Direct marketing brings customer service and personalized messages to the IMC table. Consumers will no longer accept generalized messages as incentive to buy; they want informative, personalized service, and they want their purchases to be adaptable to meet their needs. If they have a problem or need help, they want to be able to talk to someone quickly and easily. In the future, brand loyalty will be built not only on the quality of the product but on the quality of the interactivity.

The Internet allows today's savvy, educated consumers to shop from their homes, allowing them to instantly compare products. The need for additional information and research plays a particularly important role when larger, more expensive purchases are under consideration. Advertising that includes a website address or toll-free number encourages interaction and can be used as a great response device for requesting a catalog, brochure, or price list; a free consultation; a sales promotion package; coupons; or even a limited-time discount offer, to name just a few.

Consumers like direct marketing because it's convenient. Visiting retail outlets searching for the best product at the best price is becoming a thing of the past. Direct marketing comes into the consumer's home announced. Consumers decide when to shop and what messages to seek out. They are not inundated with unwanted messages or rude or pushy sales clerks. Purchasing is fast and easy, requiring only a credit card and the click of a mouse or the push of a few buttons.

The Internet has made information seeking and comparison shopping easy for today's busy consumer as previously discussed. There is little differentiation between brands in most product categories, so you have to find a way to make your client's product stand out from the competition. One way is the creative message. Strategies and promotional efforts must be unique and offer the target more than the competing brands by knowing what the target finds important, useful, and necessary. If the creative is very good, it will successfully grab and hold the target's attention and introduce him to a brand new product or service he didn't even know he needed. But the most lasting way to create product differentiation is through the development of a long-term relationship based on knowledgeable, courteous, and reliable customer service or technical assistance that is available twenty-four hours a day, seven days a week.

Once you know your options, the next step is to determine the message and the best media vehicle or combination of media vehicles needed to reach the target and accomplish the objectives.

Internal public relations efforts are critical to the success of direct marketing. The dialogue initiated between the target and customer or technical service representatives must be easy, informative, and satisfying to the target. Customer service representatives need to be familiar with any current promotions, such as sales or coupons, to knowledgeably assist the consumer and support existing advertising efforts. Good public relations efforts must be employed at all times when talking to consumers over the phone or responding to e-mail inquiries.

When print ads are used as a direct marketing device, they can be simple and direct and make the ordering process easy by attaching an order form or including a toll-free number or website address.

Newspapers are a great place to find coupons such as freestanding inserts or larger product or retail booklets. Newspapers are also a great vehicle for encouraging a visit or a trial, or as a last-minute event reminder.

Magazines are great for setting the product's image and use in the target's mind. Direct marketing can be used as a follow-up to encourage immediate purchase.

Television is ideally suited as a direct response vehicle because its ability to demonstrate allows the target to see the product in use, often in the setting in which it will be used. Because of cost, direct response television is usually found on cable. Its highly specialized programming is also better for reaching special interest groups.

## Salvations and Disasters of Direct Marketing

In order to decide whether direct marketing is right for your IMC campaign, let's look at some of the salvations and disasters associated with it.

### What Makes Direct Marketing So Great?

The more notable salvations associated with direct marketing include:

- *Personalization.* Direct marketing can personalize communications to speak to individual members of the target market by name.
- *Measurable.* Using a marketing code placed on direct marketing pieces, the marketer can tell which medium the inquiry came from.
- *Database Use.* Databases provide target information. This information allows direct marketing pieces to address specific individuals and their unique needs.
- *Customer Response.* Direct marketing builds relationships by offering two-way communication between the marketer and the target. It also allows the customer to give feedback that might affect any current or future changes in the product or service.
- *Attention Getter.* Having the right database to target the right individuals is the first step to ensure your target will open and read your direct mail piece. By creating a piece that is both attractively designed and personally and correctly addressed creates interest and encourages investigation. Once opened, the piece must hold the target's interest through entertaining and informative copy. This might be the trickiest step of all, since you do not want the piece to end up in the trash unread.

## Is There Anything Wrong with Direct Marketing?

The more notable disasters associated with direct marketing include:

- *Cost.* One of the biggest advantages to direct marketing is also one of its biggest drawbacks. The personalization of each message makes direct marketing expensive as compared to other forms of advertising. Additionally, if a company does not have its own database of names it will have to purchase a list.
- *Annoyance Clutter.* If targets are not interested in the message, they can deal with direct marketing messages in the same way they deal with other media: turn off the television, throw away the junk mail, or screen telemarketers' calls.
- *Limited Reach.* The highly personalized nature of direct marketing limits the number of consumers that can be reached with any one message.
- *Time Constraints.* Depending on the numbers required and whether the piece is a traditional letter or a more involved mailer, direct marketing can take a great deal of production time. Add the additional time needed for basic folding, stapling, envelope stuffing, and mailing, and you have months invested into pre- and postproduction.

## The Strategy behind Direct Marketing

The job of advertising is to sell to a large audience. Although the known target is a part of this large audience, there is no way to ensure the target will receive a mass message. As we now know, mass message advertising is no longer the only way to differentiate a product or service from its competition. This is where IMC comes in. IMC understands that the efforts of the promotional mix—public relations, advertising, direct marketing, sales promotion, and the Internet—properly combined, will help not only to meet objectives but assist with positioning, creating brand awareness, and building brand image and brand loyalty more efficiently and effectively than any one medium ever could.

When deciding what media mix will best reach the target and accomplish the objectives, IMC uses two different techniques: advertising, which entices the target into a sale or gets the target thinking about purchase, and promotion, which solicits immediate purchase of a packaged offer. Together, advertising and promotion can be used as building blocks in an IMC campaign: One can inform while the other encourages purchase.

Effective communication objectives that lend themselves to direct marketing as a viable medium include generating sales, building consumer loyalty, enhancing a corporate or brand image, or encouraging an inquiry or product trial.

Like advertising, promotional efforts may target both a primary and secondary target audience. Determining the need for a secondary audience will depend on the target's overall knowledge of, or past history with, the product or service and whether it can, or would, be purchased by a family member, friend, or professional associate. Additional factors affecting both the promotional mix and the strategy include how far each audience is from trial, repeat purchase, and brand loyalty.

Strategically, either a product or a consumer approach will work in direct marketing. Any of the three consumer-based approaches—brand image, lifestyle, or attitude—can flesh out the features and benefits of the product or service. Product strategies that can hammer home the product's appeal and its overall usefulness in the target's life include product feature, USP, and positioning.

The decision to use an emotional or rational appeal depends upon the product and the consumer's knowledge about the product. An emotion-based appeal allows the use of such appeals as humor and animation, fear, or slice-of-life. Rational appeals are considered a hard-sell style, so you should be careful not to go over the top and get too personal. The personal, interactive style of direct marketing walks a fine line between talking to the target like an old friend and getting too personal and inadvertently offending the target. It's important to remember that direct marketing is still a business relationship, and it should inform first and build a relationship second.

Finally, the ability to tie the key benefit to the target's lifestyle is crucial in direct marketing because it helps personalize the message.

Using direct mail to launch an IMC campaign can be very effective. Consider using it as a teaser or announcement device. Teasing the target about a top-secret new product launch or grand opening can build curiosity. Direct marketing can also be used as a status device, delivering invitations to grand openings or private sales.

Once a campaign is launched and interest begins to build, direct marketing is a great support to other media efforts and can make buying the product from home—avoiding traffic, parking hassles, long lines, and moody salespeople—easy. Detailed information can be supplied through copy and/or demonstrations, allowing any direct marketing vehicle to close the sale quickly and conveniently from the target's home or office.

## The Design of Direct Mail

Direct mail consists of any advertising material sent by mail to a targeted consumer to solicit a sale or further inquiry. The personality that is direct mail reflects a variety of diverse faces, shapes, and sizes. It is not unusual for simple direct mail kits to employ a mixture of letter formats or informally handwritten notes, postcards, scratch-off cards, die-cuts, pocketed folders, brochures, price lists, CDs, calendars, keychains, or menus.

More creative and often spectacular direct mail pieces include three-dimensional designs that use pop-ups or pop-outs or employ moving parts or sound. But not all mailings are as imaginative or expensive: Most are functional, with a strictly business appearance.

Almost 50 percent of all direct mail, known better by the derogatory name of "junk mail," is never opened. Why? Because it does not create interest or curiosity. It's considered junk for two reasons: it comes unwanted into the target's home and the overall design is junk. You can't change the former, but you can change the later—and that's the one that will get the piece opened. A typical mailer contains five basic pieces: an outside envelope, a pitch letter, a brochure, an order form or business reply card, and a return envelope for mail orders.

A direct mail kit is a design whole. One piece should not stand out alone; every piece in the kit must work together to create one visual/verbal message. The kit should reflect the key benefit and strategy as defined in the creative brief, and use the same tone of voice and reflect the same overall appearance as the other pieces in the IMC campaign of which it is a part. A direct mail kit most often includes multiple pieces that must be tied together by headline or type style, color, layout, or the use of a spokesperson or animated character. An overview of concept and creative devices will help the designer decide how to tie the kit to the rest of the campaign.

## The Outside Envelope

Use color on the outside of the envelope. If possible, use an oddly shaped envelope or one with a die cut.

Copy placed on the outer envelope of a direct mail kit is known as teaser copy. The job of teaser copy is to engage the reader's interest and attention long enough to open the piece. The envelope should include the logo and perhaps the slogan or tagline. The teaser should contain the key benefit or the *What's in it for me?* factor. The answer to that question is more likely to inspire the target to open and read the piece more quickly than a witty headline that says nothing of value ever could.

If the envelope is perceived as an intriguing piece of eye candy, you've caught the target's attention. Use your envelope like a print ad: feature a large, benefit-based headline that continues building interest after the color, photograph, or graphic image has grabbed the target's attention. The goal is to create enough curiosity that the target can't wait to see what's on the inside.

## Promotional Devices

If you are working with a tight budget, design a bright, colorful message and consider including a scratch-off card as a promotional device when design options are limited. If the money's there, create some kind of stimulating mental toy with your message inside. Design a pop-up or other three-dimensional image that raises up and off the surface when the piece is opened, such as your spokesperson or a picture of a satisfied customer who goes on to give a testimonial in the copy. Movable pieces are fun, so consider using something that reveals one part of the message at a time, allowing the reader to spin a wheel or open a window or door.

The more interactive the piece, the more time the target will spend interacting with the direct mail kit. If there's even more money, include a CD or DVD to support the written message, placed way at the bottom of the packaging to add a little surprise rewarding targets for their patience and dedication.

It's important to keep in mind that three-dimensional interactive devices are fun, but they don't make the sale—they support it. Take away the bells and whistles and you're left with the need for a strong visual/verbal message tailored to your targets needs.

## The Pitch or Business Letter

The direct mail letter should continue the same tone of voice used in the other pieces within the IMC campaign. Open by introducing the product, the key benefit, and by answering the question *What's in it for me?* The middle section should include features, uses, additional benefits, and any endorsements, testimonials, or studies. Do not be afraid to mention price; it's important to the consumer, so don't hide it at the end.

A direct mail piece opens the sale, gives a complete and detailed sales pitch, and closes the sale. The only thing the target has to do is drop the order form in the mail, pick up the phone, or boot up the computer.

Once the envelope is opened, the entire sale rests with the copy. If you've got the target this far, continue to hold her attention by providing the benefit(s) associated with your key benefit. Be specific: your copy must answer who, what, when, where, why, and how—creatively and informatively—and should help to alleviate any fears or skepticism the target may have. If it does not, the target's hard-won initial interest, created when she first opened the envelope or viewed the cover, will fade.

Copywriters must be able to take an ordinary feature and give it a personality, a new use, or a unique twist for an old use. Direct mail is a "sell the sizzle, not the steak" kind of conversation with the target.

Copy must be believable, not unimaginable. Advertising that appears in print alongside editorial matter, as in newspaper or magazines, appears credible by association. The unsolicited arrival of direct mail offers it no such advantage unless the brand or marketer name is well known and respected.

Direct mail advertising is never sought out, so it is imperative that the creative product captures the target's eye, engage the mind, and create curiosity. Long copy can be both intimidating to the eye and boring to the reader. This is where the theme you've been developing throughout the IMC campaign can shine and entertain. Well-written plot or feature/benefit-driven copy that a reader finds intriguing will be read no matter its length, and will initiate an inquiry or produce an order. Be sure to use multiple subheads to break up copy, stimulate interest, and make reading easier.

Be sure to close the sale. If you don't the target will not know what kind of action you want him to take. Make ordering or attaining more information as easy as possible. It is important to reference the enclosed order form, and provide information about how to contact customer service for more information by including a toll-free phone number, and/or a website address. One way to enhance the response rate is to limit quantities or the time the target has to purchase.

How personal should the copy get? The answer will lie in the overall price and type of product being advertised. If the product is whimsical and reasonably priced, keep your copy light and airy. If the product is expensive or a limited collectors item, the copy should be more formal in tone. Copy should sound like a letter to a friend, so use the second-person pronoun "you" to refer to the target. Whatever tone the copy takes, be sure to give the target as much information as possible, from how the product is made, designed, price, size, or color options, and credit card options.

Don't use too many different point sizes in the letter. This is the first mistake most direct mail pieces make, creating an environment rich in tacky and low in class. Use a lot of white space to make the letter appear more formal. If you have a lot of copy, consider using an opening key benefit headline, using the same style as on other print pieces, and multiple subheads to break up long blocks of copy. Use bullets to make specific points and create even more white space. Be sure to list the ordering options; let readers know whether they have to use the enclosed order form or if they can order online or over the phone. Let them know that there are operators standing by to answer any questions they may have. You have a lot of available space in direct mail just waiting for your message—in fact, more space than any other medium you will see. Use it to sell the product clearly, informatively, and without a lot of flash.

## Circulars or Brochures

Many direct mail kits include circulars or brochures. Circulars can lower the quality of the kit because of their memo-like appearance, so design them like a poster: use your visuals to say something and color to create a mood. The copy should include only the key points you want the target to take away from the kit, such as colors, sizes, prices, guarantees, and so forth.

Because of their use of color photography, illustrations, and/or graphics, brochures bring a lot more class to your kit. Brochure copy can be more creative, bringing your business letter alive with descriptive copy and visuals.

The design of a brochure is influenced by how it will be folded and eventually used. Brochures can open like a book, with panels opening from both the left and right sides, or folded like a fan, to name just a few. Panels can have small, diagonal die-cuts to hold business cards or come complete with pockets to hold additional printed material that can be removed. However the brochure folds and whatever additional information it may hold, it has to be functional and reflect the overall design.

There are many different sizes and types of brochures, but the three most popular types are tri-folds, fan folds, and double parallel brochures. A tri-fold is the most common type of brochure used in direct mail and is created from a single sheet of paper. It can be either letter size ($8\frac{1}{2}$ x 11) or legal size ($8\frac{1}{2}$ x 14) that is folded two times creating six useable panels, folding to around $3\frac{5}{8}$ to $8\frac{1}{2}$ letter or $4\frac{5}{8}$ x $8\frac{1}{2}$ legal. Fan folds, also known as an accordion fold because the panels do not close into each other but fold in and out like a fan, can be either letter or legal size, folding to $3\frac{5}{8}$ x $8\frac{1}{2}$ (letter) or $4\frac{5}{8}$ x $8\frac{1}{2}$ (legal). A double parallel brochure, also known as a double-fold, is larger and more elaborate. This brochure design also available in either letter or legal size is created by first folding the paper in half, and then in half once again, creating eight usable panels. The final folded size of the brochure is 2¾ x 8½ letter and 3½ x 8½ legal. Which do you use? Your budget will determine how elaborate the brochure can or should be.

**Reply Cards and Order Forms**  The reply card or order form should continue to reflect the kit and campaign design, perhaps through color and/or typeface, style, or layout. Use a headline to announce the offer and a few lines of copy to remind the consumer about the offer and any additional options. Be sure to include space for the consumer's name, address, city, state, ZIP, day and evening phone numbers, and e-mail address. Provide the proper boxes or lines if the consumer needs to make a color or size choice. Be sure the form has enough room to fill in the blanks and uses a type size that is easy to read. Repeat credit card information here, as well as the company's contact information.

Order forms require the consumer to fill out a structured form in order to make a purchase, receive a free sample, or request additional information. The key is to make it both easy to read and easy to fill out. No consumer wants anything so badly that they will voluntarily struggle with a poorly designed form.

The size of the response or reply card and whether it is one or two sided will vary depending on the number of items the consumer has to choose from and product details such as size or color choices. Don't forget to code the order form so the marketer knows where the sale originated.

**The Return Envelope**  Every direct mail kit should include a preaddressed, postage-paid envelope. The return envelope should be nice and plain and should have the return address and mailing address preprinted, along with postage bar codes and a statement in the stamp area that states, "No Postage Needed If Mailed in the U.S." Make sure your reply card fits inside the envelope without excessive folding or scrunching.

In the end, direct mail gets a bad name because it's usually poorly thought-out and often even more poorly designed. By following the principles outlined above, you can make your direct mail kits stand out from the crowd.

As a member of the promotional mix, direct marketing talks directly to the target and initiates a two-way dialogue, an IMC must. Messages are personalized and address the target's known interests based on past purchasing behavior. Direct marketing is less intrusive than any of the other media we have looked at so far, allowing the target to decide what message to respond to, when to respond to it, and where to make further inquiries or purchase decisions. If your goal is to introduce a new or reinvented product, employ efforts to remind or encourage retrial, or update the consumer on product changes or additions, direct marketing will reach the target in a shorter amount of time and more effectively than traditional advertising efforts.

# Sales Promotion

## The Strategic Use of Sales Promotion in IMC

Sales promotion is fun: It gives the consumer a gift or incentive to entice an inquiry or encourage purchase. Sales promotions are intended to quickly increase sales or interest through discount pricing or other motivational devices available for a limited time. By comparison, advertising takes longer to make a sale and has little personal or immediate effect on an individual consumer.

Sales promotion differs from advertising in its approach. Advertising influences attitudes and tells the consumer why they should buy, answering the question *What's in it for me?* Sales promotion gives the target an incentive to react quickly to the advertised message.

Incentives can take many different forms. Some of the most commonly used include coupons, premiums, sampling, contests and sweepstakes, in-store displays, refunds and rebates, and percent- or cents-off promotions. The choice of sales promotion vehicle should reinforce the advertised message, reflecting the strategy and both the target and product image.

---

**FIGURE 15.1**

---

## SALES PROMOTION CASE STUDY: VIRGIN MUSIC FRANCE

Sales promotion initiatives can be one quick way to generate interest in a product, service, or event. Getting something for doing little more than filling out an entry form, participating in a raffle or using instant messaging is not only interactive (a "must have" for any IMC campaign) but fun as well.

## Discussion

In June of 2003, Virgin Music France carried out a good example of how sales promotion can create excitement, with an "instant win" mobile marketing campaign. The campaign took advantage of one of the easiest, most targetable, and least expensive ways to create a promotion: the use of Short Message Service (SMS), also known as text messaging.

## The Objectives

The objectives were to create interest, build a database of fans for two specific bands and a new music fan club, and allow participants to enter a contest to win prizes, all by targeting the heaviest users of cell phones, including teenagers and young adults.

## The Promotion

Mobile marketing was the core of Virgin's promotional campaign for new singles by two British rock groups, Blue and Atomic Kitten. Through a text messaging game called M-Instant Win, fans could enter to win a variety of prizes, including a chance to meet one of the bands. All they had to do was send a text message to a special code and include the keyword for their favorite band, either BLUE or ATOMIC. Fans could also send in ideas for a new Virgin Music Fan Club. This simple type of promotion gave Virgin options as to how winners would be chosen, such as at random or by time or date of entry. Winners would be notified, again via text message, as soon as they were chosen.

Virgin worked with Mobile 365 (known as Mobileway in 2003) and its Message Moderator to collect entries and ideas for the building of the fan club. This collection of data was not only a great way to organize information, and build a database of fans and club members, but to raise brand—and band—awareness. In a July 2003 Mobileway press release, Virgin Music France's Product Manager, Boris Vedel, said the process allowed Virgin "to run a truly interactive campaign" and "build up an extremely targeted fan base."

## The Media Mix

The media mix used to inform fans about the promotion included flyers that were inserted into CD packaging as well as advertising via French television, radio, and publications.

## Future Use

Virgin could continue compiling data on fans for each band it promotes, to build fan club membership. As Boris Vedel went on to note in Mobileway's announcement, even the data from this campaign could be "used to effectively market further services and run future promotions." Vehicles for delivering messages could continue through text messaging, direct mail, or opt-in marketing such as e-mail notifications that have been requested by the recipient. In the 2003 press release, a Mobileway manager emphasized that "building up personal relationships of this kind with a whole community of consumers [is] essential to harness the true potential of effective mobile marketing."

*Sources*: Mobileway Press Release, "Mobileway Selected As Mobile Marketing Partner for Virgin Music," July 1, 2003, http://www.mobileway.com/pages/newsevents/print_pressreleases.asp?id=711, accessed January 22, 2007; "Meet Blue or Atomic Kitten: Innovative Mobile Marketing Campaign," www.mobile365.com/case_studies/virgin.php, accessed January 16, 2006.

When advertising and sales promotion are coordinated together in an integrated marketing communication (IMC) campaign, it's known as integrated brand promotion (IBP). IBP takes place when the brand's image (advertising) is integrated into the promotion (sales promotion). To do this effectively, the brand-building message of advertising has to coordinate with sales promotion's incentive to buy. For example, coupons arriving in the mail or appearing in a newspaper send a mixed message if the advertising message is elegance and sophistication. Instead, advertising efforts might direct the target to a website or toll-free number for more information or to set up an appointment. On the other hand, if the message is young and upbeat, promotional items may be distributed at concerts or in the mall.

The most distinctive characteristic about sales promotion is its intent. While public relations, advertising, and direct marketing bring a product and message to the target; sales promotion sidesteps the message and brings the target to the product, making it a great interactive device.

The basic premise behind sales promotion is to give the target something for purchasing or for remaining a brand-loyal customer. The job of sales promotion is to attract first-time buyers, stimulate impulse buys, and entice users of a competitor's product to switch brands. It's also a great tool for raising brand awareness through "try me" promotions and effectively increasing product demand using limited-time offers. This is important to IMC efforts because initiating trial is the first step on the long road to obtaining brand loyalty.

The growth of sales promotion has steadily increased over the last several years due to the overwhelming number of often indistinguishable products available to consumers in

## What Is Integrated Brand Communication?

Integrated brand communication or (IBC) is a direct result of the success of integrated marketing communication. IMC concentrates on one organized message that is heard across varied media; IBC concentrates on creating the tie that binds between the consumer and the brand. In short, IMC creates a position, while IBC works with what is already there. IBC is about positioning: What does the consumer feel about the brand? This feeling becomes the brand and defines the corporation. This feeling then dominates all advertising efforts throughout all media, consistent with IMC efforts.

IMC is one message delivered through multiple and varied mediums. IBC takes an existing symbol, image, and overall message and makes it the message. Creating a more distinctive position further strengthens this image.

Traditionally, a brand's image was built over time based on quality, reliability, and a product's desired features and overall benefits. IBC is the calculated creation of an image for a product rather than the development of an image by the consumer. Because it is more consumer focused, IBC uses more Internet-based or interactive media choices in order to interact directly with the consumer. This interaction strengthens the brand image.

any one category. By spotlighting one product, sales promotion can help consumers with a purchase decision by offering an incentive to try the product or use the service, as we saw in the sales promotion case study in figure 15.1.

## The Diversity of the Sales Promotions Voice

The success of all communication efforts rises and falls with the economy. Sales promotion can be used as an incentive to purchase when a poor economy causes consumers to purchase conservatively. However, side effects are numerous, and it's easy for marketers and their products to get caught in the vicious cycle of promotion, finding it hard to get even loyal users to buy when there is no current promotion and prompting them to simply wait for the next one.

Other side effects include the devaluation of the brand in the mind of the consumer, overall expense, and an end of promotion drop in sales. Excessive or unnecessary use of sales promotions can lead to the erosion of brand loyalty, brand image, and eventually brand equity.

When deciding whether or not sales promotions should play a part in an IMC strategy, it's important to determine whether inducing an immediate sale is a prerequisite to accomplishing your objectives. Can you build awareness or loyalty without using a form of bribery? In the end, that's what sales promotion is, and if it is overused it can tarnish the brand's image.

Although sales promotion can do a lot of things, it cannot stand alone to build brand loyalty, cover for a poorly promoted or poorly made product, or save the life of an aging brand. These objectives will require the additional and combined efforts of other media in the promotional mix to promote, educate, or reinvent a product or service's image.

There are a lot of options available when deciding on a promotional device. Some are creative, some are functional—but all are consumer motivated. Sales promotions can be broken down into two basic types: in-store and out-of-store promotions. A distinct few fall into both categories. Let's look at some of the most popular.

In-store promotions include:
- Coupons
- Bonus Packs
- Price-Off Offers
- Specialty Packaging
- Sampling
- Point-of-Purchase (POP)

Out-of-store promotions include:
- Refunds and Rebates
- Continuity Programs
- Product Placement
- Trial Offers
- Special Events
- Product Warranties or Guarantees

In-store or out-of-store promotions include:
- Contests and Sweepstakes
- Premiums
- Giveaways

## In-Store Promotions

In-store promotions are a marketer's last shot at influencing the target prior to purchase. The sales promotion devices employed are most often determined by price and purchase location.

**Coupons** Coupons come with many different offers such as cents-off discounts and two-for-one opportunities, also known as buy-one-get-one-free offers. Other offers, often for higher-priced items, might offer a percentage-off option. Whatever the offer, coupons initiate action and account for almost 70 percent of all consumer sales promotions.

Coupons can be found just about anywhere, but one of the most common places is within the Sunday newspaper, where freestanding inserts (FSIs) are found. These perforated, usually four-color, $8\frac{1}{2}$ x 11 pages offer numerous coupons for one brand of products. Coupons can also be found within newspaper and magazine ads, in the mail as a part of a direct mail kit or polypak, and as bounce-back coupons on the outside of a product or placed inside packaging. The majority of coupons can be used immediately and are known as instant-redemption coupons. Others, like those used in an FSI, might be valid over several days or weeks to encourage return visits.

Coupons can also be found on the Internet, where distribution is tracked and usually limited on a per-person basis, so it is unlikely the target will

### What Gets a Coupon Redeemed?

The better the offer, the more likely it will be redeemed. Consumers are also influenced by the origin of the coupon. On the negative side, in-store coupons require time-consuming decisions and extend the shopping experience. Other offers, such as bounce-backs or checkout coupons, cannot be used until a future visit. Polypak coupons are the least attractive because of the time required to sort through the stack of cards. On the positive side, coupons that arrive via e-mail or land on the target's front doorstep in the Sunday paper are successful because they can be looked at and organized at the target's leisure. Coupons that arrive at the point of purchase with the target are more likely to be redeemed.

Coupons never go out of fashion; they just hit their stride. Most sales or promotions occur before and during a product's peak season. It is not unusual to see a summer promotion for barbeque grills or a winter promotion for hats, coats, and gloves. This might seem a little strange because the products would most likely sell even without additional incentives. But remember, the whole point is to get consumers moving *now* in order to increase short-term sales within a specific time frame rather than waiting for them to get around to a last-minute purchase.

Believe it or not, most coupons are never redeemed, and many that are cause another problem: misredemption. This is when a coupon is accepted for the wrong product or used after the expiration date. Additionally, coupons do not always attract or reach new users and are often redeemed by consumers who are already loyal to the brand.

print coupons directly off a website. Instead, coupons are usually sent to the target by e-mail or traditional mail. A request for coupons directly from the consumer, either by toll-free number or through a website, creates an interaction between buyer and seller. The more time consumers spend actively thinking about the product or service, the more likely the product is to move from their short-term memory to their long-term memory, assisting with recall when they shop.

Technology at the checkout counter has also jumped into the coupon game. One of the most commonly used coupon systems is Catalina Marketing's Checkout Coupon. This form of coupon is distributed with grocery receipts. Which coupons are distributed is determined based on current purchases; they are often not for the same brand, but for other products in the same brand category. These checkout coupons cannot be used immediately, but may be used on the consumer's next visit. If consumers remember to bring the coupons on their next shopping visit, this is a good way to encourage trial.

Crossruffing is another coupon opportunity. Here, two mutually compatible products team up to share one promotion. For example, a coupon for Pillsbury cookie dough might be placed on a package of Nestlé chocolate chips.

**Bonus Packs** Bonus packs are very popular, giving the consumer more of a product for the price of the original size, or incluing a related bonus product in a "try me" size.

**Price-Off Offers** "Price-off offer" is a fancy term for a sale. Unlike coupons, price-off deals often appear on the packaging or are announced by shelf signage. A sale can be anything from a cents-off offer to several dollars or even several hundred dollars off, depending on the product.

**Specialty Packaging** Used to raise awareness and to attract attention, specialty packaging is often used when a product has been reinvented or repackaged. These offers are most common during holidays or in conjunction with a promotional event such as a movie premiere popular with the target audience, a celebrity endorsement, or a sponsored event (see figures 15.2 and 15.3).

**Sampling** Sampling is just what the name implies: The product is available for consumers to try at the POP. If you are looking to entice consumers to try the product, particularly if it is new or repositioned, put it in their hands: let them feel the quality, the weight, or the texture. Better yet, if it smells good, let the consumer have a taste at no charge.

Samples can also be distributed through the mail as a part of direct mail kits, bound up in the Sunday newspaper, distributed at events, or sent in response to consumer requests.

**Point-of-Purchase (POP)** POP advertising is all the advertising you see while shopping, such as store posters, signage inside and outside the store, promotional kiosks that prominently display products either in the aisle or on the endcaps, and shopping cart signs. Shelf dispensers are a popular way to distribute POP coupons that can be immediately redeemed.

**FIGURE 15.2**

The 2005 Stolichnaya Holiday Gift Scarf was created by Creative Director Michael Landou and Associate Creative Director Adam Springer from Publicis New York for Stolichnaya, Allied Domeqc Spirits. Nine different colored scarves were distributed to retailers, instantly transforming the product into a unique gift without sacrificing valuable shelf space. Image courtesy of Publicis New York.

## Out-of-Store Promotions

Out-of-store promotions can be used to reward consumers for their loyalty or for purchase, or to draw attention to a brand or service.

**Refunds and Rebates**  Both refunds and rebates give cash back to the consumer. In the case of a refund it's possible for the entire purchase price to be refunded, with or without the original sales receipt.

**FIGURE 15.3**

The 2005 Kahlua Holiday Luminary Tin was created by Creative Director Michael Landou and Art Director Casiel Kaplan from Publicis New York for Kahlua, Allied Domeqc Spirits. This limited edition tin included a LED light inside. After the bottle was removed, the die-cut tin illuminated, recasting the tin as an attractive holiday decoration. Image courtesy of Publicis New York.

The amount of return on a rebate can vary, and rebates often require the target to fill out lengthy forms and return the original sales receipt and the UPC code or model number found in or on the packaging. The target's willingness to give detailed personal and purchasing information in return for some kind of incentive is a great database-building tool.

**Continuity Programs**  One lesser-known type of sales promotion is the continuity program. Every time consumers use the program and/or make a purchase they earn points toward some kind of reward or free gift, usually associated with the program's sponsor. Most often used by restaurants or airlines, this is a great way to encourage repeat purchase and build brand loyalty.

**Product Placement**  When a name-brand product is clearly recognizable in a movie or television show, it is known as product or brand placement. The goal is to tie the product to a character image or plot in some favorable way.

**Trial Offers**  Trial offers, most often used for expensive items such as beds, larger lawn and garden tools, and exercise equipment, allow consumers to try the product in their home on a trial basis for a specified period of time, often thirty to ninety days, before buying.

**Special Events**  When a product or service attaches its name to an event, it is called special events promotion. Sponsors whose products are a good fit with the event and its target audience will experience a high degree of product awareness and recall.

**Product Warranties or Guarantees**  One of the best ways to generate trust or goodwill in a product or service is to offer a product warranty or guarantee. Consumers expect a 100 percent product warranty when shopping over the phone or the Internet, so be sure to give it to them. A warranty guarantees that if the consumer is not 100 percent satisfied, the purchase price will be refunded in its entirety.

A 100 percent product guarantee ensures consumers that they will not find the product at a lower price anywhere. If they should find a lower price, the marketer will honor the lower price, refunding the difference . Companies often require some kind of proof, such as an ad or circular with the price clearly stated, while others simply take the customer's word for it.

## In-Store or Out-of-Store Promotions

Some promotions can be used whether the target visits a store location or purchases from a website or over the phone.

**Contests and Sweepstakes**  Of all the promotions we have discussed, contests and sweepstakes are one of the few that do not necessarily require a purchase in order to participate.

Consumers love the interactive participation of games of chance. The decision to use a contest or a sweepstakes depends on the type of promotion and the desired outcome. Contests are games of skill that require participants to meet a certain set of standards in order to win. A sweepstakes, on the other hand, is based entirely on chance. Contests and sweepstakes are another great way to build up a database list; information from entry forms can be stored and used for future promotions.

**FIGURE 15.4**

A Lexus campaign (see figures 15.4a through 15.4d) in the fall of 2005 featured a large electronic billboard in Times Square with a photomosaic forming the 2006 Lexus IS. Users were encouraged to upload their own photos onto a temporary website, feeding a pool of images for the photomosaic to display.

**FIGURE 15.4a**

The IS Photomosaic execution appearing on the Reuters Sign was created by Gabrielle Mayeur, Dawn DeKeyser, and Nels Dielman from Team One. This electronic billboard appeared from September through November 2005 in Times Square, New York City, to support the launch of the all-new Lexus IS. Image courtesy of Team One and Lexus, a division of Toyota Motor Sales, U.S.A., Inc.

**FIGURE 15.4b-d**

The following web pages for the IS Photomosaic were created by Claudia Muehlenweg and Lucia Davies from Team One. This website was live from August to November 2005 and was created to drive buzz around the launch of the all-new Lexus IS. Images courtesy of Team One and Lexus, a Division of Toyota Motor Sales, U.S.A., Inc.

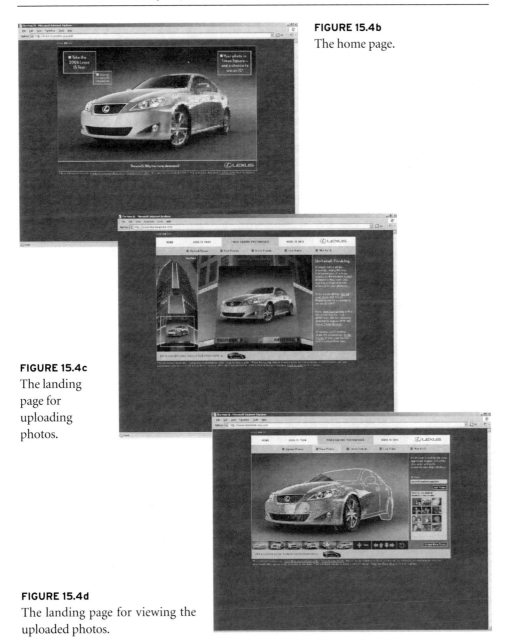

**FIGURE 15.4b**
The home page.

**FIGURE 15.4c**
The landing page for uploading photos.

**FIGURE 15.4d**
The landing page for viewing the uploaded photos.

**Premiums**  Premiums are wearable or usable gifts that are often given away at out-of-store sponsored events, through personal selling, or attached to an in-store product. Usually emblazoned with a company or product logo and/or tagline or slogan, these items include T-shirts, pens, calendars, coffee cups, and baseball caps—basically, anything that can display a logo. Not all premiums are free; sometimes a few proof-of-purchase seals and a little cash to cover shipping are required.

**Giveaways**  A giveaway can take place in or out of store. Although similar to sampling, giveaways rarely actually give the product or service away. Instead a giveaway is often something that complements the product or service. For example, a DVD player might come with an offer of free DVDs with purchase.

## How Does Sales Promotion Help IMC Be Consumer Focused?

Sales promotion brings customer contact to an IMC campaign. It can be used to reinforce an existing campaign message, stimulate trial or repeat purchase, or launch a new product.

Promotions are an interactive direct response vehicle that often initiates a one-on-one dialogue with the consumer (see figure 15.4). Products can often be tested on site, creating immediate feedback between buyer and seller. Most sales promotions are personal.

Because sales promotion, like direct marketing, is so consumer focused, it is more expensive to use than either public relations or advertising mass media approaches. Cost is also dependent upon the size and length of the promotion and the number of prizes or premiums needed. Sales promotion runs the risk of generating big losses if participation is low.

Every buyer likes a bargain, but not all consumers will respond to a bargain. Consumers who are loyal to a product will not be tempted by sales or giveaways, while others live only for the next promotion, with brand playing little or no role in their purchase decision. In between these two extremes lie the switchers, those who may be successfully tempted into switching from a preferred brand to a new brand. This is the group most influenced by sales promotion efforts.

Sales promotions are most often used in an IMC campaign to round out and reinforce the other advertising efforts that make up the promotional mix. The type of promotion used should be chosen based on the product and where it is in its life cycle. New product launches often use coupons, sampling, bonus packs, or contests and sweepstakes to encourage trial purchase. A product in its maintenance stage relies on advertising and requires little promotional assistance. The use of sales promotions is a great way to reawaken interest in a mature brand and might be used to remind the consumer of its value with crossruffing coupons, in- or on-pack offers, or flashy POP displays.

Enticing consumers to take advantage of offers is not always successful, so sales promotions cannot be relied upon as the sole way to generate interest and increase traffic or short-term sales.

## Salvations and Deterrents of Sales Promotion

In order to decide whether sales promotion is right for your IMC campaign, let's look at some of the salvations and deterrents associated with it.

### What Makes Sales Promotion So Great?

The more notable salvations associated with sales promotion include:

- *Time Limit.* Sales promotions increase a company's cash flow, since consumers are more likely to buy when they are offered an incentive, on a short-term basis, ensuring an influx of cash for a set period of time. Any kind of promotion is good for the consumer since it gives something to, or back to, the consumer. As soon as the sale or additional incentive is over, sales will drop or return to prepromotional levels.
- *Trackable.* After a coupon is redeemed or a contest winner is found, results are easily tracked. The volume of sales made during the promotion also determine success.
- *Product Visibility.* A good promotion can entice the consumer to try the product. When a product is supported by a promotion, it can increase awareness by making the product temporarily stand out from a competing brand's initiating trial purchase. Promotions can be directly responsible for convincing consumers loyal to a competing brand to switch brands based on an initial trial.

### Is There Anything Wrong with Sales Promotion?

The more notable disasters associated with sales promotion include:

- *Negative Sales Effect.* Once a promotion has ended, sales often drop as consumers move on to another product promotion. This is an unfortunate side effect of using sales promotion. In order to quickly increase sales again, another promotion will be needed.
- *Damaged Brand Image.* Overuse of promotions can damage a product's image in the mind of the consumer by cheapening its appeal. This directly affects the need to build and maintain brand loyalty. A product's image is the voice of advertising efforts, and excessive promotions can quickly erode the message, destroying consumer confidence in the brand.
- *Equity Depletion.* Excessive use of sales promotions can negatively affect the way the target views the product's image or worth, effectively depleting a brand's equity over time.
- *Cost.* Sales promotion is expensive. A relatively small number of consumers will be reached compared to other approaches, and inventory to cover prizes or premiums can be high when compared to the actual number of sales.

## The Strategy behind Sales Promotion

When should sales promotion be used? It works great as a secondary media for public relations, advertising, and direct marketing to induce trial during small or inexpensive product launches. It is a useful tool for any product where a particular feature can be proven at the point of purchase, such as taste or softness. Products in highly competitive categories with little or no product differentiation can benefit from the use of coupons, bonus packs, price-off offers, or sampling opportunities.

So how does sales promotion fit into the promotional mix? A mature product that is being repositioned might lead off with public relations, using the media to announce a new face to an old friend; advertising will then begin building awareness and introduce the new image. A coupon could be placed in almost any print medium, but would most likely be found in newspapers, magazines, or direct mail kits.

Direct marketing might use sales promotion in a direct mail kit by directing the public to a store location, a website, or a toll-free number to receive a free sample or participate in a trial offer. Incentives such as samples, coupons, POP displays, or trial offers can be used to build brand awareness for a new product or to reintroduce the target to a reinvented product.

Key benefits have nothing to say in sales promotion—but they have everything to show. The message should be your guide, along with strategy, overall objectives, and target audience as to what the image of the promotion has to do with the image of the product and the target. Sales promotion efforts should be avoided for products with a strong brand image, with the possible exception of event sponsorships or continuity programs.

Effective sales promotion objectives might include encouraging trial or product switching by nonusers, supporting a new product launch, offsetting competitor promotions, gaining a larger market share, and increasing short-term profits.

The type of strategy chosen will depend on whether you are focusing on the consumer to reward purchase or loyalty, or to promote the product. A strong product approach works on any level, as do the consumer approach options. A rational appeal is best if the execution technique employed is a competitive, product or service popularity, or news appeal. Depending on the product's life cycle stage, a good alternative emotional appeal is the reminder. If it's important to make a quick sale and increase profits for a limited time, sales promotion is a strategically good choice.

## The Design of Sales Promotion

Sales promotion must be an extension of the advertising message. The closer the visual/verbal relationship, the easier it is to excite consumer interest.

It is important to remember that in IMC there are no single messages with multiple images; only one message and one image will define a product or service's brand image across all media vehicles within the promotional mix. So it is important to carry the visual/verbal message created elsewhere in the promotional mix through all sales promotion efforts. This is often easier said than done because of the eclectic shape, texture, and size of promotional materials.

Depending on the amount of available surface space, promotional devices such as special packaging, premiums, contest and sweepstakes announcements and/or game boards, POP displays, coupons and freestanding inserts, and special event materials should take their cue from print or direct marketing materials. Consider adapting unique headline styles, color combinations, typeface and type style, a spokesperson or character representative, and logo, and slogan or tagline for use in sales promotions. POP advertising that reflects the overall visual/verbal appearance of the other IMC components can assist with product recognition should the target forget the product name while shopping.

The job of this very consumer-focused approach is to get the product into the target's hands and push for an initial inquiry, a request for follow-up information, or purchase. Sales promotion is a great way to introduce or create excitement about a new product or to reintroduce an old product, and also works well as a support medium.

If you want to entice your target through trial or gifts and games, then sales promotion is the best outlet.

# Internet Marketing

## The Strategic Use of Internet Marketing in IMC

The Internet has changed the way corporations conduct business and connects with customers. Through the Internet, advertising that once spoke to the targeted buyer can now actively interact with that buyer. Consumers can ask questions, get help or technical assistance, and make a purchase without ever leaving their home or office. The Internet allows consumers to decide when, where, and for how long they will view a message. The ease with which information can be gathered makes comparison shopping easier, faster, and more convenient, so when consumers elect to buy, they are much better educated on product use, quality, price, and/or guarantee or return policies than ever before.

It is important that when consumers initiate contact, they encounter courteous and knowledgeable customer service or technical representatives who can answer questions quickly and professionally. Often, this is the only thing that separates one product in a category from another. The quality of this interaction is often transferred to the brand or service.

The role of the Internet is still evolving. Its growth as an advertising or direct-selling tool will ultimately depend on how and why consumers use the Internet. Use as a primary vehicle requires the target to initiate contact based on a personal need that begins and ends with a search for information. In its current role as a secondary, support media source, the target is directed to a website based on exposure in a traditional advertising or promotional media vehicle.

FIGURE 16.1

# INTERNET CASE STUDY: CREST WHITESTRIPS

## Challenge

Maintain market leadership and drive sales of a complex, relatively expensive product while facing significant competition, often at a lower price point

## Solution

Leverage the power of the Internet to provide in-depth visuals and content demonstrating Crest Whitestrips' superior efficacy over the competition

## Details

To overcome the significant competition facing the at-home whitening category, Procter & Gamble (P&G) partnered with IMC[2] to develop a website (www.Whitestrips.com) to promote the leading product in the category, Crest Whitestrips. Because the product has a higher price point than its competitors, Crest Whitestrips needed to leverage the Internet to clearly explain the product's superior efficacy and demonstrate its ease of use to consumers.

To meet these needs, the Crest Whitestrips brand team and imc[2] worked together to develop a robust website for the brand, targeted toward the beauty-oriented consumer. The site uses elaborate product demonstrations that include voice over to educate consumers about how they can use the product to effectively whiten their teeth in just seven days. These demonstrations successfully de-mystified a number of pre-identified key barriers to product trial for Crest Whitestrips.

The site uses custom video testimonials to illustrate how real people use Crest Whitestrips and the success they have achieved by using it. The site also provides exclusive resources that build Crest Whitestrips' positioning as a high-end beauty product. imc[2] and the brand team also implemented an online media campaign to provide consumers with a valuable coupon and the brand team a way to grow the consumer database for future marketing. imc[2] leveraged media buys to reach the target market when they were in a need state and actively searching for information related to at-home whitening products. imc[2] is now using the database for ongoing communication.

As a result of the offline and online efforts of the Crest Whitestrips brand, it has become the undisputed leader in the at-home whitening category, owning 68 percent of the marketplace. The product has proven to have broad appeal and has been a key success for the Crest franchise of whitening products.

The brand team also tracked the direct impact that the interactive efforts played in increasing overall product sales. The web has effectively driven product trial among target audiences and increased database registration. imc[2] and the Crest Whitestrips brand team have also partnered to develop CRM programs that have shown a lift in brand awareness and purchase intent.

*Case study courtesy of www.imc2.com.*

Used together, traditional advertising and Internet marketing, also called cybermarketing, are effective at building brand awareness, initiating interactive opportunities, and educating consumers about a product or service. As an educational and informational tool, the Internet is a great place to direct the target for information on current promotions, news articles, testimonials, tests or medical results, and advice or tips from relevant experts. Many websites also sponsor chat rooms and message boards where consumers can talk to and exchange information with other product users.

After advertising, a website is often the consumer's first concentrated impression of a brand or corporation. The consumer's initial website visit is like stepping into a bricks-and-mortar store for the first time: The consumer will take notice of the furnishings, how the floor plan is laid out, and how products are displayed. A messy or haphazard appearance is a turnoff and reflects low budget and quality; a lot of white space and a clean atmosphere gives the illusion of quality and exclusivity. As we have learned, advertising in any medium is all about presentation and the way the visual/verbal message is delivered. Internet marketing introduces yet another dimension: interactivity.

Interactive media focus on creating dialogue and building relationships between buyer and seller by providing multiple channels of communication to encourage consumer interaction and/or feedback. The successful use of interactive media is an important component to an effective IMC approach.

## The Diversity of the Internet Marketing Voice

The Internet is interactive, requiring the consumer to participate in the message by scrolling or clicking to retrieve information. This participation should take little thought, and, like any other medium we have discussed, it should lead the consumer on an informative but structured journey. Interactive advertising vehicles can be as uncomplicated as a banner ad or as multifaceted as an entire website.

Advertising as we know it in print does exist on the Internet in the form of pop-ups and banners, and some Internet service providers do sell message space at the bottom of each viewable screen. This type of message is more reminder than hard sell and can be targeted to match the demographic of the viewer based on previous visits to the site. Since the message cannot be based on psychographics or the target's special interests, this type of message works best for more generic products, like shampoo or makeup for women and sports equipment for men.

Internet use is on the rise, and advertisers are still learning the ins and outs of this new medium. Making advertising interactive or participatory, rather just visually and verbally interesting, is a new challenge. To creative teams, interactive means creating an attention-getting activity that can also inform. To marketers, it is a means of creating an informational vehicle for two-way communication with the target audience.

Advertising on the Internet is less expensive than traditional advertising methods, is easier to revise, and is much more targetable and less intrusive to consumers, since they choose when and where, and for how long, they will visit a site.

**FIGURE 16.2**

The "True-to-Life Prints" online banner ad was created by Robin Tan, Jae Soh, and Justine Lee from Saatchi & Saatchi Singapore for Hewlett-Packard Asia Pacific. This banner appeared on www.asiaone.com.sg and was designed to demonstrate to home printer users the realistic quality of the prints from the HP Photosmart 8230 Photo Printer. Images courtesy of Saatchi & Saatchi Singapore.

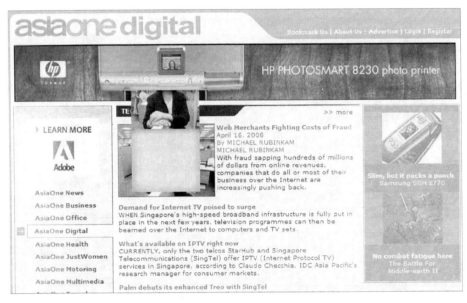

Internet advertising and promotional efforts at their simplest can take many diverse forms, such as banners and pop-ups, personalized e-mail or text messages, and opportunities to enter a contest sweepstakes or pick up a coupon or two. More sophisticated options might include streaming audio and video and interactive television.

## Banner Ads

With a click of the mouse, a banner can transport a viewer to a sponsored web page. Banner ads are mass media Internet vehicles usually found at the top of web pages. In its simplest form, a banner is nothing more than a brightly colored rectangular bar featuring a logo and a small amount of type. Vertical banners known as skyscrapers are another option, although they are not used as often. More complex banners can use moving images or blinking images to attract attention. It is important not to get so caught up in what you can do with new technology that you ignore basic design principles. It is not a big leap from animated to tacky and annoying, so use care when deciding how you want the consumer to think about your client's product the first time they see the banner.

Like traditional advertising methods, these often unpopular, intrusive, and unwanted ads are paid for by the advertiser and placed strategically throughout the Internet, usually on very active or highly visited sites. These interactive advertising messages have little type; they briefly present your key benefit and/or a slogan or tagline with an accompanying logo.

When used as a more selective targeting vehicle, banners can be placed on sites that focus on a specific market. For example, a site on dental health might have a banner for a tooth whitening system. This option allows for less waste and creates more interest.

## Pop-Up Ads

Pop-up ads are separate windows that pop up on top of a web page. Much like banner ads, these mass media ads link the viewer to another site. Pop-up ads were originally conceived as a vehicle to drive consumers to the desired website; instead, consumers consider them an annoyance, making them equally as unpopular as banner ads. Consumers are taking advantage of pop-up blockers offered by their service providers, to keep the pop-up window from opening.

For now, banners and pop-up ads make up the limited palette from which Internet advertisers can choose to deliver their message. Advertisers and marketers alike are asking: What is the look of Internet advertising? Is it more like print or broadcast? Banner and pop-up ads currently have more print characteristics than broadcast—and all the annoyance of both. Marketers are constantly working to come up with new and less intrusive ways to catch and direct the target's attention to their websites. The Internet's verbal/visual growing pains are much like television ads were in their infancy. Long and boring, they sounded more like radio ads than the creative, informative productions we see today. As knowledge of what the Internet can and cannot do, and how the consumer will interact with and react to Internet advertising, develops, creatives will be better able to define what good advertising on the Internet will look and sound like and how motion should be employed.

## E-mail Marketing

E-mail marketing is another way to electronically reach the target. E-mail makes printed copies and lengthy printing delays a thing of the past, and is an inexpensive and dependable means of reaching the target. As an effective customer service device, e-mail can be used to thank customers by name for their purchase and reinforce ways to contact the marketer with questions or comments. E-mail can also be used to verify the receipt of an order, alleviating concerns that it might somehow have been lost in cyberspace. It is also an excellent way to send a follow-up customer comment sheet, allowing buyers to comment on service, product quality, and so forth.

Like other forms of Internet advertising, e-mail marketing gets mixed reactions. When consumers elect to receive e-mail messages, it's known as permission or opt-in marketing. Elective e-mails might come from local retailers announcing sales or from airlines or hotel chains advertising discount fares or room rates. E-mail messages sent without permission are known as spam.

## CD-ROMs

CD-ROMs, one of the newest ways to get information to consumers, are not widely used. A CD-ROM holds a lot of information in a small space, reducing shipping, updating, and printing costs. For complex messages, a CD-ROM is an interactive sales device that can tell the story of the product or service in words and pictures, simplifying the message.

When electing to use a CD-ROM, it is important to make sure you tell an interesting visual story. It is not uncommon for CD-ROMs to be text-only versions of a company's website, but if you are going to spend the money, you should make it as unique as possible. Keep it visual, add some noise, and make it interactive to hold the viewer's attention.

Remember, traditional advertising is passive; interactivity brings consumers to the message and entertains them while involving them in an informational yet advertising-focused process. Any material included on the CD-ROM should be easy to access and print. Even though there is a lot of room for information on a CD-ROM, don't overdo it. This should be a quick and informative visual/verbal experience that simulates the experience of owning the product or using the service.

It is less expensive to distribute CD-ROMs at trade shows, through the mail, or as promotional devices than it is to print and distribute brochures or direct mail kits. The downside is that not all consumers can run CD-ROMs on their computers, so print is not dead quite yet.

## Streaming Video and Audio

Streaming video and audio is the Internet version of radio and television advertising. A static image or link can be clicked on and played back, creating a great opportunity to use demonstration or testimonial techniques or to give the spokesperson or animated character a role in the website. It takes a fast Internet connection to run streaming video and audio combinations, and because of technology limitations and variables it is most commonly used not as a straight advertising tool, but as an interactive supplement.

## Wireless Communication

It won't be long before regular text messaging will be routinely used by advertisers to deliver advertising via the target's cellular phone. This type of contact is known as wireless communication. About the only thing that can invariably draw people's attention these days is the cell phone. Potential customers can be targeted based on phone number, time of day, and location. Targeted consumers receive a text message and a link, and if they are interested in the product they can use the link to connect to the online sponsor.

## Interactive Television

Interactive television is a mixture of computers, television, and the Internet. Television advertising that features a link allows consumers to directly respond to a commercial message viewed on their television screen by clicking on the link using their remote control or a keyboard. Satellite television has offered interactive technology for years, allowing viewers to order movies through their remotes. The technology required to make television viable as a two-way media device is currently available, but it has yet to catch on.

## Destination or Informational Websites

The job of a website is to give company background and/or product details. There are two basic types of content sites: destination websites and informational websites.

Destination websites are the place for surfers to be. This type of site actively engages viewers using some form of entertaining activity, with the goal of building brand awareness and encouraging return visits. The ever-changing destination website can intrigue, entertain, and interact with visitors as a means of introducing a product and building brand awareness. This type of approach works great for products generally purchased more spontaneously or products that are not technical in nature and need little explanation as to use.

The novelty of this new medium, which is still being tested, is finding out what makes a surfer return to a site. A return visit requires initial interest, but the site must change constantly so that every visit is unique. Easy methods to keep a website fresh include using promotional options such as contests and sweepstakes, sponsoring chat rooms where consumers can share unique uses for the product, or simply using news and weather updates or stock quotes. The key is to find a way to make visitors bookmark your site.

Since most surfers are on the go from site to site, they like sites that load quickly and can be viewed as simply as possible. A simple visual/verbal format will be read more often than a time-intensive multimedia message. Streaming video and audio are great if consumers want to take the time to watch or listen, but even in this new medium, simple and traditional approaches work best.

An informational website's primary job is to educate rather than to entertain. This type of site showcases products or services, offers advice or promotional devices, and provides customer service or technical support. A typical page features descriptive copy with an accompanying visual. Although informational sites are not flashy, interactive opportunities exist through promotional efforts such as free gifts, additional information requests, contests, and "click and print" coupon offers.

## How Does Internet Marketing Help IMC Be Consumer Focused?

This new electronic medium called Internet marketing is voluntarily used by consumers to gather information, find entertainment, and make the occasional purchase. But most importantly, it creates interaction between the buyer and the seller.

The Internet is as consumer focused as marketing gets without resorting to personal selling. Electronic media have brought the company to the consumer and made the consumer an active participant in marketing decisions. Marketers have moved a step beyond one-way communication (the message) to two-way communication (target response). This give-and-take creates a relationship between company and target (awareness) and target and brand (loyalty).

The Internet is a great niche-marketing tool. Databases and e-mail make it easy to personally reach those most likely to be interested in a product. Advertising on niche sites is more likely to attract members of the target audience.

The Internet is the only vehicle in the promotional mix that is not readily available at the same technological level to all consumers. The costly nature of technology, subscription-based Internet access, and varied connection options limits the Internet's mass appeal. Before a consumer can go online, or interact with a company, product or service, they must first purchase access from a service provider such as NetZero, Earthlink, and PeoplePC, to name just a few. The average Internet user is generally more educated than the average consumer, will search sites based on interests, and is attracted to gadgets and any form of new technology.

Because Internet users are actively engaged in seeking information, consumer attitude is positive. Buyers choose to look at, or look for, messages; since the messages are thrust upon them, Internet consumers are less apathetic. If, when visiting a website, their attention is drawn elsewhere, they can chose a convenient time to return to the site and finish gathering information or complete an order. The Internet offers a no-muss, no-fuss shopping experience.

Internet users can also decide what they want to look at and how long they want to look at it. A poorly designed site that is confusing or difficult to navigate or read can be removed from the screen with the click of a button.

If your client's website has interactive capabilities, as it should, be sure to ask the consumer to do something: call, write, or e-mail for more information or a free sample. And don't forget that offering coupons is still a great way to encourage trial or repeat purchase. Most importantly, encourage the consumer to make a purchase or ask for assistance from a customer service representative or technical adviser. Interactive dialogue is the goal of Internet marketing.

## Customer Service Is a Must

For an IMC program that is trying to develop or maintain loyalty, customer service is critical. Customer service begins when the website launches; continues with informative messages and visuals, feedback, and ordering; and moves on to delivery, follow-up e-mails, and periodical reminder notes. Customer service and brand-building messages are the Internets keys to success.

It is important to give the consumer a way to make contact. Once a consumer clicks on a customer service button, he needs to get a response. Knowledge is power; let the consumer know how long it will take to get a response. Whether a reply is almost instantaneous or takes twenty-four hours, let the consumer know. This helps to create an environment built on trust and reliability rather than negativity and distrust.

There are two types of customer service: active interaction and passive interaction. Active interaction is live, via instant messaging, the telephone, or online chat rooms and message boards. Traditional e-mail works great for follow-up or reminder notices, order confirmations, and thank-you initiatives.

Immediate e-mail responses keep an impatient consumer happy. Consumers want their questions answered now, so be sure to incorporate contact e-mail links that will immediately connect them with a customer service or technical representative.

Toll-free telephone numbers make contact easy and familiar. Specific questions can be asked and answered with little or no effort. Many consumers are still concerned about making financial transactions on the Internet, so it is important to offer phone, fax, or mail order as options when encouraging purchase.

Chat rooms and message boards allow users with similar interests to interact and share information. Many companies sponsor chat rooms or boards dedicated to users of their products.

Passive interaction, on the other hand, involves a delayed response to questions from customer service representatives, such as receipt of a sample in the mail, or a follow-up or confirmation e-mail response.

## Salvations and Disasters of Internet Marketing

In order to decide whether Internet marketing is right for your IMC campaign, let's look at some of the salvations and disasters associated with it.

### What Makes Internet Marketing So Great?

The more notable salvations associated with Internet advertising include:

- *Individualized Messaging.* Individuals or specific target segments can be easily reached through e-mail or niche sites devoted to specific interests.
- *Database Lists.* Individuals can be reached through existing database lists or those built based on inquiry or purchase history. This allows existing customers to receive a personalized message containing customized messages and images.
- *Cost.* Relatively inexpensive to use, the Internet costs about the same as advertising in print. Although it is expensive to initially create a basic website, its overall appearance will change little over time, saving money as compared to other media. Changes and updates are much easier and less expensive than reprinting individual pieces or whole campaigns.
- *Flexibility.* Online messages offer convenient accessibility twenty-four hours a day.
- *Interactive.* Internet marketing allows for direct communication between the buyer and seller.
- *Simple Integration.* The website address can easily be promoted in other IMC advertising efforts.
- *Engaging.* Consumers look at the Internet as a communications tool more favorably because they choose when to be exposed to its messages.

### Is There Anything Wrong with Internet Marketing?

The more notable disasters associated with Internet advertising include:

- *Clutter.* There is a lot of information on the Internet, so finding a way to make your site stand out is important. Traditional advertising methods are still useful to attract readers or viewers, so the website address should appear on all advertising materials. The site itself should also be well organized and easy to navigate.
- *Niche Segmentation.* The Internet is still used mostly for information gathering and the sending and receiving of e-mail, and is not available at the same technological level to everyone. Research has shown most mass advertising efforts on the Internet, including banners and pop-up ads, are considered an annoyance and are routinely ignored; this makes attracting new audience members more difficult.

- *Reach.* The very nature of personalized data-based advertising means the message will be received by a small audience. Users tend to be more affluent and tend to browse or shop based on specific interests, leaving many sites unseen.
- *Privacy Issues.* The use of database information in other forms of advertising is also an issue with Internet marketing. The Internet has yet to fully address safety and privacy issues during purchase.
- *Measurement.* It is difficult to determine exactly how many consumers within the target audience actually visit a site. Click-through rates are not a reliable measurement tool, as they cannot distinguish between those who end up on a site accidentally and those who specifically choose to browse the site.
- *Unbalanced Technology.* Understand your customers' technical limitations and capabilities. User-friendly sites should be viewable by even those consumers with slow computers or dial-up Internet connections.
- *Cost.* Websites that feature chat rooms or message boards, which use large amounts of bandwidth, can be very expensive.

## The Strategy behind Internet Marketing

Internet marketing is an extension of traditional advertising tactics. Websites can be used to help build brand awareness, increase equity, create loyalty, and deliver an informational message. At its core, a website is no different than a brochure or direct mail kit; what makes the Internet unique is that it allows the seller to interact with the customer, creating valuable dialogue through feedback. The website represents the product through overall appearance, ease of use, and customer service options, replacing retail outlets and salespeople.

Other media used as a part of the IMC campaign should feature the website address to encourage visitation and build interest. A company, product, or service cannot survive on Internet marketing alone. It is still necessary to use traditional media vehicles to get the word out about the site.

Internet marketing efforts should reflect other advertising efforts both visually and verbally. It is important to know how the Internet fits into the promotional mix: Will it play a supporting role as an informational tool, or will it be the primary location for picking up a coupon before buying or the only location to place an order?

Promotion is a big part of Internet-based advertising. Consumers must be able to order samples, download coupons, and enter contests or sweepstakes on the website.

In public relations, the Internet can be a very effective communications tool. Timely information can be delivered to all levels of the target audience and stakeholders to announce job openings, provide information about sponsored events, or even link to other relevant sites.

Internet marketing combines elements and advantages of newspaper, magazine, and television advertising; catalogs; and sales promotion vehicles and direct mail kits, making it among the most versatile of all media vehicles. The Internet can use the strengths of each of these media vehicles to engage the viewer and successfully deliver the key benefit: print requires a visually and/or verbally dominate element, broadcast entertains, catalogs prominently highlight product features, sales promotion entices with a gift, and direct mail must be eye-catching to attract and hold the reader's or viewer's attention. Electronic media uses each of these attributes to make information gathering easy and informative, visually/verbally stimulating, and entertaining to keep a viewer from leaving the site and going elsewhere.

Media choices depend on the objectives to be met and the strategy to be used. The Internet is a good choice for building brand awareness, delivering information, and building loyal customers through interactive activities.

Effective communication objectives include developing two-way communication, making sales, building loyalty, encouraging inquiry, developing a relationship, encouraging product trial, and informing or educating.

The strategic approach can be either product or consumer based. Consumer-based approaches work well because the Internet can be used as a relationship builder. Product-based approaches should tie the product or service's features and benefits back to the consumer's self-image, lifestyle, and/or attitude. The overall style or appeal of an informational site should be rational in order to educate and inform. Rational appeals to consider might include feature or news stories.

Destination websites are consumer oriented. An image, lifestyle, or attitude approach is especially well suited to this type of site. Emotional appeals based on personal states or feelings might include stimulation, excitement, happiness, and pleasure. Additional emotional appeals based on social feelings might include approval, belonging, involvement, and status. Choice of appeal used will depend on the product or service and the target.

Possible execution techniques for an informational site include testimonials, the product as a star, straight fact, technical information, science, or news. Possible execution techniques for a destination site might include humor, animation, or fantasy.

## The Design of Internet Marketing

A typical website should tell the story of a company, product, or service. It must take consumers on a visually and verbally stimulating trip that creatively informs and educates them about the benefits of the product or service. Accessed through an address called a URL, each page of the site is like a section of a map that can be used to find product information.

Each website is assigned a domain name or address with one of the following suffixes: .com, .net, .edu, .org, or .gov. This makes access to information easy and foolproof. The message is organized into pages that lead the viewer logically through the information. A table of contents or navigational tool is often located on the left side or top of each page. This menu highlights specific sections of the site, allowing viewers the option to jump quickly around a site without having to scroll through to find information each time they visit.

Although the Internet can work like a television, featuring sight, sound, and motion, it is important to lay pages out as you would a print ad. It is just as important to keep the connection speed of your end user in mind when designing a website. Not everyone has a high-end computer system or fast Internet access, so it is important to design for both the low-end and high-end viewer. Nothing is more annoying than having to wait for a site to load. Remember, a company's website is its online storefront; it is the first impression many consumers will have of the product or company. Graphic-heavy sites take longer to load than copy-heavy sites. Features such as streaming video are great for demonstrations, but should be kept short and have a point. Streaming video takes more time to load and view than the consumer may want to invest, so make it an option. Don't waste the target's time with creative executions that do not hammer home an answer to the question *What's in it for me?*

At the top of a basic web page is a page header that includes the company logo, site, and/or page name. A page footer, located at the bottom of the page, may have copyright information or numbers for page jumps. The sidebar, usually located on the left side, displays the table of contents or navigational toolbars for the site.

Following the basic design used in print advertising, a website should have a headline, subhead(s), visuals, copy, and a consistently viewable logo. A headline can be used to shout the key benefit; the message can be interspersed with visuals that demonstrate use and/or act as links the target can click on access streaming video or audio. The website should reflect the same tone of voice and visual cues as the other pieces in the IMC campaign. To improve readability and legibility, a site with a lot of copy will need a lot of white space and increased leading, or the amount of white space that appears between lines of text.

Good websites are current and ever changing, recognizing that news is old at the end of every day. A website should pique and maintain the target's initial interest, build excitement, create need, and encourage action.

## Designing for a New Medium

From a design standpoint, the Internet is part print, part television. At its simplest, it is pure text with visual accents; at its most complex, it is sight, sound, and motion. However, the Internet is neither print nor television, so it has its own set of rules that must be followed to effectively accomplish the objectives and strategically highlight the key benefit. Keep it simple, keep it clean, make it interactive, and think of the page layout as print and the delivery of information as television.

Like print, Web design requires a lot of white space to be readable and legible. It requires the use of typefaces that are easy to read at a glance, increased white space, and color. Copy should be informative, creative, and intermittently interspersed with subheadings and visual images, whether traditional photographs, illustrations or graphics, or streaming video.

Don't get caught up in what can be done electronically; do what should be done to inform consumers. They are visiting the website, first and foremost, for information; only after you've kept them from clicking away to another site will they plan on making an inquiry or purchase.

## The Creative Website Options

This discussion will concentrate on the section known as the main text area or the message area, where your key benefit will first be featured. The key benefit and visual and verbal elements should reflect the other pieces in the IMC creative series. In order to brainstorm ideas about how the website should look, the creative team needs to know the purpose of the site. Will it be a destination or informational site? Will there be any customer service or technical representatives available? Will consumers be able to order from the site, or can they request additional information only? Will they be introduced to promotional opportunities? Will there be a chat room, a survey, or a customer feedback area? What about follow-up e-mails? Will there be a way to send information quickly? The marketer needs to commit to these devices by having enough staff to manage service or technical sites twenty-four hours a day, every day. If the service is provided it must be done to the customer's satisfaction in order to build brand loyalty and ultimately brand equity.

Storyboard thumbs are used to work out the overall look of the pages, before the final, full-size storyboard rough is completed. The goal is to keep each page consistent throughout the site.

Each site will require specific categories or subject heads where topical information will be placed. These categories will vary from site to site depending on the function of the site and role it will play in the IMC process. However, most sites include the following categories.

---

- Home Page
- Navigational Aids
- Menu Options
- Links
- Main Menu Links
- Text-Only Format Option

- Press Releases or Relevant News Articles
- Frequently Asked Questions (FAQ)
- Annoying Banners
- Contact or Customer Service Options
- Back Button
- Printer-Friendly Option

---

**Home Page**  Every website has a home page, or the main page of the site. The home page is a corporation's resume; it should introduce the business and its philosophy, and reiterate or strengthen its brand identity. The design should reflect this identity or philosophy. This page is the first impression the viewer will receive about a product or corporation. It should creatively deliver information about a product or service. It is important when developing a website that the design match existing IMC efforts. The home page should highlight the key benefit and tie in with existing IMC efforts. Be sure to keep the side panel or navigational system consistent from page to page. Organize the site into logical sections that match the menu options. Consider adding visuals to the remaining pages; anyone who gets past the home page is interested and will read the copy while waiting for the visuals to open.

The overall layout should follow print principles. Announce your key benefit in a headline. Use subheads to break up longer blocks of copy. Keep copy light and relatively short, and keep visuals to a minimum to help the site open quickly: Any delays could cause viewers to "click out" to another site. Consider using larger headlines to announce different areas within the site. Bold headlines, as in newspaper design, work as an announcement and capture attention. All text should be the same face and style used in other pieces within the IMC campaign. Keep lines of text to around 6 inches to create much-needed white space and make reading off a computer screen easier. Use short sentences and multiple paragraphs to assist with readability and legibility.

If you have to give product steps or a list of product attributes or features, consider using bullets to attract attention and break up the page, rather than listing them in sentence form. Another option is to place them in a graphic box.

The target is at the site for one of two reasons: to gather information or to place an order. Potential orders depend on the consumer knowing how much something costs, including tax, and any charges for shipping and handling. Do not be afraid to prominently list prices. Consider making them bold or including them as a part of the page design, as in newspapers. However you handle them, if you want the target to purchase, don't hide them.

Color use should also reflect other IMC pieces and/or packaging. Use color as an accent, for headlines, or on top or side banners. If you must use a colored background, make sure it's light and make the type large enough to read over it. Many sites use too much color, giving them a garish or circus appearance. Keep print in mind here: The proper placement of color can call attention to an area or topic, but if you use too much nothing stands out.

Visuals of varying size interspersed within or around copy are a great way to break up a gray page and draw a viewer's attention. Consider using a rebus style approach to the page. Visuals that show the product or the product in use, or in a setting, are critical to informational websites. However, if it's not relevant to what's being said, don't include it. Streaming video is a great way to demonstrate a product or present testimonials from current users or professionals such as engineers or scientists.

Writing for the Internet is often handled as if it were a business document, full of facts and little else. This style completely ignores the fact that the target must be both visually and verbally stimulated if you want to hold their attention.

Creatively written copy can tell the story of the product or service and clearly give the facts, but in a more memorable and attention-grabbing way. Remember the discussion on direct mail: readers will read long copy as long as it's interesting.

**Navigational Aids**  A website needs to be easy to get around in. Navigational tools can be either text or graphics that allow the viewer to move around the site with ease. When working with large amounts of text or with multiple pages, the bottom of each page should include a footer with page numbers the viewer can click on to jump to another page. These helpful links appear in the same place on every page. The most common navigation tools are buttons labeled home, next, previous, and help. Consumers do not want to waste their time scrolling through a site to find topics or answers, so be sure to include navigational buttons that allow the viewer to jump quickly around the site.

**Menu Options**  Think of the menu options as a table of contents that will logically lead the reader to specific sections within the site. Menu options, also known as site maps, are navigational tools that take the viewer to specific sections within the site. These links are most often graphic bars located on the left side of the screen or on tabs stretching across the top of the page that can be clicked on to move to a specific topic or section. Be sure there are enough menu options to make getting around the site quick and easy, so the viewer doesn't have to scroll to find information.

**Links**  A website should offer links to help the viewer quickly find additional information such as chat rooms or product testimonials, endorsements, surveys, tests, customer service, frequently asked questions, or ordering information.

**Main Menu Links**  At the top and bottom of each page, be sure to include a link for viewers to click on in order to quickly and easily return to the main menu.

**Text-Only Option**  Some consumers may not have the technology to open image-heavy pages or streaming video or audio quickly. No one wants to wait for a site to open, so offer a text only option. This option allows viewers to decide if and when they want to view any visuals. If the target decides to open a visual by clicking on it, creatively written copy will hold their attention while waiting for the visual to load.

**Press Releases or Relevant News Articles**  A website is a great place to find information about a company, product, or service. Any events, sponsorships, informative news or feature articles, testimonials, awards, or new product releases should be announced on the website.

**Frequently Asked Questions (FAQ)**  Many times consumers have similar questions and concerns. If the answers are posted in one place, consumers can easily find the answers they need to make a decision to purchase.

**Annoying Banners**  Nothing is more annoying than having something flashing or moving in your peripheral vision while you're trying to concentrate. Banners that move should be avoided. If you must have them, place them at the bottom of the page, where they can be hidden below the viewable frame.

**Contact or Customer Service Options**  Be sure to offer as many ways as possible for consumers to contact customer service or technical representatives, including instant messaging, e-mail, toll-free numbers, fax numbers, or traditional mail.

**Back Button**  Many times when searching for information a viewer will want to jump back to the previous page. Make it easy by including a back button.

**Printer-Friendly Option**  Make sure the site is easy to print. Many consumers still like to read from hard copies. If the site uses a lot of color or images, be sure to include a printer-friendly option so that the consumer can print a page that contains only the relevant information.

Finally, be sure to give the site return appeal with visually and verbally interesting and creative content. The site's design should reflect the overall image and tone of voice projected in other IMC pieces. Be sure it's easy to get around in and can be quickly downloaded and easily revised on a consistent basis.

The Internet connects the target, the product, and the seller through information and dialogue. It is the only member of the promotional mix the target actually seeks out for information on a product or service. It is important that this contact, whether initial or ongoing, is a positive one and is considered meaningful and productive to the target. This type of one-on-one contact with customer service representatives or techs is great for building loyalty beyond knowledge of the product. Website design should reflect the product's image both visually and verbally; offer some kind of interactive activity such as instant messaging, order forms, or coupons; and continue the overall message reflected in other IMC pieces.

# Glossary

**Advertising**  A paid form of nonpersonal mass media in which the sponsor of the advertised message is clearly identified. Advertising uses persuasion to sell, inform, educate, remind, and/or entertain the target about a product or service.

**Announcer**  An individual who is both seen and heard on camera delivering the dialogue.

**Assorted Media Mix**  An assorted media mix uses more than one medium in a campaign.

**Banner**  An announcement device in the shape of a black or dark-colored bar that is often placed at the top of an ad. Banners can also be used as page dividers and feature either white or a light-colored type.

**Banner Internet Ads**  Mass media Internet vehicles usually found at the top of a web page.

**Behavioristic Profile**  A profile that breaks down the target audience by looking at how a person buys.

**Big Idea**  A creative solution that sets a product/service off from the competition while at the same time solving a client's advertising problem.

**Body Copy:**  The descriptive copy that works to make a sale or create an image. Body copy focuses on copy features such as color, price, and size, and features a visual/verbal message.

**Callout**  A small amount of copy that appears alongside or below an individual image to which it is connected by a small line.

**Camera Instructions**  Instructions tell the camera what to do or how to move in a shot.

**Clip Art**  Publicly available line art drawings that can be used without specific permission.

**Cognitive Dissonance**  The guilt or anxiety associated with decisions concerning extravagant or excessive purchases.

**Command Headline**  A headline that firmly tells the reader what to do.

**Communication Objectives**  A set of goals the client needs communication efforts to achieve. Communication objectives should describe what it is you want the target to think, feel, and do after exposure to the message.

**Cooperative Advertising** Two individual but compatible clients pair up to share the cost of advertising and to encourage consumers to use their products or services together.

**Concentrated Media Mix** A concentrated media mix places all advertising efforts into one medium.

**Creative Brief** Also known as a *copy platform*; a document developed from the marketing plan and creative strategy and defines the big idea or unique selling proposition. The creative brief also looks at the individual features and benefits of the product or service, outlines tactics, and redefines the target market.

**Creative Concept** An idea that imaginatively solves the client's advertising problem.

**Creative Strategy** The part of the marketing process that outlines the creative approach needed to accomplish marketing goals and/or objectives.

**Creative Team** A team made up of at least a copywriter and an art director that is responsible for developing the creative idea for the IMC program.

**Cropping** The removal of any unnecessary part(s) of a photograph, allowing the designer to dispense with information that is not necessary to the design.

**Cybermarketing** Use of the Internet as a sales device.

**Databases** Collections of individual customer data that are developed from previous interaction with a company, such as a purchase or a request for more information. Databases help marketers personalize the communication message.

**Demographics** Defines the target audience in terms of age, income, sex, marital and professional status, education and number of children, and other relevant factors.

**Detail Copy** Small copy that features addresses, phone numbers, store hours, website addresses, credit card information, e-mail addresses, store hours, parking, and other relevant information.

**Direct Headline** A headline that delivers the key benefit with little or no creative flair.

**Direct Mail** Also known as *junk mail*; a direct marketing tool that includes an outside envelope, a personalized pitch letter, an informational brochure, an order form, and a return envelope for mail orders.

**Direct Marketing** A marketing strategy that uses databases and multiple media to talk to members of the target market individually.

**E-mail Marketing** The use of e-mail to communicate directly with the target.

**Embargo** A news release that is sent in advance to an editor or broadcaster.

**Flag Headline** A headline that talks to a specific group by calling out to them to catch their attention.

**Focus Group** A representative sample of the target, usually ten to twelve people, that gathers together to use or try a product in a controlled environment.

**Font** A typeface's catalog of upper and lower case letters, numbers, and punctuation.

**Formal Surveys** Surveys that include closed-ended questions where participants choose from a predetermined set of responses such as strongly agree, agree, disagree, and strongly disagree.

**Frame Transitions**  Directions that tell the director and postproduction editors of a television ad how to get out of one frame and into the next.

**Freestanding Inserts (FSIs)**  Also known as *supplemental advertising*; full-color ads that are inserted into the newspaper, usually featuring coupons and/or to announce special sales or promotions.

**Geographic Profile**  A profile that breaks down the target audience by looking at where a person lives.

**Guerilla Marketing**  The use of any non-traditional clean, printable surface to deliver a message.

**Headline**  The largest copy in an ad, focusing on highlighting the ad's USP or big idea.

**Home Page**  The first or opening page of a website.

**How-To Headline**  A headline that tells the reader how to do or find out something.

**Indirect or Curiosity Headline**  A headline that tantalizes consumers with just enough information to make them curious for more information.

**Infomercials**  Thirty- to sixty-minute television commercials that allow the target to order immediately from information provided on the television screen.

**Informal Surveys**  Surveys that include open-ended questions, allowing participants to give their opinions.

**Integrated Brand Promotion (IBP)**  An IMC campaign that uses advertising and sales promotion in a coordinated effort.

**Integrated Marketing Communication (IMC)**  Also known as *relationship marketing*; a marketing method that uses databases to interactively engage a specific individual with a specific message through specific media outlets. The goal of IMC is to build a long-term relationship between buyer and seller by involving the targeted member in an interactive or two-way exchange of information.

**Internet Marketing**  Use of the Internet as an interactive medium to allow the target to come to the product or service. Consumers can place an order or talk to a customer service or technology representative from the comfort of their own homes.

**Key Benefit**  The one thing or product feature/benefit that will be stressed in an IMC campaign.

**Leading**  A specific numerical value for the amount of white space that appears between lines of text.

**Legibility**  The ease with which an ad can be understood when viewed quickly.

**Letter Spacing**  The amount of space between letters.

**Line Art**  Black-and-white line art consists of a line drawing that has no tonal qualities.

**Line Spacing**  The amount of white space between lines of text.

**Logo**  The symbol of a company or a product.

**Magazine Advertising**  A highly targetable member of the media mix that often uses color images to set a tone, mood, or image.

**Major Benefit Headline**  A headline that highlights a USP as the key benefit.

**Marketing Mix**  Also known as the *4-Ps*; a brand's marketing plan of action, including product, price, promotion, and distribution, or "place." Each of the *4-Ps* plays a vital role in message development.

**Marketing Plan**  A client's business plan. The marketing plan outlines the company's strengths and weaknesses as well as the opportunities and threats affecting the product or service. It determines marketing objectives, profiles the marketing strategy, and looks at budget issues and evaluation tactics.

**Marketing Public Relations (MPR)**  The selling of a corporate or brand image to a specifically defined target audience.

**Media Kits**  A direct marketing media option that can include a news release, fact sheet, backgrounder, and head shot. These kits are prepared for members of the press.

**Media Mix**  The media mix breaks the promotional mix down to specific media vehicles, such as newspaper, magazine, direct mail, and so on.

**Metaphors, Similes, and Analogies Headline**  A headline that uses metaphor, simile, or analogy to compare a product to something else.

**News or Announcement Headline**  A headline that tells the target something newsworthy about the product.

**News Release**  A document that contains the latest news and information about the product or service in the form of a finished news article.

**Newspaper Advertising**  Also known as *retail advertising*; uses bold headlines and prominent prices to announce various types of sales.

**Niche Marketing**  Advertising efforts that concentrate specifically on winning the attention of a small group of mostly affluent consumers loyal to one specific product.

**Outside Influencers**  Individuals or groups of individuals trusted by the primary target audience and who can influence their purchasing decisions.

**Overline Subhead**  A subhead that appears above the headline as a teaser or attention getter.

**Personal Benefits Headline**  A headline that promises something to the target.

**Play-on-Words Headline**  A headline that manipulates words, often giving special meaning to words to match a campaign theme.

**Pop-Up Internet Ads**  Mass media Internet ads that pop up over a website and contain a link directing the target to another site.

**Psychographic Profile**  A profile that breaks down the target audience down by looking at a person's lifestyle.

**Practical Advice Headline**  A headline that tells the target how to do or achieve something.

**Primary Data**  Data that is gathered through original research from a variety of sources, such as surveys, interviews, focus groups, observations, or experiments.

**Problem/Solution Headline**  A headline that promotes the solution rather than the problem.

**Product Name Headline**  A headline that features the name of the product. Product name headlines work best for new product launches or reinvented products.

**Promotional Mix**  A promotional mix includes any combination of public relations, advertising, direct marketing, sales promotion, and/or Internet marketing.

**Public Relations**  A mostly nonpaid form of communication that builds relationships with both internal and external audiences through communication efforts that reinforce, defend, or rebuild a corporate or product image.

**Qualitative Data**  Information presented in a verbal or narrative way.

**Quantitative Data**  Information represented by statistics, numbers, or comparative scales.

**Question Headline**  A headline that asks the target a question, requiring the target to think and thus participate.

**Radio Advertising**  A relatively inexpensive member of the media mix that uses dialogue, sound effects, and music to reach the consumer.

**Readability**  The ease with which an ad can be read at a glance.

**Reason-Why Headline**  A headline that gives the target a good reason, or a list of reasons, to use a product or service.

**Repositioning**  A strategy to change the way a product is positioned in the mind of the target.

**Retail Advertising**  Another term for newspaper advertising.

**Return on Investment (ROI)**  The profit realized after advertising and other costs have been deducted.

**Roughs**  Also known as *layouts*; full-size representations of the final piece, with all elements in place and tightly rendered in black and white or color. Conceptual devices such as headlines, subheads, and visuals are readable and viewable.

**Sales Promotion**  A marketing strategy that gives the consumer a gift or incentive to entice an inquiry or to encourage purchase.

**Sans Serif**  A typeface that has no feet or appendages.

**Scenes**  The visual aspects of a television commercial.

**Screen Tints**  Tonal areas, ranging from very light to medium to dark to very dark, that can be used as highlights or shadows.

**Script**  The copy sheet used in radio and television that indicates sound, camera instructions, and any spoken parts.

**Secondary Data**  Data that has already been collected and is available from external sources such as the public library, the Internet, trade associations, and the U.S. Census.

**Serif**  A typeface that features feet or delicate appendages that protrude from the edges.

**Slogan**  A statement that represents the company's philosophy or a product or service's image and that is usually placed above or below the logo.

**Sound Effects (SFX)**  The noises we hear in radio and television ads, such as doors slamming, dogs barking, or babies crying.

**Spot Color**  The use of a spot of color to highlight a detail in a black-and-white photograph.

**Stock Art**  Existing photographs of all varieties that can be purchased and used in an ad.

**Storyboards**  An illustration of the visual portion of the commercial and the timing sequence between what is heard and what is seen, one frame at a time.

**Super Comprehensives**  Also known as *super comps*; representations of an ad created from the final roughs. Super comprehensives are generated on the computer and include all headlines, subheads, visuals, and a logo—and, for the first time, completed body copy in place, simulating exactly how the design will look and read.

**Talent**  The individuals who will be seen on camera or heard on radio reading the copy or dialogue.

**Target Audience**  Also known as *target market*; the group of people research has determined is most likely to buy the product or use the service. A target audience can be broken down based on demographics, psychographics, geographics, and behavioristics.

**Television Advertising**  A very expensive member of the media mix that uses sight, sound, and motion to reach the target.

**Testimonial Headline**  A headline that quotes a satisfied customer.

**Thumbnails**  Small, proportionate drawings that are used to get concept ideas down on paper.

**Typeface**  A specific style of type.

**Type Style**  The form of a typeface used, for example, boldface, italic, or roman.

**Type Weight**  The thickness or thinness of a typeface's body.

**Underline Subheads**  A subhead that appears below the headline and explains in more detail what the headline is saying, elaborates on the statement or comment made, or answers the question posed.

**Unique Selling Proposition (USP)**  A consumer benefit that is unique to a client's product or service or a commonplace feature promoted as unique.

**Viral Marketing**  The use of interactive and/or entertaining Internet advertising, often delivered via e-mail or on a website, to inform and "infect" the receiver with enough interest about a product or service to visit the host website.

**Visual**  A basic design element that can take the form of a photograph, an illustration, line art, or graphic design.

**Voiceover**  Dialogue read by an announcer who is not seen on camera.

**Warning Headline**  A headline that acts as a warning to the target audience.

# Bibliography

Allen, Gemmy, and Georganna Zaba. *Internet Resources for Integrated Marketing Communication.* Orlando, FL: Harcourt, 2000.

Avery, Jim. *Advertising Campaign Planning.* Chicago: Copy Workshop, 2000.

Bangs, David H. *The Market Planning Guide.* 5th ed. Chicago, IL: Upstart Publishing, 1998.

Bendinger, Bruce. *The Copy Workshop Workbook.* Chicago: Copy Workshop, 1993.

Blake, Gary, and Robert W. Bly. *The Elements of Copywriting.* New York: Simon & Schuster, 1997.

Blakeman, Robyn. *The Bare Bones of Advertising Print Design.* Boulder, CO: Rowman & Littlefield, 2004.

Book, Albert C., and Dennis C. Schick. *Fundamentals of Copy and Layout.* 3rd ed. Lincolnwood, IL: NTC Contemporary Publishing, 1997.

Burnett, John, and Sandra Moriarty. *Introduction to Marketing Communications.* Upper Saddle River, NJ: Prentice Hall, 1998.

Burton, Philip Ward. *Advertising Copywriting.* 7th ed. Lincolnwood, IL: NTC Contemporary Publishing, 1999.

Clow, Kenneth A., and Donald Baack. *Integrated Advertising, Promotion and Marketing Communications.* Upper Saddle River, NJ: Prentice Hall, 2002

Duncan, Tom. *IMC: Using Advertising and Promotion to Build Brands.* Boston: McGraw-Hill, 2002.

Evans, Joel R., and Barry Berman. *Marketing.* 4th ed. New York: Macmillan, 1990.

Guth, David W., and Charles Marsh. *Public Relations: A Values-Driven Approach.* 2nd ed. Boston: Allyn and Bacon, 2003.

Hafer, Keith W., and Gordon E. White. *Advertising Writing.* St. Paul, MN: West Publishing, 1977.

———. *Advertising Writing.* 2nd ed. St. Paul, MN: West Publishing, 1982.

Hester, Edward L. *Successful Marketing Research.* New York: Wiley, 1996.

Jakacki, Bernard C. *IMC: An Integrated Marketing Communications Exercise.* Cincinnati, OH: South-Western College Publishing, 2001.

Jay, Ros. *Marketing on a Budget*. Boston: International Thomson Business Press, 1998.

Jewler, A. Jerome, and Bonnie L. Drewniany. *Creative Strategy in Advertising*. Belmont, CA: Thomson Wadsworth, 2005.

Jones, Susan K. *Creative Strategy in Direct Marketing*. 2nd ed. Chicago: NTC Business Books, 1998.

Krugman, Dean M., Leonard N. Reid, S. Watson Dunn, and Arnold M. Barban. *Advertising: Its Role in Modern Marketing*. 8th ed. Fort Worth, TX: Dryden, 1994.

Malickson, David L., and John W. Nason. *Advertising: How to Write the Kind That Works*. New York: Charles Scribner's Sons, 1977.

McDonald, William J. *Direct Marketing: An Integrated Approach*. Boston: Irwin/McGraw-Hill, 1998.

Moscardelli, Deborah M. *Advertising on the Internet*. Upper Saddle River, NJ: Prentice Hall, 1999.

Ogden, James R. *Developing a Creative and Innovative Integrated Marketing Communication Plan: A Working Model*. Upper Saddle River, NJ: Prentice Hall, 1998.

O'Guinn, Thomas C., Chris T. Allen, and Richard J. Semenik. *Advertising and Integrated Brand Promotion*. 3rd ed. Mason, OH: Thomson South-Western, 2003.

Parente, Donald, Bruce Vanden Bergh, Arnold Barban, and James Marra. *Advertising Campaign Strategy: A Guide to Marketing Communication Plans*. Orlando, FL: Dryden, 1996.

Percy, Larry. *Strategies for Implementing Integrated Marketing Communication*. Chicago: NTC Business Books, 1997.

Peterson, Robin T. *Principles of Marketing*. Orlando, FL: Harcourt Brace Jovanovich, 1989.

Shimp, Terence A. *Advertising Promotion: Supplemental Aspects of Integrated Marketing Communications*. 5th ed. Orlando, FL: Dryden, 2000.

Sirgy, Joseph M. *Integrated Marketing Communication: A Systems Approach*. Upper Saddle River, NJ: Prentice Hall, 1998.

Throckmorton, Joan. *Winning Direct Response Advertising*. 2nd ed. Lincolnwood, IL: NTC Business Books, 1997.

Vanden Bergh, Bruce, and Helen Katz. *Advertising Principles*. Lincolnwood, IL: NTC Contemporary Publishing, 1999.

Wilcox, Dennis L., Glen T. Cameron, Philip H. Ault, and Warren K. Agee. *Public Relations Strategies and Tactics*. 7th ed. Boston: Allyn and Bacon, 2003.

# Index

# About the Author

**Robyn Blakeman** received her bachelor's degree from the University of Nebraska in 1980 and her master's degree from Southern Methodist University in Dallas, Texas, in 1996.

Blakeman began teaching advertising and graphic design in 1987 with the Art Institute. As an assistant professor of advertising, she taught both graphic and computer design at Southern Methodist University. As an assistant professor at West Virginia University, Blakeman held several positions, including advertising program chair, coordinator of the integrated marketing communication online graduate certificate program, and coordinator of student affairs and curriculum, in addition to developing the creative track in layout and design. She was responsible for designing and developing the first online integrated marketing communication graduate certificate and online integrated marketing communication graduate program in the country.

In the years 2002 and 2004, Blakeman was nominated for inclusion in *Who's Who among America's Teachers*. She was included in *Who's Who in America* in 2003, has received the Kappa Tau Alpha honorary from her peers, and was voted best journalism professor of the year for 2001–2002.

She is also the author of *The Bare Bones of Advertising Print Design* (2004) and currently teaches design at the University of Tennessee.